How To Rebuild and Modify Your
Manual Transmission

How To Rebuild and Modify Your
Manual Transmission

Robert Bowen

MOTORBOOKS

First published in 2005 by Motorbooks, an imprint of MBI Publishing Company, Galtier Plaza, Suite 200, 380 Jackson Street, St. Paul, MN 55101-3885 USA

The information in this book is true and complete to the best of our knowledge. All recommendations are made without any guarantee on the part of the author or Publisher, who also disclaim any liability incurred in connection with the use of this data or specific details.

This publication has been prepared solely by MBI Publishing Company and is not approved or licensed by any other entity. We recognize that some words, model names, and designations mentioned herein are the property of the trademark holder. We use them for identification purposes only. This is not an official publication.

Motorbooks titles are also available at discounts in bulk quantity for industrial or sales-promotional use. For details write to Special Sales Manager at MBI Publishing Company, Galtier Plaza, Suite 200, 380 Jackson Street, St. Paul, MN 55101-3885 USA.

ISBN-13: 978-0-7603-2047-1
ISBN-10: 0-7603- 2047-0

Editor: Peter Bodensteiner
Designer: Christopher Fayers

Printed in China

Author bio: Robert Bowen is an automotive writer and photographer from Los Angeles. He is best known for his technical articles in *Grassroots Motorsports* and other publications. Other than a short detour to travel and earn an MA in linguistics, he has spent most of his life working in the automotive industry in some capacity, including a stint as a technician in a busy garage and race prep shop, and as a technical editor for a major automaker.

CONTENTS

ACKNOWLEDGMENTS

This book would never have happened without the help of many industry professionals, personal friends, and family members who offered encouragement, advice, and more than a few last-minute favors. There isn't enough space on this page to list them all, but there are a few that were instrumental in getting the manuscript and photographs finished on time and accurately.

I would never have started this project without the support and encouragement of my family, including my wife Nichole and my parents. I come from a long line of gearheads, and I owe a good part of my enthusiasm for greasy parts to my father, Don, and my uncle Lee. I probably wouldn't know a gear from a bearing if I hadn't been underfoot in the shop from a young age.

Mike Long of G-Force Transmissions and Dirk Starksen of Advanced Clutch Technology were two great sources of detailed information on their respective fields. My conversations with both of them helped ground much of the theoretical information contained in Chapters 1, 2, and 8. Dirk also played excellent host at ACT's great facility in Lancaster, California.

Robert Ramirez of Road/Race Engineering helped out with several extended loans of rather expensive new transmission parts, including those used for the cover shot and some of the images in Chapters 3 and 4. Also, Richard Walker was instrumental in getting the cover and many detail shots by providing his lighting equipment and workshop "studio" for some late-night photo shoots.

The hands-on chapters, 5 and 6, represent a small portion of the knowledge given to me by the guys at two very professional shops—Gearspeed and Anaheim Gear. James Ornelas of Gearspeed allowed me into his shop to photograph the expert work of Jason Wishmeyer, and checked the B-series gearing data for accuracy. Monte Griffin of Anaheim Gear shared his extensive experience with the T-5. Both men were very patient with my constant questions and intrusive photography. I also appreciate the T-5 specifications and diagrams provided by Jim Averill of TTC (TREMEC's U.S. arm).

Peter Bodensteiner, my editor, gave me this project in the first place and prodded me to increase my meager output speed and avoid "feature creep," to borrow a term from the software industry. He was great to work with, and the book—by definition—wouldn't have happened without him.

The staff at *Grassroots Motorsports* magazine has also been consistently encouraging and inspiring, particularly my editor, David Wallens. His flexibility on more than a few occasions over the past year helped me avoid conflicting deadlines.

And although I've never met any of them personally, I'd like to thank Fred Puhn, Carroll Smith, David Vizard, and all the other technical writers whose books not only distracted me from my homework as a teenager, but also inspired me to follow in their footsteps. I won't pretend to approach their level of knowledge, but I hope that what I've written teaches you half as much as what they taught me.

INTRODUCTION

This book is an introduction to the fascinating technology of automotive manual transmissions, as well as a hands-on guide to repairing, rebuilding, and modifying any transmission, transaxle, or clutch. Until now, the only books available have been either dry, theoretical texts intended for engineers, or factory repair manuals intended for experienced technicians. This book will bridge that gap and give you, the home mechanic, a clear picture of how transmissions work, what causes them to stop working, and how to repair them.

Transmissions have more in common than you might suspect, so even if your specific car or transmission isn't mentioned, 90 percent of the information in this book will still apply to your situation. Because of this general approach, this book is not a substitute for the factory shop manual, but rather a companion to it. It covers information that is glossed over or completely ignored in most manuals, such as detailed troubleshooting procedures that could save you valuable time and labor costs.

Chapters 1 and 2 cover the basics of manual transmissions and transmission terminology. The later chapters assume that you understand those basics, so it helps to read the early chapters before jumping to the rebuild section. Even if you're comfortable with manual transmission technology, the discussions of gear design and lubrication technology should be informative.

Chapters 3 and 4 discuss the procedures and techniques used to properly diagnose and repair transmission problems, while chapters 5 and 6 put that information to use. Chapter 5 presents a rebuild of the popular TREMEC T-5, which is a fairly typical example of a rear-wheel-drive transmission. Chapter 6 covers the Honda B-series transaxle with the same depth, and can be used as a guide to the process of rebuilding a front-wheel-drive transaxle.

Chapters 7 and 8 introduce the topics of manual transmission modification and clutch technology. Chapter 7 is a good starting point for choosing modifications or discussing the finer points of racing transmission setup with your builder. Finally, Chapter 8 gives you the ammunition you need to select a clutch that will meet your demands without breaking your budget or your car.

CHAPTER 1
TRANSMISSIONS: THE BASIC CONCEPTS

The inner workings of a manual transmission can be intimidating. Amateur mechanics who have never worked on a gearbox are often afraid to tackle rebuilding or modifying one because of the jumble of gears, bearings, linkages, and shafts that confront them after pulling the cover or splitting the case of a modern transmission. Luckily, the situation isn't that bad: transmissions are confusing only if you don't know what you are looking at. Despite their appearance and reputation for complexity, transmissions are simple mechanical devices that can be rebuilt and modified like any other part of a car. In some ways they are even simpler internally than components that are modified more often, such as cylinder heads and carburetors or fuel injection systems.

The first chapter explains the basic concepts of automotive power transmissions in general and manual transmissions in particular. If you have a technical background it might seem a bit simplistic, but I hope that there is something here that can be used by anyone, particularly the section on gearing. If it seems too basic, feel free to skip ahead to the more specific chapters.

THE NEED FOR GEARING

Transmissions are necessary because of the nature of internal-combustion engines. All engines produce different amounts of twisting force, or torque, at different engine speeds. Starting from almost nothing at idle, torque increases with engine rpm, reaching a peak and then decreasing beyond that point to the engine's upper speed limit. Even the most flexible powerplants produce useful torque in only a limited range of engine speeds. A typical street engine produces maximum torque between 2,500 and 4,000 rpm, for example, and may have a redline (upper engine speed limit) of 6,000 rpm.

Unfortunately, the torque requirements of a vehicle are more varied than an engine's torque output. Torque is the force that accelerates a vehicle by overcoming inertia and friction between the road and tire; more or less torque may be required depending on vehicle speed, weight, and acceleration. Something is needed to mediate between the engine and the tires, allowing the engine to run at its most efficient speed even while the vehicle's speed varies and its torque demands change.

The most common and efficient method of varying the speed between an engine and the wheels in an automotive drivetrain is via gears, although chains and belts have been used as well. An important principle of power transmission is shared by all of these methods—they not only reduce the rotational speed of the engine's output, but they also multiply the available torque to increase acceleration. To understand how this happens, it helps to look at what torque really means, and how it relates to the mechanical principles of **force**, **work**, and **power**.

The **force** produced by an internal-combustion engine is measured in terms of torque, the standard measure of rotational force. Torque can be visualized as the force exerted by the end of a lever centered on a turning shaft (the engine's crankshaft). It is really a two-part measurement, defined as the distance from the center of the shaft (the length of the imaginary lever) times the amount of force measured. In the United States, the customary unit of force is pounds, and length is measured in feet, so torque is described as "pounds-feet" (lb-ft). The metric equivalent is "Newton meters" or N-m.

Since torque is force times length, producing more force simply requires a longer lever. This comes from the principles of mechanical advantage and should be readily apparent to anyone who has used a "cheater bar" on the end of a wrench to apply leverage to a frozen bolt—30 pounds of force on the end of a 3-foot-long breaker bar exerts the same amount of twist (90 lb-ft) as 90 pounds of force on the end of a 1-foot ratchet handle. Thirty pounds of force is a lot easier to produce than 90, at least for most nongorillas. The cheater bar allows a mechanic to apply less force with the same result—90 lb-ft of bolt-loosening torque.

In this example, before the bolt moves, there is no difference between the two lever lengths. Both produce the same amount of static torque. When the bolt finally breaks free, however, the 30 pounds of force applied to the longer lever (the cheater bar) will need to be applied over a greater distance (through a larger arc) to achieve the same amount of rotational movement as the ratchet handle. The same amount of **work** (force times distance) has been done in both cases—90 lb-ft of torque at the bolt over the same number of rotational degrees—but the force and distance have changed inversely. This relationship between force,

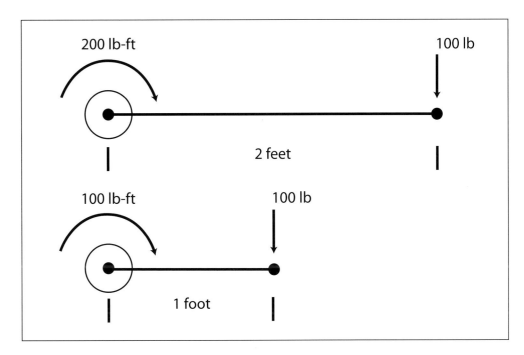

To visualize torque measurement, it helps to think literally in terms of distance and weight. The longer the imaginary lever arm between a pivot and a force (or weight), the greater the torque. This works in reverse, too. If the engine is producing 1 lb-ft of torque, the force at the end of a 1-foot lever is 1 pound, while the force at the end of a 1.5-foot lever is 1.5 pounds. Like the breaker-bar example in the text, a longer lever allows the engine to move more weight, or do more work.

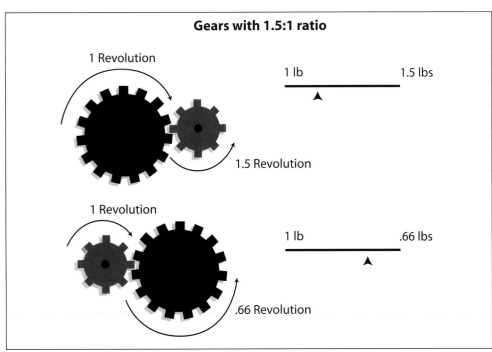

Gears are simply elaborate levers. A gear with 20 teeth driving a gear with 30 teeth is the same as a lever with a pivot 30 inches from one end and 20 inches from another. The smaller gear acts like the longer lever arm, and the larger gear the shorter. If the larger gear is driven, the distance traveled by the smaller gear (in revolutions) is greater but the torque is less. On the other hand, if the smaller gear is driven, the distance is less but the torque is greater.

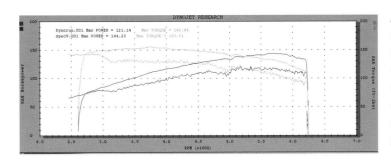

All internal-combustion engines have this characteristic in common: they produce more torque at higher speeds up to a point, and then less torque beyond that point. This "torque curve" means that some method must be used to vary vehicle speed while the engine is producing the necessary amount of torque. Notice that on this chart from a dynamometer session with a real car, the horsepower and torque numbers are the same at 5,252 rpm. This occurs because of the way power is calculated, taking into account torque and engine speed.

distance, and work is the key to the function of the transmission in an automotive drivetrain.

Gears are simply an elaborate method of using mechanical advantage—imagine a pair of gears as a lever with a pivot along its length. A small gear driving a larger one works like a lever with a pivot nearer the output end—a large movement of the smaller gear (the long end of the lever) translates into less movement of the larger gear (the short end), but with more force (torque). The larger the difference between the gears, the more mechanical advantage the small gear has over the larger.

Because of the principle of work, gears can only change the relationship of force (torque) to distance (rotations). A gear train that multiplies the input torque must also lower the output speed to compensate—a given amount of work can only produce more force over less distance or more distance with less force.

The term "gear ratio" refers to the number of teeth on the output gear divided by the number of teeth on the input gear. This determines the speed differential between gears, and thus the torque multiplication factor of that gear train. The smaller of a pair of gears is usually called the pinion, and the larger is called the wheel, although this terminology is not always used in shop manuals and the like.

If the pinion is the driven gear, then the output speed will be lower than the input speed, and the output shaft is said to be underdriven. The inverse is true as well: in overdrive gear trains, the wheel is driven, and the output shaft turns at a faster speed than the input shaft. The lower, underdriven gear ratios increase torque from the input shaft to the output, while the high, overdriven gears actually decrease torque (but increase speed).

The final piece of the gearing and transmission design puzzle is **power**, defined as the work done over a set period of time, or force times distance times time. Power is important in engine and gearing design because it reflects not only the work that the engine can do but also the rate at which it can do that work.

In autocross racing, the courses are very short, less than one minute per lap, and speeds are kept lower than 60 miles per hour. In such a short course, the less shifting the better, since each shift reduces the amount of time that the engine can accelerate the car. To choose the best gearing for autocross, most racers choose a final drive ratio (if it can be changed in that class) that allows the engine to hit the highest speed on course in second gear. This reduces the number of shifts to one, since the driver simply shifts into second after the start and doesn't shift again.

Gearing for road racing is somewhat more complicated. If the transmission gears can be changed individually, the best strategy is to arrange them so that first gear is needed only on the very slowest corner on course, while the high gear will allow the engine to hit the rev limiter in top gear just past the end of the longest straight. If the other gears are reasonably spaced, the resulting gear spread will maximize the ratios over the operating conditions. If only the final drive ratio can be changed, the best strategy is to ignore first gear, and arrange the gear ratios so that second through fifth are used each lap.

In the United States, the power of engines is measured in units of horsepower, which can be very easily calculated by multiplying an engine's rpm by its torque at that point on the curve and dividing by 5,252. Because of the multiplication factor, torque and horsepower of any engine are always the same at 5,252 rpm (although correction factors may change this somewhat on a live dynamometer printout).

Since horsepower considers both engine speed and torque, it is clear that the faster an engine is turning at any point on the torque curve, the higher the horsepower will be at that point. The key to taking advantage of this higher engine speed is gearing. Gears can only multiply torque by reducing speed, so torque made at high speeds is more useful than low-speed torque because it allows gearing to increase the torque output even further without reducing the output speed too much. Similarly, the faster an engine is turning, the more speed is available to take advantage of gearing. The same low gears that are necessary to reduce engine speed to a useful range also increase torque by the same amount.

Horsepower is even more important in racing because the goal of most forms of racing is to beat the clock, or, in other words, to do the most work in the least amount of time. The more power an engine has, the more work it can do over a given time, like a lap of a racetrack or a run down a dragstrip. The range of vehicle speeds is also narrower than on the street, so the optimal gears can be chosen to maximize the engine's power output without the compromises necessary for the street.

Theoretically, at least, power does not change through gearing since gears give up one part of the equation (speed) to increase another (torque), and vice versa. A perfect chain of gears (in the sense of having no frictional or inertial losses) will have no effect on horsepower, while modifying engine torque and output speed to be more useful. In the real world, however, the friction between gears and transmission bearings absorbs some power by converting it to heat, depending on rotational speed and gear ratio.

This cutaway shows a typical rear-wheel-drive transmission in neutral. All three of the shift forks (the two aluminum wedges visible on top of the transmission case, and the aluminum fork on the far left, outside the rear countershaft bearing) are in their central positions. They are engaged with the grooves in the synchronizer sleeves, but the sleeves are not locked to either gear. The input gear (upper right) is turning as long as the clutch is engaged, and so is the countergear and thus all of the speed gears.

THEORY OF GEARING

Ignoring wheel spin, lower gears allow faster acceleration because of their torque multiplication. The lower the gear, however, the lower the top speed of the vehicle. A car with a single low gear accelerates very quickly to the engine's torque peak and more slowly beyond that point. At the engine's redline, the car stops accelerating. To continue accelerating, the car needs another ratio to drop the engine back into its torque peak. Each successive gear allows the car to continue accelerating until the power needed to drive the car at the current speed (because of friction between the tires and road and air resistance) is greater than the output of the engine.

Only simple vehicles with high power-to-weight ratios and a limited range of speeds—like racing karts or sprint cars—can get away with single-speed gearing. Even then, a centrifugal-activated clutch (as in a kart) or wheel slip (as in a sprint car) allow the engine to turn faster than the car

is moving in some situations. The engine's rpm and torque output can stay relatively constant, while the slipping clutch or tires allow the car speed to "catch up" with the engine while accelerating out of a corner. For most other vehicles, more than one gear is necessary.

Engineers solved this problem in the early days of the car by developing transmissions with multiple gear ratios and a shift mechanism to choose between them. As materials technology and manufacturing processes improved, gear trains became stronger and lighter, and car manufacturers added additional gears and synchronizers to select gears without grinding.

Modern production transmissions give engineers the ability to include five, six, or more gears, which means they can accommodate many factors when deciding on the gear ratios for a new engine/chassis combination. Engineers make gear choices on the basis of the vehicle's intended use,

The shift linkage engages the first/second shift fork (the left fork inside the case) when the driver moves the lever to the left. When the driver pushes the lever forward, the linkage moves the fork back and engages the splines of the first/second synchronizer sleeve with the dog teeth on first gear (the leftmost gear inside the case). Engine power now flows from the input shaft to the countershaft, and from the countershaft to the first speed gear on the mainshaft.

the engine's power characteristics, the vehicle's weight, and fuel economy.

Street cars often have low first through third gears and a high fifth or sixth gear because of fuel-economy concerns. Engines operate most efficiently near their torque peak, so the gearing is optimized to keep the engine near that point as much as possible. The gears needed to accelerate the vehicle (first through third or fourth) are low, giving the engine more mechanical advantage and allowing more efficient engine speeds (nearer the engine's torque peak) in stop-and-go driving. The cruising gears (fifth or sixth) are high to keep the engine rpm low at cruising speeds. Low engine speeds during times of low power demands (like freeway cruising) increase mileage and lower noise.

Depending on the weight of the car and the final drive ratio, this kind of ratio spread is not particularly bad for street performance, either. Low transmission gears make a

car more fun to drive by adding to the "seat-of-the-pants" feel and low-speed acceleration, since the lower the gear, the more torque multiplication and the more acceleration. The low gears help heavy street cars accelerate off the line, and high cruising gears keep rpm down for good fuel economy.

Choosing gears for a race car is another matter entirely. True racing transmissions allow swapping ratios, so racers can juggle gears to match the chassis and engine to each track. Although gearing strategies vary widely in racing, the goal is to tune the gear ratios so that the engine doesn't drop out of its torque curve or hit the rev limiter during a lap or run down the strip. Also important is controlling the number of shifts required to maintain the engine in the most powerful part if its torque curve. Each shift causes the car to lose a tiny amount of time because there is no power being transmitted to the wheels when the clutch is in. Of course if each shift takes .020 second, that does not automatically add

All of the lower gears work the same way—as one is locked to the mainshaft (like second gear in the picture above), it begins to transmit power. Each gear also makes use of the reduction in the input gears to reduce output speed and increase output torque. In a front-wheel-drive transaxle there are no input gears, so each gear pair must do all the gear reduction. This means that each gear in a front-wheel-drive transaxle must be larger in diameter to achieve the necessary high-gear reduction. The drive gears for first and second gear, in particular, must be very small and the driven gears very large.

.020 per lap or run—the car is still moving during the shift, so the real time penalty is much less.

In road racing, there are several schools of thought regarding gearing, but most mechanics set the car up so that the engine revs to just past the power peak at the end of the longest straight in the highest gear. That ensures that the other gears can be chosen to optimize acceleration in the important corners. Second gear is usually chosen so that the engine is not turning too slowly to accelerate the car quickly out of the slowest corner, while the other gears split the difference between these two extremes. Road race gearing is so predictable, in fact, that modern F1 teams choose gearing on the basis of computer simulations of the course.

In autocross racing, the most important factor influencing gear ratios is avoiding excess shifting. Most autocross courses do not have straights long enough to reach more than 65 miles per hour, so there is no point concentrating on gearing above this speed. The time lost on each shift adds up quickly on a 30-second course, so given the choice, most builders of production-based autocross cars choose gearing so that second gear is higher than average to avoid shifting into third. With a wide power band and well-chosen gearing, most cars can be shifted into second right after the start, and not shifted out. In general, assuming a usable first gear, the higher the car speed at redline in second gear, the better.

Gearing for drag racing is somewhat more complicated. There are several factors that influence gear choice. Drag racing, in a sense, is a competition between traction and acceleration. Driven wheels of a given size and weight loading will support only so much acceleration before the friction between the tire and the track surface breaks down and wheelspin occurs. First gear is therefore a delicate balance between acceleration and wheelspin. This problem is worse when there is less weight on the drive wheels during acceleration (like the effects of weight transfer on a front-wheel-drive car), and with high-powered cars.

Once the tires hook up, however, the most important consideration is the drop in engine speed between each shift. Given a limited number of speeds, each one should be chosen so that as the engine reaches just past its power peak in each gear, shifting to the next gear will put it as near as possible to the torque peak. The exact shift point will vary, but generally the target is 200 to 300 rpm past the horsepower peak. This allows the drivetrain to convert the maximum amount of torque into acceleration with the minimum number of shifts—maximizing acceleration with the given number of gears.

With optimal gearing, the car will go through the traps (the timing lights at the end of the strip) at redline in the highest nonoverdrive gear (generally fourth gear), to avoid another shift and make more power available at the end of the run. If a race car uses a modified street-car transmission, overdrive gears like fifth or sixth gear may not be used. Many racers lock out fifth gear since it involves a pair of gears that are often not as well supported on bearings as the lower gears, and because it lowers torque and engine rpm at high speeds.

The final drive ratio is much easier to change than transmission gears on rear-wheel-drive cars, so this is the focus of significant discussion and modification for both race and street cars. The final drive ratio chosen is often a compromise if transmission gearing is fixed, since all of the transmission gears are lowered or raised the same amount. An excessively low final drive will result in low gears that are too low, and a very high final drive will result in unusable high gears and poor acceleration in the low gears. Every final drive gearing choice is a compromise between off-the-line acceleration and cruising rpm, or between low fuel economy and sluggish low-speed performance.

TRANSMISSION DESIGN

The modern multispeed manual transmission is the result of years of gradual evolution, and it is a remarkably strong, efficient system. Many different methods of shifting gears and achieving the necessary ratios have been utilized over the years, including dozens of synchronizer and shifter designs, clutched planetary gear sets like automatic transmissions (and the Model T Ford), and sliding gears. Most of these innovations died with the transmissions they were used on.

Not counting electronically shifted or "clutchless" manual transmissions, the internals of all currently produced manual transmissions and the overall flow of power from the engine through the transmission to the driveshafts is remarkably similar. Part of the reason for this standardization relates to the small number of transmission manufacturers that supply units for the world's auto manufacturers; many modern cars use an off-the-shelf transmission customized for the application.

The clutch is technically not part of the manual transmission, but it is an important part of the drivetrain and the source of many transmission difficulties. The flywheel and pressure plate, bolted to the end of the engine's crankshaft, transfer torque to the transmission through friction with the clutch disc. The disc is clamped by springs between mating faces on the engine-driven parts and has internal splines that mesh with an externally splined shaft to drive the transmission.

All modern street and racing transmissions are constant-mesh, meaning the gears are always engaged, and collar-shift, meaning that gears are selected by sliding collars. With the exception of reverse gear, the gear pairs (the drive and driven members of each speed gear) in a transmission are always in contact and always counterrotate. The gears themselves do not move into or out of mesh. In order to shift the transmission from one gear to the next, one of each pair of gears can run freely on a bearing or be locked to the splined steel shaft that it rides on. The other gear of each pair is permanently locked to its shaft, either through splines or by being forged from the same piece of steel.

The floating gears are locked and unlocked to their shafts by a system of large-diameter internally toothed sliding collars or sleeves. The collars are driven by large splined synchronizer hubs that are splined, pinned, or pressed onto the center shaft. Collars cannot turn relative to the hub and shaft they are riding on, although they can move axially (along the length of the shaft) to engage and disengage the speed gears. The collars' inner teeth match a large, narrow ring of teeth called dog teeth on the face of each gear.

When a transmission is shifted into a forward gear, the collar for that gear slides on its hub and engages the gear's dog teeth. That gear is then locked to the center shaft through the collar and hub. In neutral, or in a different gear, the collar's inner teeth are not engaged with any gear, and it is free to rotate at a different speed than the shaft that it rides on. Often each collar is shared by two gears, and has three positions; at each end of its travel, the collar engages a different gear, and in the center it engages neither.

Any time the engine is running with the clutch engaged, the two gears on either side of the collar are spinning at different speeds. If the car is moving, the inner shaft is turning at yet another speed. If there were no method of matching these speeds, the transmission would be very difficult to shift—the collar teeth and gear dog teeth would be

spinning at different speeds and would not match up. Gear changes can only happen when the collar and gear are turning at exactly the same speed.

To get around this problem, modern street transmissions utilize a blocking ring synchronizer system that prevents the sleeve and gear from engaging until the rotating elements are turning at the same speed. This allows the dog teeth and internal splines to mesh without grinding. The Blocking rings use friction to increase or decrease the speed of the transmission's input shaft to match the rotating speed of the chosen gear pair during the blocking process.

FINAL DRIVES AND DIFFERENTIALS

The final link in an automotive powertrain is the final drive, which uses gears to distribute torque to the wheels. Most of the gear reduction in an automotive powertrain takes place in the final drive, with ratios between 1.5:1 and 5:1. To achieve this reduction, a small pinion gear drives a large-diameter ring gear.

Incorporated into the final drive is a differential unit that allows the driven wheels to rotate at different speeds. A differential is necessary because when a car makes a turn, the inside and outside tires turn at different speeds. The outside tire follows a larger-diameter path and therefore must turn faster to get through the corner in the same amount of time as the inner tire. If both wheels were locked together, one would have to slide in order for the car to turn.

REAR-WHEEL-DRIVE TRANSMISSIONS

Rear-wheel-drive transmissions generally utilize three main shafts to transfer power from the engine to the driveshaft or final drive. The third shaft allows the input and output shafts to turn in the same direction, despite the necessary gear reduction, and reduces the size of the gears necessary to get sufficient torque multiplication. The splined input shaft (also sometimes called the first motion shaft) transfers power from the clutch to the gear train. It rides inside the transmission case on a large-diameter ball or tapered roller bearing called the input shaft bearing. The outer end of the shaft may ride on a small needle or plain pilot bearing in the end of the engine's crankshaft. The gear on the end of the input shaft, the input gear, turns the transmission's second shaft, the countershaft (sometimes called the layshaft). The countershaft normally has several cast-in-place or splined gears, one for each of the lower speed gears.

In a rear-wheel-drive transmission, once fourth gear is selected, the input shaft is locked to the mainshaft by the third-fourth synchronizer sleeve. No gear reduction takes place, and the ratio is therefore 1:1. Fifth gear works like the other gears, but since the ratio must be higher than 1:1, and since the input gears lower the ratio before it gets to the overdrive gears, they must be larger than the other gears on the mainshaft. In a sense, the fifth gear pair in an overdrive transmission (the gear to the left outside the main case in this picture) is working against the input gears.

The countershaft is supported at both ends by bearings mounted in bores in the transmission case, or inside the hollow countershaft. Each countershaft gear drives one of the freely rotating mainshaft gears, which are the gears selected by the shift collars or synchronizer assemblies. The end of the mainshaft (also known as the output shaft or third motion shaft) nearest to the engine runs on a small needle or tapered roller bearing called the mainshaft pilot bearing that is located inside the end of the input shaft. The driveshaft end runs on the center support bearing near the rear of the main transmission case.

In most transmissions, engine torque travels through the input shaft and input gear to the countershaft, and in turn to each of the mainshaft gears. Some transmissions also have one direct gear, where the countershaft does not transfer any power to the output shaft. In this gear, the input and output shafts are locked together by synchronizer teeth on the input shaft gear. A direct-drive gear is used both to make the transmission more compact (since it does not require an extra gear) and to increase efficiency, since no power is lost to friction between gear teeth.

To make shift linkage easier to design, many transmissions have the lower gears arranged in order along the mainshaft, starting with fourth and ending at first. Gears normally share a synchronizer with the next consecutive gear in the shift pattern, with first-second, third-fourth, and fifth-sixth synchronizers, but this is not always the case.

Although most modern transmissions incorporate fifth and sixth gears onto the mainshaft, some designs isolate them behind the center support bearing, or in a separate part of the transmission case. In some cases, the overdrive gears are designed with the synchronizer assembly mounted to the countershaft, rather than the mainshaft as with first through fourth gears. This simplifies linkage and can make the transmission more compact, at the cost of some shift speed in the upper gears (which aren't shifted into all that often).

Reverse gear requires a third gear to make the output shaft turn the same direction as the input shaft and reverse the direction of the vehicle. The reverse idler gear is driven by a gear on the countershaft and drives another gear located somewhere along the mainshaft. The reverse idler gear is brought into mesh with its drive and driven gears by its shift fork, which makes it the exception to the rule that transmission gears do not move into mesh.

The end of the mainshaft is splined to accept a slip yoke or flange on the end of the driveshaft, which transfers the engine's torque from the transmission to the rear end in a rear-wheel-drive powertrain. The outer diameter of the slip yoke is ground smoothly, and it rides on a large-diameter bushing. The rear part of the transmission that supports the mainshaft and shift linkage is called the extension housing, or tailshaft housing.

FRONT-WHEEL-DRIVE TRANSAXLES

The term "transaxle" simply describes a transmission with built-in final drive. Transverse front-wheel-drive transaxles and rear-wheel-drive transmissions have more similarities than differences, but there are a few general points of divergence. Front-wheel-drive transaxles make use of a very similar architecture but with only two shafts (input shaft and output shaft) instead of three. Because the final drive unit is incorporated into the same case and involves another change of rotational direction, there is no need for the output shaft to turn the same direction as the input shaft. A transmission with this arrangement of shafts does not have the option of locking the two shafts together, so it does not necessarily have a direct (1:1) gear.

The other main differences between transmissions and transaxles are the shift linkages. In most modern transmissions, the shift linkage is incorporated into the transmission extension housing, while transaxles use some form of rod or cable linkage to operate the shift forks.

The biggest difference between a transmission and transaxle is the incorporation of a final drive unit and differential into the same case. The final drive in most front-wheel-drive transaxles is a large gear pair similar to the speed gears in the transmission. The pinion gear is sometimes machined integrally with the output shaft, and drives a helical ring gear. The differential drives two axles with constant-velocity joints at both the inner and outer ends. The joints allow drive torque to be transmitted even while the wheels are moving up and down with suspension movement and from left to right as the steering is turned.

Longitudinal front-wheel-drive transaxles (like Audi transmissions), rear-engine transaxles (like VW transaxles), and rear-mounted front engine transaxles (like the Porsche 944) are all variations on the same design. In most cases, these transmissions have only two shafts, like a front-wheel-drive transmission, and incorporate a helical final drive like a rear-wheel-drive rear end. In all three cases, the gear shift linkage is remotely mounted.

FOUR-WHEEL DRIVE

There are two general types of four-wheel drivetrains: all-wheel drive (AWD) and four-wheel drive (4WD). An AWD system is designed for use on paved roads in all conditions. The system is constantly engaged, and all four wheels are driven at all times or as dictated by the powertrain control computer. A 4WD system is selectively engaged by the driver when the vehicle is taken off of the road. FWD drivetrains also generally feature longitudinally mounted engines and are based on rear-wheel-drive vehicles.

Transmissions for four-wheel-drive vehicles are not very different from either rear-wheel-drive or front-wheel-drive transmissions, but they incorporate a transfer case to transmit power from the transmission to axles at both ends of the vehicle. A transfer case is a simple device similar to a single- or two-speed transmission, although some use planetary gear sets or chains instead of externally toothed gears. Some transfer cases bolt to the transmission in place of an extension housing. In the transfer case's neutral position only the rear wheels are driven by the engine and transmission, but there may be another mode with additional gear reduction.

Since a 4WD system is not designed for use on paved roads, the transfer case can be locked to distribute torque equally to both axles, and a center differential is not necessary. A center differential is necessary on pavement because the front and rear axles must travel at different speeds through a corner, just as the wheels on the left and right side of the vehicle do. With a locked transfer case, the front wheels have to slip slightly to allow the vehicle to turn.

An AWD transfer case includes a center differential to allow the front and rear axles to turn at different speeds. In this application, only some form of limited-slip differential will work, since an open differential would prevent the vehicle from being driven if one wheel were to lose traction. The most common type of center differential is the viscous coupling, which utilizes a heat-sensitive silicone fluid to drive both axles. Modern AWD systems (and some 4WD systems) incorporate extensive electronic controls, with a computer that determines the optimal torque split for the front and rear axles for the present conditions.

CHAPTER 2
THE INTERNAL PARTS OF A MANUAL TRANSMISSION

GEAR BASICS

Gears are deceptively simple mechanical devices. Gear design is a complex and fascinating science, but luckily, most of us who work with gears don't have to design them. It does help, however, to have a basic understanding of gears if you plan to work on automotive drivetrains. There are really only three types of gears you are likely to find in a modern transmission or final drive: spur gears, helical gears, and hypoid gears.

SPUR GEARS

The simplest and most basic form of gear has straight teeth around its radius, which is the tooth profile that comes to mind when most people think of a generic gear. Gears with

Spur gears have straight, wide teeth that come together suddenly rather than gradually. The wide base (called the root) of each gear tooth makes spur gears strong, and the minimal contact between two mating teeth does not create as much friction and absorb as much power as helical gear teeth. The noise of the constant tooth contact makes them unsuitable for street use.

Helical gears, like this front-wheel-drive pinion gear, have teeth that are "twisted" along the axis of the gear's shaft. The angle of the twist can be varied by the gear designers to optimize strength and decrease noise.

this kind of teeth are known as spur gears (also sometimes called straight-cut gears by racers). Spur gears are the easiest to manufacture, and they were the first type of gear widely used in automotive transmissions. Spur gears are still used in many low-speed industrial applications and in racing transmissions, but they have some disadvantages.

Spur gears are not often used in manual transmissions because they are noisy when driven at high speeds. As a pair of spur gears turns together, each tooth on the drive gear knocks into its companion on the driven gear. The full width of the contacting teeth comes together at the same time, causing a tiny "click." Multiplied by the number of teeth on the gears and the speed the gears are turning, these little clicks together create a loud, high-frequency whine.

HELICAL GEARS

Modern street transmissions get around these problems by using gears with teeth that are not straight. Instead, each tooth is cut on an angle to the gear's axis. Each tooth twists from one gear face to the other, following a curved path. As the teeth in each gear pair come into mesh, the curved teeth contact one another gradually rather than suddenly. This kind of gear is known as a helical gear.

Since each pair of helical teeth slides into full contact before the previous pair is completely out of mesh, the angled gear teeth reduce transmission gear noise compared to spur gears. Helical gears are also stronger because the number of teeth sharing the torque load (referred to as the contact ratio) is greater. With all gears, more than one tooth

transmits the torque traveling through the gear pair, but helical gears have higher contact ratios than spur gears of the same size. The sliding motion and gradual meshing make each tooth less likely to foil because they decrease the shock load on each tooth.

There are a few trade-offs with helical gears. The biggest downside is increased thrust or axial (along the length of the shaft) forces that put outward pressure on the bearings supporting the transmission shafts. Another is increased spreading (opposing radial) forces. As helical gears turn together, the input torque creates forces that attempt to spread the two gears apart, stressing the shafts, bearings, and transmission case. In addition, the gear teeth create friction by sliding against one another, which creates heat and makes helical gears slightly less efficient than spur gears. All of these effects become worse with higher gear speeds, higher torque levels, and steeper gear-tooth helix angles.

Helical gear teeth can be cut on almost any angle, but most gears used in manual transmissions have angles between 20 and 45 degrees to the shaft axis. Below 20 degrees there is not much improvement in noise over a spur gear, and above 45 degrees the gears become inefficient. Even more interesting, transmission manufacturers generally use a different helix angle on each gear. In the lower gears, the input torque is high and output speed is low, so shallower angles transmit torque more efficiently with an acceptable level of gear noise. In the higher gears, the helix angles tend to increase, since the speed of the output shaft is higher and the torque being transmitted is less. The teeth

The twisted teeth of two helical gears come together gradually. Notice that the teeth on the two gears are twisted in opposing directions. Also notice that more than one tooth is in contact at the same time—this increases strength by allowing multiple teeth to share the torque loads across the two gears.

Reverse idler gears in transmissions without a reverse brake or synchronizer are generally spur gears, because the gear must slide into mesh with both the mainshaft and countershaft reverse gears. In this cutaway, the reverse idler gear is hidden behind the mainshaft and countershaft. The small spur gear on the countershaft drives the reverse idler gear, which in turn drives the first/second gear slider through the spur teeth machined around it.

on each member of a pair of helical gears are cut in opposite directions—a right-handed gear requires a left-handed mate, and vice versa.

There is one exception to the general rule that street transmission gears are helical—the reverse idler gear. An idler gear is simply an additional, freely rotating gear that allows the input and output shafts to turn in the same direction.

In many designs, a sliding gear is brought into contact with its mates in the transmission, and it must have straight teeth to be able to mesh with the other gears. It is driven by teeth on the countershaft, in turn driving the outside diameter of the first and second gear shift collar. This eliminates the need for another gear on the mainshaft, and it works well since full engine torque is not normally applied while the transmission is in reverse. Some modern designs have reverse idler gears that are in constant mesh like the other speed gears, but many are still straight-cut spur gears.

Many race transmissions (though not all) use spur gears for a couple of reasons, including ease of manufacture and a reduction in the thrust loads and frictional losses that come from helical gears. Straight-cut spur gears are extremely noisy, however, and can be weaker than an equivalent helical gear.

GEAR STRENGTH

As with anything made of metal, there are two kinds of gear strength: fatigue strength and ultimate tensile strength. Fatigue strength is the gear's ability to resist cracking and damage over many cycles of use, while ultimate tensile strength is the gear's maximum-torque handling ability. Since most transmission gear failure occurs because of metal fatigue—even those that appear to be sudden—fatigue strength is by far the more important.

Each revolution of a gear pair causes the teeth to be constantly stressed and released, and this working back and forth will eventually break transmission gears. There are many factors contributing to a gear's fatigue strength, some of which can be changed after the transmission is designed and some of which cannot. The most important are gear and tooth size, gear material, and manufacturing processes.

Gears in automotive transmissions are usually made from a steel alloy that is later heat-treated to be more resistant to fatigue, and then surface-hardened to resist wear. The surface hardening does not go all the way to the core material of the gear; if it did, the gear would be too brittle to absorb the continuous stress of transmitting torque. Gears can also be stress-relieved or otherwise treated to help with the ability to resist fatigue stresses that build up over time.

The biggest factor contributing to gear strength is the size of the gear teeth. It's a pretty obvious assumption that larger gears are stronger because their teeth are larger. What's less obvious is that there are two parts to tooth size: pitch and tooth width. Pitch is a measure of gear-tooth size defined as the number of gear teeth per inch of gear diameter. Width is measured from face to face along the root, or bottom, of each tooth, giving helical gears (with their longer teeth at the same gear width) yet another advantage over spur gears.

The problem here is that large teeth require large gears. There is a lower limit to the number of teeth that can be used on a gear of a certain diameter before the geometry of the two gears meshing becomes impossible to correct. The larger the teeth (the lower the pitch), or the smaller the gear diameter, the larger this problem becomes. Also related to gear size is the contact ratio of the gears. Larger gears have better contact ratios (more teeth share the task of transmitting torque) and are stronger for the same pitch and width.

So if larger teeth are stronger, and larger gears are stronger, why aren't all gears made with huge teeth? In automotive transmission design, engineers are always trying to balance the conflicting requirements of gear strength and gear size. Larger gears are stronger, but they are heavier, more expensive, and require larger transmissions. Drivetrain inertia is another factor since gears that are larger than necessary take excessive amounts of power to accelerate.

The larger in diameter each gear is, the farther apart the centers of a gear pair becomes. This is one of the primary factors in transmission design—the farther apart the center of each gear must be, the farther apart the centers of the two transmission shafts must be located. This distance from center to center is called the shaft center distance and determines transmission size, torque capacity, and efficiency.

The larger the shaft center distance of a particular transmission, the more power the transmission can transmit, all else being equal. It's a pretty intuitive concept that larger transmissions are stronger than small transmissions, and center distance is a good way of quantifying the size and strength of one transmission compared to another.

SHAFTS AND SPLINES

Transmission gears run on two or three steel shafts. Half of the gears are splined to the shaft on which they turn, and the rest are free to turn on their shaft. The free-running gears usually rotate on small-diameter needle bearings between the inner bore of the gear and the transmission shaft, although in older designs, the inner bore runs directly on the shaft.

From the standpoint of an engineer, transmission shafts are essentially long, straight springs. They bend and twist with the torque and thrust loads being placed on them,

Gear strength is determined by width, as well as the "pitch," or number of teeth, per inch of diameter of a gear. Lower-pitch gears have thicker teeth roots, which makes those teeth stronger. The gear on the left is from a Mitsubishi front-wheel-drive transaxle used with a four-cylinder engine, and the one on the right is from a late-model TREMEC T-5 used behind a Ford V-8. It should be obvious which one is stronger.

The greater the distance between the centers of a transmission's shafts, the larger the gears can be made. Since larger gears can have larger teeth (lower pitch) for the same gear ratio, they are stronger than smaller gears. This has a greater effect on transmission strength than gear width or gear material. To roughly compare the strength of two transmissions, take a look at the shaft center distance. Here, the shaft center-to-center dimension can be determined by measuring between the shaft bores in the transmission case.

despite their appearance as solid shafts. This bending and flexing absorbs some of the vibrations and irregular torque patterns that are produced by internal-combustion engines and acts as a "shock absorber," preventing overload damage to the transmission gears.

This is a feature intentionally utilized by engineers. Two well-known examples of a flexible steel shaft are the World War II–era Rolls-Royce Merlin V12 aircraft engine and the 1960s Chevrolet Corvair. The 1,000-plus-horsepower Merlin had a small, hollow steel driveshaft that ran from the back end of the crankshaft to the supercharger drive. The shaft reduced speed variations and vibration from the huge cylinders to increase supercharger bearing and rotor life.

The 100-horsepower Corvair, on the other hand, used a long, thin steel input shaft from the clutch disc to the transmission to make up for the loss of a driveshaft and transmission output shaft in the rear-engined car. Standard rear-wheel-drive transmissions have long output shafts that serve the same purpose—to minimize vibrations that are passed on to the axles, suspension, and body of the car.

To make the most use of the shock-absorbing properties of transmission shafts, most are intentionally designed to be smaller and more flexible than absolutely necessary for optimal power transmission. The constant flexing is a design feature, but it makes shafts very vulnerable to fatigue damage (that is, work-hardening and the cracks that result from it).

Rear-wheel-drive transmissions have long output shafts that act like torsion springs. The shaft twists and absorbs harmonic and torsional vibrations that would otherwise be transmitted through the engine mounts into the passenger compartment. The two driveshafts of a front-wheel-drive car act similarly.

Transmission shafts could be a lot smaller in diameter if there was a way to avoid splines, diameter changes, and retaining ring grooves. The sharp edges of these machined-in features act like "tear here" perforations at the top of a pad of paper. Without exception, shaft failures occur at these weak spots.

If transmission shafts were simply straight bars of steel, they would be almost unbreakable. As it is, they must have cuts and diameter changes to provide things like bearing seats, keyways, and drive splines. These cuts and cross-sectional changes make the shaft weak. Sharp corners, cross-sectional changes, and splines leave "stress raisers" that concentrate stress in one area and make the shaft weaker.

To reduce stress raisers, transmission shafts are (or should be) carefully machined and heat-treated. Wherever the diameter of the shaft changes, the change must be gradual, and all corners should be rounded (known as a fillet radius). In addition, wherever splines are required on the shaft, that part of the shaft should be a larger diameter than the surrounding metal to eliminate the small notches that would occur at the end of splines in a straight shaft. This has the same effect of not concentrating stress in one area and makes the shaft more resistant to stress failures. OEM manufacturers do not always follow these requirements

Notice how splines are not square—the so-called involute spline shape is actually stronger than a straight-sided spline. Also look carefully at the ends of the spline—they taper off into the metal of the shaft with no sharp edge. These splines are not cut; rather, they are pressed into the metal of the shaft before it was hardened, which is the strongest way to make splines.

because properly made shafts may be too expensive, and the stresses they are asked to cope with are not very high.

The design of the splines also contributes to the strength of transmission shafts. Contrary to first appearance, most transmission splines are not, in fact, square in profile. Most have an angle on each face, like the teeth of a spur gear, and are called involute splines. The angle varies, but it is generally 30, 37.5, or 45 degrees. Generally, the more splines, the stronger the connection between the shaft and gear, but this is not always true. Like gears, splines have a pitch that refers to the number of splines per inch of diameter, and assuming the same pitch, more splines mean a larger shaft and more strength.

Another part of the shaft/spline system in manual transmissions is the retaining ring. The rings themselves are not particularly exciting—they locate gears, synchronizer hubs, and bearings along the shaft axially—but they have significant impact on the strength of the shafts. Retaining rings are seated in narrow grooves cut into the shaft's outer diameter. These grooves have sharp corners that concentrate stresses and shorten shaft life.

BEARINGS

Any time a shaft turns in relation to a surrounding part, the interface between the two surfaces forms a bearing. The bearing area supports the shaft and allows it to turn. An ideal bearing would reduce friction at the same time it supports the shaft, and minimize the wear of both parts. There are many different kinds of bearings in a drivetrain, each with different characteristics and specifications. Transmission designers use these bearings according to the speed, load, and cost of the rotating parts.

There are two different kinds of forces, or loads, acting on the shafts of a transmission that the bearings must be able to cope with. The most significant loads are radial, or at 90 degrees to the centerline of the shafts. As the engine drives the gears inside the transmission, the torque tries to force them apart, applying pressure to the shafts that they run on. These forces are carried to the shaft bearing, which are held rigidly by the transmission case and must absorb these radial forces while allowing the shaft to turn freely.

The second kind of load in a transmission is axial, or thrust load. Helical gears, as mentioned above, produce axial loads as they rotate against one another, forcing the gears in opposite axial directions. The axial loads travel down the shafts, again ending at the rigidly mounted bearings. The direction of the axial loads depends on the direction of the helical gear teeth on the driven gear, but it will always be opposite on two parallel shafts.

The most widespread use of plain bearings in a manual transmission is the reverse idler gear hub. This particular bearing is bronze, and it has dimples to hold oil between the bearing and shaft surface. This reduces wear and increases transmission reliability over a nondimpled or grooved bearing.

Plain Bearings

The most common types of bearings found in manual transmissions (and most other machines) are plain, ball, roller, tapered roller, and needle. Plain bearings, like those found in the lower end of an engine, have no moving parts. Instead, a steel shaft rides directly on a metal surface, most often an aluminum or bronze insert but sometimes in a hardened steel race where stresses and speeds are not high. Plain bearings were used on early transmissions because ball bearings were prohibitively expensive at the time, and are still used when cost is a factor.

There are very few plain bearings in a modern transmission because they wear quickly and do not support small-diameter shafts very well. Plain bearings are rated for the surface speed of the shaft, so a large shaft can use a plain bearing only at low speeds; a small-diameter shaft might be fine at higher speeds in the same type of bearing.

Contrary to appearance, plain bearings do not allow the shaft to run directly on the surface of the bearing metal. Rather, an oil film develops, and holds the two parts apart. The oil acts as a cushion, and reduces friction. The only time that the oil film is not present is when the transmission is first turned, and that is why most plain bearings are made of a soft material. The soft bearing surface allows impurities to embed and allows metal-to-metal contact to occur for a very short time without damaging the bearing surface of the shaft.

The most common use of plain bearings in manual transmissions is in the shift linkage. Shift rods and forks usually bear directly on the case, but the loads and rotational speeds of these parts are very low. Plain bearings are also often used in the extension housing of rear-wheel-drive transmissions with sliding yoke–type driveshafts. The low speed and multiple-direction movement of the yoke inside the transmission are perfect for this kind of bearing. Some light-duty and old transmissions have plain bearings in the speed gear hubs on the mainshaft. Since there is plenty of oil present, the bearings are simply hardened steel running on hardened steel.

Ball Bearings

Ball bearings are some of the most common bearings found in transmissions. They are simple, reliable, and very good at tolerating combinations of radial and axial loads, particularly when the radial loads are large. They can also tolerate a small degree of misalignment between the inner and outer race without serious problems.

In a ball bearing, an inner race and an outer race, both with a narrow, semicircular groove around the circumference, are held apart by a series of hardened steel balls. The outer and inner races are also made of hardened steel. The balls are usually contained and held a fixed distance apart by a cage of plastic, pressed sheet metal, or machined brass.

There are four common variations of the rolling-element bearing found inside manual transmissions and transaxles. From lower left, they are ball, needle roller, plain roller, and tapered roller. The last three are really all variants of the same basic design. Each bearing has different load-carrying capabilities, which engineers exploit to increase shaft stiffness, bearing life, and cost.

There are two common types of ball bearings in manual transmissions: radial contact and angular contact. Radial-contact bearings have an inner and outer race that have shallow grooves that are the same on both sides. They can withstand significant radial loads, but very limited axial, or thrust loads because all the forces must pass through the relatively unsupported edges of the balls.

Angular-contact ball bearings are designed to cope with combinations of radial loads and moderate thrust loads. In an angular-contact bearing, the outer race wraps around the balls, providing a thrust surface on one side of the bearing. These bearings are not reversible and cannot be exchanged for standard radial-contact bearings.

In manual transmissions, ball bearings were the dominant type of shaft-supporting bearing for many years because of their cost and ability to cope with radial loads. Many modern heavy-duty transmissions use different bearings that can withstand heavier axial loads, so that the shaft assemblies can be preloaded and made stiffer. Ball bearings are not often used inside gears because of space constraints.

Roller Bearings

A roller bearing is similar to a ball bearing, but instead of balls, hardened steel pins, known as rollers, are used. The rollers can bear either on an inner and outer race or directly on a ground shaft. Roller bearings are better than ball bearings at supporting radial loads for a given size, but they are not as good at supporting thrust loads. Strong axial pressure bears on the ends of the rollers and can cause them to get hot and gall on the race or shaft.

Small-diameter roller bearings are often referred to as "needle roller" or "needle" bearings. Needle roller bearings are most commonly seen in manual transmissions between the driven gears and the shaft that they ride on. Needle roller bearings are used here because there is very little load at this point. When the gears are carrying a load, they are splined through the synchronizers to the shaft, and the shaft and gear do not rotate in relation to each other. When a gear is turning on the shaft, another gear is engaged and almost no torque passes through the rotating gear.

These bearings are important because of the high speed differential between the gear and shaft. When the transmission is in a high gear, for example, the speed differential between first gear and the mainshaft is very high. The higher gears have less of a speed differential between the gear and shaft, so they are not as critical. The needle roller bearings withstand these high-speed differences without causing excessive heat or friction.

The needle roller bearings can be either loosely packed into the gear hub or caged, with a pressed steel housing that holds them together. Since these bearings are not heavily loaded, the caged bearings are more than adequate for most applications. Some rear-wheel-drive transmissions also feature a small needle thrust bearing between the end of the mainshaft and

Most transmissions use caged needle roller bearings like these between the speed gears and the mainshaft. This is a high-speed but rather lightly loaded application, which is perfect for small needle bearings like these. Older designs use plain steel gear hubs running directly on the shaft. This is fine for low-speed use, but high-revving engines demand needle bearings.

the bore of the input shaft to reduce friction caused by thrust loads. These needle bearings are shaped like flat washers with several rollers radiating out from the center.

Roller bearings with tapered bearing races are called tapered roller bearings, and they differ from plain roller bearings in some significant ways. Tapered roller bearings are very good at coping with combinations of severe thrust and radial loads; this type of bearing is often used in wheel bearings.

The tapered inner race and rollers (known as the cone) transfer axial loads from the shaft directly to the bearing bore through the outer race (known as the cup) without damaging the rollers and races. Tapered roller bearings are most often used in pairs, because the opposing cone angles support each other and allow the two bearings to share the loads on the shaft.

Tapered roller bearings are most common on both ends of the mainshaft and countershaft in heavy-duty rear-wheel-drive transmissions. They absorb the axial forces generated by the helical gears in the transmission, while at the same time keeping the shafts in good radial alignment with their high strength and stiffness. Some transmissions also use a tapered roller bearing between the end of the mainshaft and input shaft. The only disadvantage to tapered roller bearings is slightly increased friction over ball bearings, because the rollers contact a greater combined surface area on the races than do the balls in a ball bearing.

BEARING FITS, CLEARANCE, AND PRELOAD

Ball and roller bearings in manual transmissions are usually installed with the inner race pressed onto the shaft. This makes them difficult to remove, but it makes the gears run more accurately and quietly since the shafts (and thus gears) are more constrained in their locations. In addition, the more perfectly the bearing races fit on their shafts, the more support the races have and the longer the bearings will last. Outer races are sometimes pressed into their housings, but it is more common for them to be a tight "slip fit" into the transmission housing. Snap rings and locating collars machined into the shaft or case locate bearings axially in most transmissions.

With ball and roller bearings that absorb both radial and thrust loads, the way the bearing is installed is important. By controlling the length of the shaft with shims or spacers, or changing the location of a bearing in the transmission housing, bearings can be installed with more or less internal clearance. The greater the internal clearance of a bearing, the more the shaft it supports can move axially. Clearance allows lubrication to get into the bearing elements and lowers friction in the bearing. On the other hand, too much clearance also allows the shaft to move more than necessary and can make the transmission jump out of gear or rattle in neutral.

This assembled synchronizer (the blocking rings have been omitted for clarity) shows the splines on the inside of the sleeve, as well as the three inserts and one spring. This synchronizer is for first and second gear, and the teeth around the outside edge drive the reverse idler gear. The splines in the center of the hub keep the assembly in place on the mainshaft.

Bearing internal clearance can actually be reduced beyond zero. Bearings that can accept axial loads, like ball and tapered roller bearings, actually perform better when they have a slight axial load. This installed pressure is known as preload. This force helps to make the shaft assembly stiffer and somewhat counteracts forces that act on the bearings when the transmission is running. The more preload on the bearings, the stiffer the assembly and the more shock loads will be transferred to the bearing outer races and thus to the transmission case—a tightly preloaded shaft will be stronger than a loosely installed shaft, all else being equal.

Tapered roller and radial contact ball bearings are usually installed with a very small amount of preload to help the bearing last longer. A small preload keeps the bearings in place and helps them cope with thrust and radial forces better without adding unnecessary friction to the transmission.

SYNCHRONIZERS

At the heart of a modern manual transmission are the synchronizers. The synchronizers match the rotating speed of the gear and the shaft so that the gear can be locked to the shaft without grinding. The synchronizer and sleeve also do the work of locking the gear to the shaft so that power can flow through the selected gear pair. All modern transmissions use synchronizers on the forward gears. Most modern transmissions also have reverse gear synchronizers, but they are less effective because synchronizers require rotation to function, and reverse is normally engaged when the vehicle is not moving.

The collars and their hubs are usually splined onto the mainshaft of a rear-wheel-drive transmission, or divided equally between the input and output shafts of a front-wheel-drive transaxle for packaging reasons, although the end result is the same. Setting aside the Porsche-type split ring synchronizers used before the mid-1970s, most transmissions use a variant of the "BorgWarner" cone-type synchronizer. This synchronizer is also sometimes known as the block type, or "baulk ring" synchronizer. Like all synchronizers, it uses friction between the gear and the synchronizer assembly to slow down or speed up the gear that it contacts and allows shifts without grinding.

Synchronizer assemblies consist of the previously mentioned hub and sleeve, as well as a blocking ring (or synchronizer ring), and three inserts or spring-and-ball detents. The outside diameter of the sleeve has a machined groove that the shift fork rides in, and it is a loose sliding fit on the hub splines. The hub has three axial grooves on its outside diameter, which the inserts or detents ride in.

The inserts can slide back and forth in the grooves and have a small ridge on their outside surface. To keep the sliding collars in the neutral position, the insert ridge or detent balls engage a radial groove on the inside of the collar. The inserts are held against this groove by springs. In neutral, the balls or inserts are extended into the groove and increase the force needed to move the collar from the center position.

The important parts of the synchronizer are the blocking rings, which fit between the synchronizer hub and the face teeth of each gear. The inner surfaces of the blocking

The disassembled synchronizer (including blocking rings this time) gives you a better view of (clockwise from right) the two insert springs, all three inserts, the hub, single-cone blocking ring, multicone blocking ring, and the sleeve. This is a pretty typical design, used by dozens of manufacturers around the world.

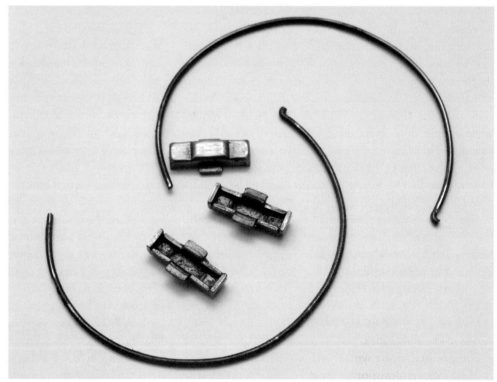

The synchronizer inserts drive the blocking rings—they project into recesses in the outer circumference of the rings. As the transmission is shifted into gear, the inserts push against the rings before the sleeve splines contact the ring. The inserts also provide positive locking action to keep the sleeve engaged with the gear dog teeth. Not all blocking ring synchronizers have inserts—Honda is fond of using an external spring and a few long splines on the hub, for example.

rings are conical and match synchronizer cones on the face of each gear. These surfaces of the blocking ring are the friction surfaces of the synchronizer and do the work of slowing the gear to match the synchronizer speed. Around the outside diameter of the blocking ring are a set of pointed teeth that exactly match the dog teeth on the face of each

gear. These teeth block the sleeve while the gear and synchronizer are still turning at different speeds.

As the synchronizer sleeve is moved toward a gear by the shift forks, the inserts move with the sleeve via the sleeve's internal groove. As the inserts move, they push the blocking ring toward the gear's synchronizer cone. When the

From top: The sleeve with groove, the hub (inside the sleeve), blocking ring, gear dog teeth, and gear teeth. When the shaft and gear are turning at different speeds, there is relative motion between them. When the blocking ring grips the gear cone, it turns slightly and its external splines don't line up with the sleeve's internal splines, as shown here. Once the gear and shaft are turning together from the frictional drag of the blocking ring, the pointed ends of the sleeve splines can push the blocking ring to one side or another and engage the gear dog teeth.

blocking ring makes contact with the film of oil coating the gear's synchronizer cone, the oil film begins to transmit torque to the gear, slowing it down or speeding it up to match the speed of the synchronizer. The drag of the oil film rotates the blocking ring slightly, so its teeth do not align with the internal splines of the sleeve. This prevents it from advancing onto the gear's face teeth.

Continued pressure from the sleeve squeezes the oil out of the space between the synchronizer cone and the gear cone, and the blocking ring contacts the gear to slow it even further. As soon as the speed of the gear and sleeve matches, the chamfered edges of the synchronizer sleeve splines rotate the blocking ring out of the way and continue on to the gear face teeth. At this point, the sleeve's internal groove releases the inserts, and the gear is locked to the shaft through the synchronizer and hub. The synchronizer ring is stuck to the face of the gear and pulls the sleeve into closer contact. The shift fork is no longer contacting the side of the groove around the synchronizer.

When the transmission is shifted out of a gear, the shift fork pulls back on the sleeve, and it simply slides back to the neutral position over the blocking ring. The inserts drop back into their groove, and the gear is again free to rotate independently. When in gear, the sleeve is held in position by the friction between the blocking ring and gear, and in neutral, the inserts or detent balls hold the sleeve centered on the hub. The shift forks and linkage only provide the push to get the transmission into or out of each gear.

BLOCKING RINGS IN DETAIL

Nearly all modern road transmissions and transaxles employ these cone-type blocking ring synchronizers. Cone-type synchros are popular because they are very efficient. The conical shape of the friction surfaces increases the locking force between the cone and gear for a given amount of pushing force from the sleeve. The cone clutch (of which the synchronizer is a variation) is a kind of wedge. A small amount of axial force on the synchronizer ring creates a larger force at the friction surface.

In addition, the conical shape increases surface area over a flat surface, giving the synchronizer better heat resistance. The angle of the cones may be varied, with more angle providing more grip and friction, but possibly less synchronizer life.

The engineering challenge in designing an effective conical synchronizer involves balancing the somewhat opposing demands of squeezing the most friction possible out of a small space and making sure the shift quality stays constant in varying temperatures and driving conditions, and throughout the life of the transmission. This tradeoff is no different from that of clutch or brake friction material design.

Cone-type synchronizers are also common because they are cheap. The technology is well developed, and millions of transmissions already in service use the same type of synchronizers. Traditionally, synchronizer blocking rings were made from brass. The hard material wears well and has frictional characteristics that make it a good choice for such applications.

These three blocking rings are lined with a composite material made from carbon fiber and powdered metal. The lining is bonded to the brass ring through a brazing process. Lined blocking rings have a higher coefficient of friction than unlined blocking rings, and they increase synchronizer efficiency. Some transmissions have available aftermarket or OEM lined blocking rings that can be installed to improve performance.

Compare these plain blocking rings with the ones above. Their inner surface is machined brass. The grooves and channels cut into the inner surface clear the oil film away from the gear's synchronizer cone so that the blocking ring can grip it more tightly. As the sharp edges of the grooves wear down, the synchronization process slows down and the transmission shifts less smoothly.

Recently, however, lined sintered-metal blocking rings have become the most common blocking rings used for new designs. The rings are lined like a brake shoe or automatic transmission clutch plate with phenolic (a kind of plastic reinforced with fibers) or carbon friction material. These blocking rings have a higher coefficient of friction than plain brass rings, so they slow the gear train more quickly for smoother, faster shifts. In addition, the carbon material (carbon fibers embedded in a matrix of carbon) has high heat resistance and wears much better than brass or phenolic.

In order to squeeze more friction surface into the same space, improving shifting and blocking ring life, most modern transmissions have moved to multicone synchronizers on some gears. Instead of a simple toothed conical blocking ring, these synchronizers have a three-part blocking ring assembly. The outer ring has the external teeth and tapered friction surface of a traditional synchronizer ring, but a larger diameter. The middle ring is made from thin steel with several bonded friction pads around its circumference on both the inner and outer surfaces. The edge of this ring

This is a pretty typical three-piece synchronizer blocking ring. The inner brass ring on the right has three recesses around the inner lip that engage the three projections on the outer brass blocking ring. The projections keep the two rings turning at the same speed. The steel friction ring in the middle is driven by the gear through the three projections on the outer lip. This ring takes the place of the gear cone in a single blocking ring synchronizer. Functionally there is no difference between the two types—the multipiece blocking ring simply works better because there is more friction area.

This three-piece blocking ring assembly is designed opposite the one above. The inner and outer cones are made from sintered (powdered and brazed together) steel with no lining. The middle ring has friction surfaces on the inside and outside. The four projections on the middle ring are driven by notches in the face of the gear. The large splines inside the inner cone are driven by splines on the mainshaft. The inner and outer cones are always driven at the same speed, but are not connected as in the assembly above.

has several large fingers that engage matching slots in the face of the gear. The innermost ring is a tapered sintered steel ring with fingers that engage the inner edge of the outer ring.

The speed gears do not leave synchronizer cones like traditional single-cone synchronizer gears, although they have drive notches for the middle friction ring. The benefit of dual-cone synchronizers comes from their dual-sided middle ring. Twice the contact area means nearly twice as much friction will be built up by the same amount of side force, matching gear speed more quickly and allowing for easier shifts.

The multiple surfaces are the downside of dual-cone synchronizers as well. Theoretically, with twice as many surfaces to wear, dual-cone synchronizers would be expected to wear twice as fast, but modern, durable friction materials alleviate this problem.

On the subject of synchronizers, some transmissions have pressed-on synchronizer cones on the speed gears. This makes them easier to repair and saves ruining the gear with

The face dogs on a racing transmission are much, much larger than the fragile dog teeth of a synchronized transmission, and take a lot more abuse. Notice how the engagement "windows" in the slider on the left match up with the dogs—they fit loosely around the dogs and allow for some speed variation between the slider and gear.

a bad blocking ring, but it is more expensive. Most transmissions have gears that are machined in one piece with the synchronizer cones and dog teeth.

DOG RINGS

A synchronizer delays each shift very slightly as the gear train is accelerated or decelerated, and while this delay is nearly imperceptible, this is one of the reasons true racing transmissions do not use them. Instead, the gears and shift collars have larger, stronger dog teeth that lock positively with no synchronization. Compared to synchronizer dog teeth, the dogs in a dog ring transmission are much more resistant to wear and breakage. The dogs are larger than the dog teeth on a synchromesh gear, so they can absorb more force without damage. Also, since they are larger, it takes more wear to affect their functioning. Dog ring–shifted or nonsynchromesh transmissions are not really suited for street driving—they can only be shifted quickly and firmly and can be downshifted only by double-clutching to match the input and output shaft speeds.

The dog teeth on the gears of a dog ring transmission are called face dogs. The spaces between the matching teeth

on the shift collars are wider than the face dogs, which allows the dog teeth to mesh even while there is some variation in shaft speed. The shape of the teeth in top profile (that is, looking down on the two parallel gear shafts) can be varied to suit different kinds of racing. In drag racing, for example, the teeth may be machined on an angle away from the direction the gear is turning (called "back cut" dogs)—since the transmission is not designed to be downshifted, the dog teeth and sliders are optimized to stay in gear under power. For road or oval tracks, the dogs are often back-cut on both sides to keep the transmission from popping out of gear during downshifts.

Dog rings are essentially the same thing as a synchronizer sleeve, and they are commonly used in street car transmission conversions for racing since it is easy for the designer to replace the synchronizer assemblies with a set of dogs and splined rings. The shift sleeves in a nonsynchronizer transmission can be made much narrower and each gear wider since there is no need for synchronizer cones, springs, and inserts. This makes the gears stronger. This type of conversion allows the converted transmission to use the same linkage and shafts as the donor. The dog rings can have either

These two gears and their dog ring are from a racing conversion for a Mitsubishi street transmission. Notice that the slider is significantly thinner than a synchronizer and sleeve. This means that each gear can be made wider, which makes the teeth stronger. Also notice that the gears are straight spur gears—these would likely be too noisy for street use.

mirror-image face dogs to mesh with the gear dogs or recesses that fit over the face dogs on the gears. Generally, the internal dog rings are most commonly used in dedicated transverse racing and motorcycle-type transmissions in order to reduce the total length of the stack of gears. This correlates with a narrower transmission case and is very desirable from a packaging standpoint in many race cars. Motorcycle transmissions often use circular dogs, but the higher-torque demands of automotive engines and the relatively higher weight of an automotive drivetrain make them too weak to use in a racing transmission.

SHIFTING MECHANISMS

Normally, two adjacent gears on a transmission shaft share the same synchronizer assembly and shift fork. Of course, there is no requirement that the synchronizers be shared this way, but it is cheaper and easier to build street transmissions with the least number of synchronizers possible since that also reduces the number of shift forks and control linkages needed. Since only one gear will ever be engaged at a time, there is no need for each gear to have its own engagement system.

Shift forks (also sometimes called shifter forks) move the sliders into engagement with each gear in a manual transmission. The forks' rubbing on the grooves in the synchronizer sleeves creates friction and wear. To reduce the friction and make them live longer, most street transmissions have

shift forks made of brass or soft steel. In addition, the forks are sometimes machined with small wear pads on the ends of each fork arm. The wear pads take most of the abuse. Some transmissions' shift forks have plastic inserts that serve as wear pads. The plastic inserts wear more quickly than steel would, but they are easy to replace and reduce friction against the synchronizer sleeve.

Generally, shift forks are mounted on shift rails in the transmission. The shift rails move the forks axially to shift gears. On some older manual transmissions, the shift forks

Shift forks sometimes have wear pads on the tips. The pads wear more quickly than a steel shift fork might, but they prevent galling of the synchronizer sleeve and are cheaper to replace than an entire fork.

Shift forks are usually mounted to some kind of shift rails. This clearly shows the grooves for the detent springs that keep the rail (and thus fork) in each of its three positions. At the other end of the shift rail are shift fingers that allow the linkage and interlock to operate each rail in turn.

A hardened steel ball and spring like these bear against a groove or dent in the shift rails shown above. This gives the shifter a positive "detent" that keeps the transmission in gear and lets the driver know that a gear has been selected. Some detents are found in blind holes, but the one shown here has a separate plug in the side of the case.

were mounted in short levers in the side cover, and the operating linkage was mounted on the outside of the case. For the most part, modern rear-wheel-drive transmissions have internal shift rails and linkage, except for some drag-racing and circle-track-only designs. Front-wheel-drive transaxles have external shift controls, but the rails and forks are internal.

While the details of internal shift mechanisms vary, there are at least two common elements necessary for quick and safe gear selection. The first are positive detents to keep the shift linkage aligned and prevent the forks from rubbing against the sides of the synchronizer sleeves. Most detents are the ball-and-spring type, with a steel ball pressed against a groove in the shift rails by a spring and retainer. Detents

do not keep the transmission in gear under power. With insert-type synchronizers, the inserts act as positive detents holding the synchronizer sleeves engaged with each gear. Nonsynchronized transmissions need detents to prevent the shift forks and rails from moving and disengaging the sleeve from the gear dog teeth under engine braking (the dogs are back-cut to hold them together under power).

The second important part of an internal shift linkage is some kind of mechanical interlock that prevents two gears from being selected at the same time. If the transmission is in a gear, the interlock does not allow shifting into another gear. There are a number of different interlocks in common use, some using ball-and-spring detents with a sleeve to hold the balls apart, or a flat detent key that drops into slots in the shift rails in each gear.

REMOTE SHIFTERS

When the transmission is front- or rear-mounted, some kind of external shift linkage is necessary. There are two general types of shift linkage—rod-operated and cable-operated.

Rod-operated transmissions have a shift linkage that connects to the shift lever through a system of rods and joints. This is the most direct system, since it gives the driver better feedback from the transmission's internal shift linkage.

The drawbacks of the rod-operated shift linkage are the amount of space that the system takes up, the wear that occurs at each pivot, and the vibrations and noise that are transmitted from the transmission to the shifter. As each pivot or bushing wears, the shifting gets looser and more difficult, and the solid steel rods are very good at transmitting noise and vibration to the passenger compartment of a road car.

Cable-operated remote shifters are controlled by a lever and cable stops mounted near the driver. Two thick cables

All shift linkages incorporate some way of ensuring that more than one gear cannot be selected at the same time. This Honda interlock has two parts—a shift selector finger that moves the shift rail and fork, and a sheet-metal interlock that prevents the other two shift forks from moving. The interlock also prevents the finger from selecting a gear if any of the shift rails is moved from the neutral position. This eliminates the possibility of a bent or damaged shift linkage destroying the transmission.

travel from the lever to the transaxle: one for the forward and back motions of the shifter and the other for the left and right motions of the shifter. The cables are stiff in compression and tension, but flexible enough to allow the engine to rock on its mountings and prevent vibration from entering the passenger compartment.

Cable shift linkages have a significant disadvantage in precision and shifting "feel," however. With each movement of the shift lever the cables bend more than the equivalent rod linkage would, which absorbs some of the movement of the shift lever and makes each shift less precise from the standpoint of the driver.

Race cars with remote-mounted shifters nearly always have a solid, direct shift linkage connection to the transaxle. The stiffer the shift linkage—from the driver's perspective—the better, since each shift is easier to control, and less force is required to complete each shift.

SEQUENTIAL SHIFT LINKAGES

Motorcycle transmissions and sequential transmissions used in some formula cars make use of a different scheme for actuating the forks and changing gears. In these transmissions, a complex machined drum engages each gear in turn. Each fork is moved by a follower that rides in a groove machined into the drum. The grooves are shaped so that as the drum is rotated, it moves one fork into engagement and the opposing fork(s) out of engagement. The drum is

rotated by a pair of ratchets that allow a single lever to turn the drum forward (down a gear) and backward (up a gear).

In some racing series like Formula 1, this technology has been taken a step further—an electrical, hydraulic, or pneumatic (air-operated) actuator turns the drum to select gears far faster and more precisely than a human can. The "paddle shifters" popular in F1 work this way: One paddle instructs the actuator to move the drum clockwise and the other moves it counterclockwise. An electronic control unit controls the timing of the shift actuator when the driver requests a shift.

A drum is a very fast and precise method of changing gears, but it does have some drawbacks. Chief among these are wear and drivability issues. As the groove in the drum wears, more friction occurs between the shift forks and the drum, and the more effort it takes to turn the drum. Also, as the clearances between the fork and drum increase, shifts become less and less precise. If the clearances get large enough, the slop can cause the gears to crash between shifts.

The shift pattern and incompatibility with synchronizers make drum-shift or sequential transmissions difficult to use for street applications. In a sequential transmission, each gear can only be selected in turn and cannot be skipped, since the drum can only turn from gear to gear. Neutral is at the "bottom" of the shift pattern, before first gear. Most drivers (unless they are familiar with motorcycle practice) would not be happy with a transmission that cannot be shifted directly into neutral from any gear. In addition, it would be very difficult to add synchronizers to a sequential transmission. The drum forces each shift fork into gear indiscriminately—there is no slop in the system to allow the synchronizer time to slow the gear or shaft.

RACING SHIFTERS

Dedicated drag and circle-track racing transmissions usually have simple, nonsequential shifters with external rod linkages. Shifters can either be H-pattern units with an external control, mounted on the extension housing, or have multiple levers controlling individual forks. With individual levers, one lever shifts from first to second and another lever from third to fourth (assuming the box has four speeds). This makes the linkage simple, stiff, and reliable. Each shift can also be made faster since the driver does not have to move the lever sideways to shift into third.

Sometimes each gear has its own fork and slider, to make shift linkage design easier and shifting faster. These transmissions (like the G-force and Lenco units) also have optional pneumatic shift linkages, with an air cylinder for each gear. A "black box," or air-distribution manifold, sorts out the shift order and speed. An air-shifted dog ring transmission can shift extremely fast, since each dog does not have to pass through the neutral position to engage the next gear. As one dog becomes disengaged, the next is already in position. The slight overlap eliminates all delay in each shift.

FINAL DRIVES

In a rear-wheel drive, four-wheel drive, or any car with an inline-mounted engine, the final drive both changes the direction of the power flow and adds further gear reduction to the powertrain. This is usually done through a special set of helical gears known as hypoid gears, which have tapered helical teeth on both the pinion and ring gear. Vehicles with transverse-mounted engines do not need hypoid gears since there is no need for the power flow to change direction. Interestingly, nearly all of the hypoid gears in use today are cut using machines and technology from the Gleason Corporation, who invented this gear form in the 1930s.

Hypoid gears are used because their gradual tooth engagement makes them quiet, like helical gears, and their geometry allows the pinion to be located above or below the center of the ring gear. In a rear-wheel-drive powertrain, this allows for a lower driveshaft, which leads to a lower center of gravity and more space in the driveshaft tunnel. In a longitudinal front-wheel-drive or midengine powertrain, hypoid gears allow the transaxle input shaft to be above or below the axles, making packaging easier for the vehicle designer.

Hypoid gear strength comes from the same factors described above, but instead of center distance and gear width, the important measurement is ring gear diameter. Hypoid pinion gears have geometric limits on the width of each tooth (for a given reduction ratio and hypoid angle), so the only way to make larger teeth is to increase the size of both gears. The larger the diameter of the ring gear, the larger each tooth on the pinion can be made.

Hypoid gear strength is also affected by the angle of the gear teeth on the pinion. The hypoid angle of the teeth on the ring gear is indirectly related to the distance from the ring gear centerline and the centerline of the pinion gear. The closer the pinion is to the centerline of the ring gear, the less hypoid angle and the more efficient the gear set. Higher-angle teeth are stronger, but they consume more power and generate more heat than low-angle teeth.

Some commonly used designs (including the Ford 9-inch and various Porsche/VW transaxles) have very high hypoid angles and can cause significant power loss. Many racing transaxles (including the leading Formula 1 designs), on the other hand, reduce power loss by eliminating hypoid gears and using straight-cut bevel gearing to change the direction of power, with a secondary gear reduction achieved through parallel final drive spur gears.

The ring gear is mounted to the differential with a few bolts around its diameter, while the pinion rotates in opposing tapered roller bearings to absorb the axial thrust loads that are generated by hypoid gears. The differential is also usually supported by opposing tapered roller bearings, since the loads on these bearings are very high (cornering loads from the tires and wheels are absorbed in these bearings).

LUBRICATION

The most important part of a manual transmission—the lubricating oil—is probably the least considered and certainly the least understood. The lubricant, by keeping the gears wear-free and cool, impacts transmission life, synchronizer performance, noise, temperature, and power-handling ability. That is a lot to ask from a simple lubricant, so modern gear oils have been developed as a complex blend of various additives and base oils to improve their overall performance.

Although at one time it was almost universal, not all manual transmissions are filled with gear oil. Factory fill in a modern gearbox can be automatic transmission fluid, gear oil, engine oil, or a specially formulated lubricant. In each case, lubrication needs vary depending on the unit's internal design, synchronizer material, and intended use—delivery-truck transmissions require stronger lubricant than car transmissions, for example.

Commercially available automotive lubricants are usually categorized according to viscosity (a measure of pouring thickness) as well as standards set by the American Petroleum Institute (API). The viscosity numbers refer to Society of Automotive Engineers (SAE) categories of thickness at certain oil temperatures, and the API standards tell the consumer about the proper application for a given oil. Engine oil viscosity uses a different system than transmission gear lube, so the numbers are not directly comparable. 30w crankcase oil has approximately the same viscosity as 85w gear oil, for example.

LUBRICANT FILM THICKNESS

The most important factor when talking about lubrication is oil film thickness, more properly known as "elastohydrodynamic lubricant" (EHL) film thickness. This simply refers to the properties of the oil film that prevent wear and friction between metal surfaces. Oil does this by flowing over and sticking to those surfaces, separating them from each other and allowing them to move without actually touching. The EHL film thickness varies with several factors, but the most important are the oil viscosity, base stock (mineral or synthetic), temperature, and the pressure between the two parts in contact.

A thin EHL film increases the rate of gear wear because it is easily squeezed out of the space between two gear teeth by pressure, allowing metal-to-metal contact more often than a thick film. The slower the gears turn, the longer the sliding contact and the more pressure squeezing the film out from between the gear teeth. Microscopic lumps and roughness on the surface of each tooth (known as asperities) break through a thin EHL film and can contact similar asperities on the mating part.

The asperities "microweld" together from the frictional heat that is developed by sliding gear contact, and tear apart as the gear teeth move out of contact. This damages the tooth surface and encourages the development of small pits (micropits) and cracks. The cracks reduce the fatigue life of gear teeth by propagating through the gear (from the constant stresses) until they get under the surface case hardening and the tooth fails. With thick EHL films, small asperities on each tooth surface do not have as much of a chance to contact one another, and the small pits that do develop are much less likely to develop into larger pits or cracks.

The vitally important EHL film thickness varies significantly with the viscosity of the oil. High-viscosity (thick) oils generally have thicker EHL film thicknesses than thin oils of the same formulation and temperature. As with everything else in engineering, however, there are tradeoffs with high-viscosity lubricating oils. High-viscosity oils

cause drag on the transmission gears, which robs engine power, creates heat, and decreases fuel mileage. Today's manufacturers use thinner lubricants to help reduce power loss and increase fuel mileage, but most older transmissions specify fairly thick lubricants.

As the temperature of the gear teeth and oil increases, the viscosity (and thus EHL film thickness) decreases, and the advantage of the thicker oil begins to disappear. More viscosity results in higher temperatures, which results in thinner EHL film thicknesses. Because they run hotter, transmissions with high torque transfer requirements and slow gear speeds require thicker oil than light-duty transmissions for the maximum possible EHL thickness under their usual operating conditions.

OIL BASES

All automotive lubricants are formulated starting with a "base stock" of plain oil, either mineral or synthetic. Mineral oil comes from crude oil that is pumped out of the ground and refined, while synthetic oil is chemically manufactured from base molecules. Synthetic base stocks have advantages over natural oil base stocks, but there are many different kinds of synthetic and it is not always easy to tell which kind is sold by a particular company.

Of the more common synthetic oil bases, the ester (E), polyglycol (PAG), and polyalphaolefin (PAO) bases are more expensive and have more of the positive qualities associated with synthetic oils. Of the three, PAG has a slight, though disputed, edge. Petroleum-based synthetic bases (like those used in some "synthetic" motor oils) are cheaper, however, and have better lubricating properties than nonsynthetic bases.

All synthetic oils tend to stabilize the relationship between viscosity and EHL film thickness, and they require less compromise in viscosity to achieve the required EHL film thickness. They tend to have thicker, more stable EHL films than mineral oils of the same viscosity, and their viscosity and EHL film thickness change much less with temperature. This means that a synthetic oil with lower viscosity should protect the gear teeth as well as a high-viscosity mineral oil, while at the same time reducing power loss and heat production.

Viscosity-modifying additives are usually added to mineral oil bases to reduce the EHL film thickness variation with temperature. Yet the viscosity/temperature/EHL film thickness relationship rarely approaches that of a good PAG synthetic oil. The biggest advantage of mineral oil lubricants is their cost—if cost is an issue and the extra performance of synthetic oil is not necessary, mineral lubricants are usually chosen.

COMMON MANUAL TRANSMISSION LUBRICANTS

API GL-4

American Petroleum Institute (API) performance specification for lubricating oil for manual transmissions and transaxles. Does not have the high levels of AW additives needed for a hypoid final drive gear. This is the preferred lubricant for manual transaxles because the lower additives level allows synchronizers to work more efficiently.

API GL-5

API performance specification for lubricating oil for hypoid final drive gears. Has approximately double the AW additives of GL-4. Should not be used in place of GL-4 in manual transaxles since it will degrade synchronizer performance and may lead to increased blocking ring wear. This is the preferred lubricant for dog ring–shifted transmissions without synchronizers.

API GL-1 to 3

Obsolete API classifications for gear lubricant with minimal levels of AW additives. Generally only used in some tractor and farm implement gear change boxes or other industrial applications. Should not be used in any automotive transmission.

API SH/SL (Engine Oil)

Engine oil is classified under a different set of standards than gear oil. Generally has only a low percentage of AW additives. Some manufacturers recommend engine oil as transmission fill (Honda, for example), but generally the same transmissions will wear much longer with a lightweight, synthetic GL-4 gear oil.

Automatic Transmission Fluid (Dexron/Mercon/Type F)

Special fluid designed for the needs of hydraulically operated automatic transmissions. Different manufacturers have different specifications. ATF has a significant percentage of friction modifiers to help the clutch plates in an automatic transmission, as well as AW additives to reduce wear to the planetary gear train. ATF is recommended by TREMEC for the T-5, and people have successfully used it in other manual transmissions. Do not use it in differentials with hypoid gears—there are not enough AW additives for this demanding application.

"Synchromesh" fluid

This is a special transmission fluid designed for certain manual transaxles and transmissions used by General Motors and Chrysler. It has EP wear additives yet is formulated to be kind to yellow metals as used in synchronizer blocking rings. The base stock is essentially motor oil; it is not synthetic. Synchromesh fluid works very well in non-GM or Chrysler transmissions, although it is not recommended for them. You can also buy it at GM dealers under Part No. 12345349 or 12345577. Chrylser dealers know it as Part No. 4874464.

OIL ADDITIVES

The API standards for lubricants do not depend on the viscosity or base oil; they can be met by many different formulations and each manufacturer has a proprietary oil "recipe." Oils of any base can be formulated to meet a particular API standard by adding a different mixture of chemical additives. The most common API oil classifications for gear oil (as opposed to Automatic Transmission Fluid or motor crankcase oil) are GL-4 and GL-5. Both contain a significant percentage of so-called Extreme Pressure (EP) additives, although they differ mainly in the percentage of these additives.

EP additives make thinner EHL film thicknesses less important, since they use chemical and mechanical action to protect metal surfaces from one another. Most EP additives are composed of chemically reactive compounds of sulfur, phosphorus, and sometimes chlorine that bond with the base metal to form the protective film. They adhere to the base metal under conditions of high pressure and heat, which occur between the asperities on two metal surfaces.

The deposits formed by EP additives are softer and smoother than the underlying metal, so they wear first, which protects the metal during extreme pressure conditions. In addition, EP additives encourage the metal parts to become smoother and polished over time by their chemical and mechanical action. These compounds give gear oil its characteristically bad smell. Chemical EP additives are generally corrosive to so-called yellow metals such as brass, copper, and bronze.

Some EP additives are not chemically reactive. Rather, they are solid particles that protect the metal surfaces by adhering to them without forming strong chemical bonds. Molybdenum disulfide (also known as "moly"), borate, graphite, and fluorinated polymers (e.g., Teflon) are all commonly used nonreactive solid EP additives. Solid EP additives are less corrosive than standard EP additives, which has advantages in some applications.

The problem with EP additives is their effect on synchronizers. Active EP additives corrode brass blocking rings and can degrade synchronizer performance. The same properties that make them necessary for lubricating gears make them bad at promoting synchronizer action. Inactive and solid EP additives do not corrode brass blocking rings, but they do tend to make the oil too slick, so the blocking rings have trouble gripping the gear cones to slow the gears. API GL-4 gear oil is formulated for just this purpose. Gear oils in this classification contain enough EP additives to combat wear and damage to helical transmission gears without negatively impacting synchronizer action.

Hypoid gears, like those found in rear axles, require a different oil formulation. The teeth of hypoid gears slide across one another more than the teeth of simple helical gears at the same angle, so lubrication is very important. The sliding contact produces high contact pressure that tends to wipe the oil off the teeth of each gear, flattening the EHL film. The high pressure and thin film require more EP additives than transmission gear oil. GL-5 is the API oil classification for lubricant formulated for hypoid axles, and using it in a transmission that calls for GL-4 oil is a recipe for poor shifting and bad synchronizer performance because of the EP additives.

PUMPS AND COOLING

The vast majority of manual transmissions used in street cars are "splash lubricated." The gears and bearings are lubricated by an oil mist flung around by the spinning gears that contact the surface of the oil reservoir in the bottom of the transmission case. In some designs, small catch wells are set up in strategic locations to funnel the splashed oil to important parts of the transmission like the input and output shaft bearings.

Some street transmissions are pressure-lubricated, with a pump located along one of the shafts. Pressure-lubrication increases transmission bearing life, although the pump robs some power from the engine. Manual transmission pumps are generally gear-rotor pumps like an engine oil pump, but they are designed with larger internal clearances. Small chips and flakes of steel from the gears and bearings in a transmission pass through the pump, which must have enough internal clearance to pass them without damage. The output from the oil pump is usually directed down the shafts to the transmission bearings and gears. Sometimes small spray nozzles are pointed at each gear to keep them lubricated and cool. Transmissions, transaxles, and final drive units used in racing usually incorporate some kind of pump, whether external and electrically driven, or internal.

The heat produced by helical gears is radiated into the oil, which in turn carries the heat to the case. In street transmissions, this cooling path works pretty well—the transmission case absorbs the heat and is cooled by the air flowing past it. Race cars and some high-performance street cars require more cooling than this simple radiant system can provide. For better cooling, they incorporate a small air-to-oil heat exchanger (a.k.a. radiator) in the oil circulation system. Of course, this also requires an oil pump and fluid plumbing.

The two drilled holes in this section of shaft (part of a Honda pinion shaft) are for lubrication purposes. Oil thrown up by the gear teeth dipping into the oil reservoir at the bottom of the case is collected by special metal scrapers and directed to the center of the shaft. From there, drilled holes like these ensure that the gear hub bearings and synchronizers get all the oil they need.

CHAPTER 3
PROBLEMS AND DIAGNOSES

Gears are inherently reliable mechanisms, but like all mechanical things, transmissions eventually wear out. Unlike automatic transmissions, however, total failure is unlikely unless some other contributing factor is at play, such as a lack of oil, racing, or abuse. Noise, leaks, and hard shifting are much more common complaints, but most transmission problems actually stem from related external parts, including the driveshafts, shift linkage, and clutch.

Any of these is more likely to be a source of trouble than the transmission itself, and they can cause serious internal problems if they are not caught right away. An ignored clutch problem, for example, can lead to damaged synchronizers, while bent linkage rods or cables can result in bent shift forks inside the transmission.

Because fixing a worn linkage is a lot easier than pulling a good transmission, the first step in diagnosing any noise, shifting problem, or other transmission difficulty is to check those parts located outside the transmission. The second step is to check the oil level, because unlike engines, transmissions do not usually have dip sticks and oil lights.

One of the most common causes of transmission failure is lack of lubrication or improper lubrication. Even if you normally run something different from what the manufacturer recommends, fill the transmission with a fresh load of the recommended stuff and warm it up before doing any diagnosis. Knowing that the transmission has enough of the right kind of oil will prevent a lot of frustration and possible catastrophic failure.

NOISE

Noise is the first warning sign of a transmission problem and a good signal of impending troubles in most other parts of the drivetrain too. Small noises turn into larger ones, and ignoring them can result in broken parts. Despite this progression from harmless noise to harmful failure, transmissions are remarkably sturdy—they can howl and grind for many, many miles before they fail completely. The sooner the problem is caught and repaired, however, the better: fewer parts will be affected and any repairs will be less expensive.

Bearing, gear, and shaft wear are the most common causes of noise. As gear tooth faces and bearing races wear, they develop grooves and small pits that are nearly micro-

scopic at first and gradually become larger. As they grow, these small surface imperfections cause more and more noise. Ball and roller bearings are the most susceptible, with their tight internal clearances, but other parts can cause just as much noise. Until you've experienced it, it's hard to appreciate the amount of noise that a failing bearing or gear can make.

Every mechanical device is going to make some kind of noise, particularly one with as many moving parts as a manual transmission. Some of these noises are normal and some are not —the key to diagnosing transmission trouble is separating the normal noises from the abnormal ones. Unfortunately, all the descriptions in the world won't help your accuracy. The way one person hears a sound is very different from the way another person hears the same sound, so written descriptions can give you little more than a guideline to diagnosing the source of the problem. While the noise descriptions given below can be helpful, there really is no substitute for an experienced ear.

Some of the experience comes from a general familiarity with mechanical things—the more accustomed you are to

Bearing races that look like this cause horrendous amounts of noise. This one happens to be from a countershaft bearing—it made a low-pitched grinding noise as though there were a handful of rocks inside the transmission case. The damage appears to be flaking (called "spalling" in bearing terminology) caused by water in the lubricant. The water corroded the surface of the bearing and normal wear tore off flakes of rusted metal to leave the pattern shown.

The underside of your car is another place to check for strange noises, drive problems, and vibration. Front-wheel-drive CV joints, in particular, have a habit of failing in noisy ways that are often confused with transmission noises. Check them out by driving the car in tight circles before you give up and remove the transmission.

the sounds that any mechanism makes, the better you will be at diagnosing transmission sounds. The process of elimination is the same in any case. Keep your ears open and rule out wrong answers and you can't go wrong. If all else fails and you are having trouble identifying a strange noise, find a helpful ear in a local mechanic or racer, and ask for a second opinion.

There are several types of drivetrain noise with different causes and symptoms, and determining the likely source can be a pain. Always verify that the noises are coming from the transmission and not from some other part of the car. Sources of noise close enough to the transmission to cause confusion include broken or collapsed motor mounts, clicking CV joints, a loose flywheel, or bad driveshaft U-joints. Other undercar noises (such as from a loose exhaust or even bad wheel bearings) can appear to originate in the transmission. Hypoid final drives are a common source of noises, so make sure that you have ruled out the rear end in a rear-wheel-drive car before assuming a problem with the transmission.

Sometimes it can be very difficult to isolate the source of a particular sound. To help track down the noisy parts, take careful notes while you diagnose any drivetrain problems. Note whether the sound occurs when the car is moving or stationary, or if it only occurs when the engine is running. See the sidebar in this chapter for a step-by-step

procedure for isolating and diagnosing each internal part of the transmission in turn.

The most common transmission noises are described below in more detail, along with the most likely causes and conditions for each.

CLICKING AND CLACKING

Many transmissions make a slight rattling or knocking noise while the engine is running and the car is stationary with the transmission in neutral and the clutch out. The noise sounds like rocks being lightly shaken around inside a container, or like faint metallic tapping. The noise usually only occurs while the engine is idling and goes away as soon as any torque is transmitted through the transmission.

The rattling or knocking sound is caused by individual gear teeth inside the transmission knocking back and forth with no load on them. Since there is no torque being transmitted (neither drive torque from the engine nor braking torque from the wheels), there is no force keeping the teeth of each opposing gear tight against the teeth on its mate. The teeth rattle back and forth, causing the noise. The more space (known as backlash) between the gears, the more noise. Larger gears inherently require more backlash than smaller gears, so transmissions with large center distances and large gears are noisier than small transmissions.

43

A gear with a tooth that looks like this might make an annoying tapping or clicking sound as power is transmitted through this gear. It's unlikely to cause much noise in other gears, or when in neutral, however. You could probably reuse a gear like this, as long as the edges of the damaged tooth are not sharp.

The bad news about gear rattle is that there is no cure. Rebuilding the transmission is unlikely to make any difference. The noise is simply the result of clearance between the teeth of each speed gear, and there is no way to eliminate it, short of selecting pairs of gears that mesh with the least amount of backlash with the given shaft center distance. The good news about gear rattle is that it is harmless. Gear rattle does not indicate a more serious problem with the transmission, and it will not cause any problems by itself.

Gear rattle occurs only during idle. Tapping or knocking while the car is in gear and moving is likely caused by a more serious problem with the transmission. A gear with one broken or bent tooth will make a light clicking noise when that gear is selected, and a lighter, tapping noise when the transmission is in neutral. A broken or bent tooth will cause knocking and tapping that gets louder as more power is transmitted through the gear pair.

A sound like gear rattle in some cars is actually from the flywheel. One way that car manufacturers reduce drivetrain noise and isolate engine torque spikes is through dual-mass flywheels. Dual-mass flywheels are made in two parts. The outer ring of the flywheel is a heavy weight that is separate from the flywheel's hub, mounted to the end of the crankshaft. Between the hub and outer weight are springs or rubber blocks that dampen drivetrain torsional vibrations. This is similar in function to the sprung hub of some clutch discs.

This setup works well until the parts start to wear. The constant movement between the inner and outer parts of the flywheel wears away metal until play develops in the pivots. Play in the pivots allows the outer ring to rattle back and forth, creating noise at idle. The clacking noise from a worn dual-mass flywheel sounds suspiciously like gear rattle, although at a lower frequency. This problem is common on newer BMWs, as well as Corvettes, the manual-transmission Cadillac CTS, some Nissans, Ford diesel pickups, and a few others.

The only cure for a worn dual-mass flywheel is replacement. Most are riveted together and are not designed to be disassembled and rebuilt. A solid flywheel can be used in some cases, but this may increase gear rattle and drivetrain noise. Whenever replacing a dual-mass flywheel with a solid one, be sure to replace the solid clutch disc with a sprung-hub part. Without any springs to absorb torsional vibrations, the transmission may have problems with gear and bearing damage.

While on the subject of loud clicking noises, a clicking noise while driving is almost always from CV joints if the car is four-wheel drive or rear-wheel drive with independent rear suspension. To test this, make a low-speed turn. Bad CV joints will become louder while the wheels are turned and the joints are at their most extended, with no noise in a straight line.

continued on page 48

EXTENDING TRANSMISSION LIFE

Although it sounds like a cliché, the durability and long-term performance of a manual transmission depend significantly on how it is treated. If you insist on not changing the oil, powershifting the gearbox through the gears, and dumping the clutch from every stop, don't be surprised when your transmission gives up the ghost after only a few thousand miles. Any street transmission can last for 200,000 miles if it is properly cared for and driven with at least a hint of respect.

Maintenance is crucial to long life. No matter what the manufacturer claims, transmission oil must be changed at some point during the life of the vehicle. Bearings, gears, and synchronizers like clean, fresh oil.

Although many manufacturers recommend oil changes as infrequently as every 50,000 to 100,000 miles, this interval varies somewhat with the load placed on the transmission and the service life expected from the bearings. A daily driven car with street tires and a stock engine can easily get away with long oil-change intervals, but the harder the use, the shorter the expected transmission lifespan for a given oil-change interval. If the transmission sees much track use, changing the oil at least yearly, or every 15,000 miles or so, will significantly extend the useful operating life of the gears and bearings. The old axiom, "Changing oil is cheaper than changing parts," still holds for manual transmissions—as well as anything else.

The second part of maintenance is checking the adjustment of the clutch and external shift linkage. A clutch that does not release completely is one of the most frequent causes of excessive wear and bad transmission performance. If the clutch does not release fully, the synchronizers have to fight the clutch drag and will wear much faster, if they can work at all. For this reason, check clutch adjustment frequently and make sure that the cable, pushrod, or hydraulic system is in good shape and properly adjusted. The same goes for external shift linkage—check it every time you check the clutch.

The second aspect of proper transmission treatment is shifting technique. The easier you make the synchronizers' job, the better. Synchronizers wear a little with each shift. The greater the speed difference between the gear and shaft, the more they wear. To extend the life of your synchronizers, push the clutch all the way in with each shift, and shift firmly but gently—don't bang into the stops on every shift. The synchronization process takes

only a fraction of a second to complete, and forcing a shift before the blocking rings have gripped the gear cone will cause the gear and sleeve to bang together and wear out.

It isn't necessary to "double-clutch" on every downshift, but a quick tap on the throttle pedal while the clutch is in can go a long way toward reducing the speed differential between the input shaft and gears. To pull this off takes some practice, but the rewards in transmission life and reduced maintenance are worth it. The entire subject of downshifting on the street is somewhat controversial—most cars have plenty of braking power to slow the car before entering a turn, and some people never downshift when coming to a stop to save wear on the transmission and clutch.

It should go without saying that if you want your stock transmission to live, avoid drag racing at all costs, especially if you have a rear-wheel-drive car with a lightweight transmission. The shock loads resulting from a dumped clutch can be high enough to rip the teeth right off the gears. A transmission strong enough to survive thousands of miles of road racing (assuming flying starts) will be much too light for drag racing with any kind of reliability.

Some cars (the Lancer EVO comes to mind) actually have transmission protection built into the clutch hydraulic system. A small-diameter restrictor in the clutch line on these cars slows the rate at which hydraulic fluid returns to the master cylinder, which in turn slows the release of the slave cylinder and clutch fork. Since the clutch cannot release quickly, it slips slightly and acts as a "fuse," dissipating some of the power that might otherwise shock the transmission. Of course, this reduces clutch service life somewhat, but clutch plates are cheaper than transmission gears and driveshafts. Take a lesson from the Mitsubishi engineers—a slipped-clutch start won't be as dramatic, but it will keep your transmission alive much longer.

All of this only applies if you aren't racing. If you're on a track, anything goes as long as you get to the finish line without breaking anything. Race transmissions should have frequent fluid changes, at least as often as the engine, or every other race weekend. This also helps you keep an eye on the level of metal chips in the oil—when you start seeing large flakes, it's time to pull the cover and check on the gears. Nonsynchronized transmissions can take a

continued on next page

lot of abuse. The proper shifting technique for a dog ring box is exactly the opposite of a synchronized transmission. Shift quickly and positively. Do not hesitate—the dogs do not have a varying engagement point the way synchronizers do.

There are two ways to shift a dog ring trans-mission—with the clutch and without. Without using the clutch is the faster way. To upshift, start by resting your hand on the lever and applying slight pressure away from the gate toward the next gear. Release the throttle slightly to disengage the dogs and drop the lever into the next gear as quickly as you possibly can. Get on the throttle as soon as the linkage hits the stop. This will lock the dogs together and keep the transmission from jumping out of gear.

Downshifting requires matching the engine rpm with the gear you are going into. This usually requires the clutch, but it can be done without. The procedure is to press the clutch and drop the transmission into neutral as you come into the corner. Keep pressure on the brake pedal, but roll the ball of your foot over to blip the throttle. As the engine revs come up, slot the lever into the lower gear and release the clutch. Done properly, there will be no lurch or change in the car's attitude in the corner. Apply power and accelerate away from the apex.

One additional, often-ignored caveat applies to all manual transmission–equipped vehicles—avoid towing with the drive wheels on the ground for long distances. The mainshaft and its bearings are designed to be lubricated by the oil thrown onto them from the rotating countershaft (in a rear-wheel-drive transmission) or final drive (in a front-wheel-drive transmission). When a car is towed with the transmission in neutral and the engine off, the countershaft is not turning. The mainshaft bearings are therefore not receiving sufficient lubricant, and they will eventually fail from the heat and scant lubrication. Front-wheel-drive transaxles are less sensitive to this problem, but the small needle bearings in the hub of each gear are just not designed for extended periods of constant, high-speed rotation. Short distances (10 miles or so) at low speed are no problem, but very long tows should be avoided.

TRANSMISSION NOISE — ISOLATION AND DIAGNOSIS

With the exception of an obvious total failure, careful testing is necessary to diagnose transmission problems (or any other problem, for that matter). Before jumping to a conclusion about the cause of a transmission or final drive problem, try to use the process of deduction to isolate and locate the source of the problem. Since most manual transmission problems start with a noise of some kind, the first step in diagnosis is isolating each part of the transmission in turn and listening for the noise by testing the transmission under different operating conditions. An accurate assessment of where a sound is coming from is incredibly useful when it comes time to disassemble the transmission and repair or rebuild it.

The following step-by-step guide demonstrates one way of seeking out various whining, howling, growling, and grinding noises. These are the most difficult noises to track down and diagnose because they tend to travel through the transmission and gear shifter into the passenger compartment. Since they can be indistinguishable, these noises require careful testing to separate.

Isolate each part of the transmission in turn for testing by using the clutch and different gears following the steps outlined below. Listen carefully for signs of the noise at each stage. Even if it seems like you've found the source, continue with the checklist to definitively rule out other parts of the transmission. This will save time and work later in the rebuild stage by allowing you to concentrate on the likely causes of the trouble and will lead your inspection to the right gear pair.

IDLING NOISES:

• First, set the parking brake, place the transmission in neutral, and start the engine. With the engine running, and with the clutch engaged, listen carefully for any noises.

• If the noise appears at this stage of testing, rev the engine a few times and listen for a change in its frequency. If the noise does not seem to change, it may be from another part of the engine or drivetrain (such as the fuel pump or smog control equipment). If it changes in frequency or loudness, it could be engine- or transmission-related.

• Now, press the clutch pedal in. If the noise goes away or becomes quieter as the clutch is depressed, it is very likely something inside the transmission. It may be in a part of the transmission that is rotating in neutral, including the input shaft and bearing, counter gear or output shaft, and idling gears on the mainshaft. A growling noise heard under these conditions is a classic symptom of a bad input shaft bearing, but it could also be the countershaft bearings in a rear-wheel-drive transmission.

• If the noise becomes louder as the clutch pedal is pressed in, this suggests that it is related to the clutch. One nontransmission noise that becomes louder is a chirping or rattling sound in the bell housing that changes loudness or frequency as the clutch pedal is slowly depressed. This is a classic symptom of a bad clutch fork pivot or linkage. A squealing or grinding noise that increases in proportion to the clutch pedal travel is likely to be a bad clutch release bearing.

• With the clutch pedal still depressed, put the transmission in gear. A howling or squealing noise that occurs when the clutch pedal is depressed and the transmission is in gear is often caused by the pilot bearing supporting the transmission input shaft in the end of the crankshaft. Needle roller bearings and bushings in this location dry up and seize from the lack of lubrication.

• With the clutch in, the car stationary, and the transmission in gear, the transmission gears and shafts are not moving. Any noise at this point must be coming from the clutch or engine. There is no way the noise could be caused by the transmission.

ROAD TESTING:

• The next step is a road test to check for noises in each of the speed gears. Let out the clutch and listen for new noises. Shift through each gear in turn, listening for noises at each point as you accelerate. Noises that occur only while the car is driving, or in a certain gear, are almost certainly caused by parts inside the transmission.

• If the source of the noise is one or more of the main shaft bearings, it will occur in all gears. With the transmission in gear and driving, a bad output shaft bearing will make a low-pitched noise that increases in volume and frequency as the car moves faster. If the noise disappears at idle with the car stopped, it is definitely in the output shaft.

• If a rear-wheel-drive transmission makes a growling noise in neutral that occurs in all of the speed gears, the countershaft bearings may be the suspect. If the growling noise appears in neutral and each of the lower gears but goes away in fourth (direct gear), it is very likely that the mainshaft pilot bearing inside the input shaft gear is bad.

• To diagnose a whining noise, note which gear(s) it occurs in. Let off the gas with the transmission in each gear in turn and allow the car to coast down in speed. Listen for a change in the frequency of the noise in each gear—sometimes only one side of the gear teeth is damaged and the sound will be louder in one direction (acceleration or coast).

FINAL DRIVE:

• If the same whining noise is present in all gears it is most likely not caused by transmission gear noise. It would be very unlikely for all of the gears in the transmission to become worn or noisy at the same time. A whine in every gear is probably from the final drive.

• To isolate engine noises from drivetrain noises, put the transmission in neutral and allow the engine to idle while the car is going down the road and see if the noise changes. If it does not change, it may be in some part of the drivetrain such as the driveshaft and final drive.

• To check for pinion bearing wear, accelerate to a medium speed and then decelerate—if a whining noise comes from the final drive, and changes pitch in acceleration and deceleration, the pinion bearing is a likely suspect. If the noise is louder on acceleration and disappears on deceleration or coasting, the cause is probably a worn ring gear in the differential.

• To check for a bad wheel bearing, give the engine just enough gas to keep the road speed steady—neither accelerating nor decelerating. The final drive will not be loaded, and a noise coming from the rear of the car may be a wheel bearing. A bad wheel bearing will tend to get louder as the car's speed increases.

Make sure any howling or whining noise isn't coming from this area. Clutch forks can become loose on their pivot studs and rattle, pilot bearings (which this transmission doesn't have) can seize and squeal, and throwout bearings can howl and grind. A simple process of elimination should rule out most of these causes before pulling the transmission.

WHINING AND HOWLING

A steady, high-pitched noise coming from the transmission is generally gear whine. Whine varies in frequency and loudness with speed and the gear selected—louder and higher pitched at higher speeds, and in the lower gears. Gear whine is common with many transmissions, and it is another sound that may not be curable. Some types of gear whine, especially those that appear suddenly, are related to transmission problems, but other types are simply the result of particular gear tooth shapes, oil, or wear.

As mentioned in the section on gear geometry, gear whine caused by the straight teeth on spur gears cannot be eliminated in these gear sets. In addition, new helical gears very often whine until they have "bedded in" or worn together enough to reduce the asperities on both gears. For this reason, if the transmission or gear set is new, give it at least 1,000 miles of varied driving before assuming that the noise is a problem.

Sometimes, gear whine will become noticeable after rebuilding a transmission or final drive with some new and some used gears. This is due to a phenomenon known as "tolerance stack-up." When gears are manufactured, the tolerances for each gear are carefully controlled to produce nearly optimal tooth contact against a wide range of mating gears. However, in some cases, the tolerances of a pair of gears can add up and produce a pair with imperfectly mating teeth. Some transmissions have more problems with this than others since they have looser manufacturing tolerances. It is another form of whine that cannot easily be avoided, although the probability of postrebuild whine can be reduced by replacing transmission gears in pairs.

Hypoid final drive gears are very sensitive to this—never mix a pinion and ring gear from a mismatched set. During manufacturing the gears are lapped together with a fine abrasive to create a perfect match. Any noise from a freshly installed hypoid gear set is probably due to an incorrect setup, since the gears are so carefully mated. With an older set of hypoid gears, whine is most often caused by worn pinion support bearings—as they become loose, the pinion bearing rocks up and down in relation to the centerline of the ring gear as power travels through the gear set. This will eventually destroy the gear teeth on both gears and result in gear failure. Worn ring gear teeth will whine during acceleration only. Helical final drives in transverse front-wheel-drive transmissions can whine, but not as much as hypoid gears.

If the whine appears suddenly and becomes very loud in a short time, it can be indicative of damage to the gear teeth or gear hub bearings. A shortage of lubrication is the most likely cause of such damage—if the oil film on the gear teeth gets too thin, the teeth wipe against one another and "microweld" from the friction. This destroys the smooth surface on the face of each tooth and causes them to mesh roughly. This can

Corrosion of the gear occurs when water gets into the lubricating oil. The most common cause of water in the oil is condensation—if the car isn't driven often, a small amount of water can collect in the oil and eventually cause corrosion damage. Change transmission oil yearly, no matter how many miles are on the transmission, to avoid this problem. This gear could probably be reused in a street-car transmission, but the tooth is definitely weakened and could fail if stressed.

be caused by an insufficient oil level, oil that is too thin for the application, or even overheated oil. In all cases, even if the fluid is replaced, the gears will never recover.

Other sources of gear tooth damage include corrosion, vibration, and wear. Water in the gearbox oil attacks the steel surface of each gear, causing pitting and abnormal wear. Transmissions used on the street often do not get hot enough to burn off all of the water present from condensation, so this can be a particular problem in humid areas. Changing the oil often is a good way to avoid corrosion wear. As for vibration, this is a problem only in some street transmissions used for racing behind solid (unsprung) hub clutch discs. The torsional vibrations from the engine smack the gear teeth against one another, causing surface damage. Wear of the gear teeth is inevitable and unavoidable. The rate of surface wear can be greatly decreased, however, by ensuring that the gears have lots of clean, suitable lubricating oil at a low temperature.

RUMBLING AND GROWLING

Low-pitched growling or rumbling noises when the engine is running are usually a sign of a bad rolling-element (ball or roller) bearing. These bearings have very tight internal clearances and require that all of the contacting surfaces be very smooth and well lubricated. They are extremely sensitive to small bits of metal or dirt in the lubricant film between the bearing elements. A small piece of foreign matter inside a bearing causes the rollers or balls to "skid" or drag across the surface of the race. After the wear reaches a

certain point, the surface becomes rough enough to cause further skidding and more wear, until the bearing becomes noisy and eventually fails. The more foreign material in the oil, the worse the skidding and the faster the bearings wear.

Manual transmissions are very unkind environments for bearings because of this, and bearings normally wear out more quickly than most other parts in a transmission, with the exception of the synchronizer rings. The meshing of the gears, the friction between synchronizer rings, and all of the steel-on-steel bearings produce lots of small chips and flakes of steel and brass inside a transmission. These chips and flakes end up in the oil, which distributes them to every corner of the case as it is whipped around by the gear train. Some of these small particles migrate into the bearings and wear them out quickly. Since most transmissions do not have pressure-lubrication systems or filters, the dirt does not get flushed out of the bearings right away.

Transmissions with pumps and cooling systems may incorporate a filter into the system, but this is not common. Unlike the inside of an engine, there are no carbon deposits from burning fuel that must be removed from the oil, but there are plenty of steel particles. Most transmissions incorporate a magnet somewhere in the bottom of the case (sometimes in the drain plug) to trap the small bits of steel, but not all of them are caught, and any non ferrous (not steel) particles do not stick to the magnet.

Another factor that influences the (short) life of transmission bearings is the viscosity and type of oil that is used and the way it is delivered. For the most part, helical gears

Shielded ball bearings, like this one on a Honda differential, last longer in some applications. The metal shields keep out larger pieces of metal that might be circulating in the oil. Since particles in the lubricant are the chief cause of bearing failure, the cleaner the oil inside the bearing the better.

like thick oil that provides them with a thick, strong oil film at high temperatures. The slower the gears are run, and the more torque is transmitted through them, the thicker the oil should be for maximum gear life.

The problem with this is that bearings depend on oil being available inside the bearing races. Thick oil flows more slowly than thin oil, so it tends to reach the bearings last and least. This results in reduced bearing life because the bearings are lubricated less than they optimally should be. The hub bearings inside each gear suffer particularly badly in transmissions with no oiling system—the only reason they last at all is that they are not heavily loaded.

To combat the problems of dirty transmission oil, some manufacturers specify sealed or shielded bearings some shaft bearings. The shields or seals keep out most of the large particles and help the bearings last much longer, despite the fact that the seals reduce the flow of lubricant. This works best for bearings that are "buried" deep inside the transmission case, where there is plenty of lubricating oil.

The growling of a bad transmission bearing, like the whine of a bad gear, will eventually get louder and louder until the bearing seizes or falls apart, with catastrophic results. One of the functions of the bearings in a transmission is to maintain the proper clearance between pairs of gears. If the bearings begin to wear and get loose, the gears can start to mesh improperly and become damaged from the crooked tooth contact.

If the bearing falls apart, the results are equally bad. Small pieces of steel from the broken bearing will travel through the transmission and may get caught between gear teeth. Smashed gear teeth and damaged gears are the eventual result. If one of the bearings seizes, chances are high that it will take the transmission case with it.

Sometimes the poorly lubricated needle bearings between each gear and the mainshaft will seize from the high revolutions in a racing application. The needle bearings will burn the shaft and gear bore, destroying both. This can be avoided somewhat by careful assembly and clearance monitoring.

BUZZING AND HISSING

If the shifter or shift linkage makes a hissing or buzzing noise while the car is moving (particularly while accelerating or decelerating), the cause could be as simple as a loose bolt or worn rubber isolators in the shift linkage. Other causes of these high-frequency noises include bent shift forks, shift rods, or interlocks, or even excessive in the synchronizer sleeves. In all of these cases, the cause of the noise is the shift forks contacting the grooves in the sleeves. This causes a hissing noise that travels through the shift linkage to the shift lever.

When diagnosing buzzing shifter noise, first make sure that all linkages are adjusted properly, and then check to see that all original shifter bushings are in place and not torn or damaged. If the linkage appears to be in good shape and the noise persists, it might be time to look inside the transmission at the forks and sleeves.

Pay particular attention to any stops that prevent the shift forks from going past the engaged position in each

The clearance (or lack of it) between the shift forks and synchronizer sleeves is important. If the clearance is nonexistent, the fork and sleeve will wear very quickly. While the parts are rubbing, a faint hissing noise may come up through the shifter into the passenger compartment. This is usually the result of faulty assembly or a bent shift fork—it doesn't happen through wear.

gear. When the transmission is in gear, there should be some clearance (the exact amount varies between transmissions) between the face of the shift fork and one edge of the groove in the sleeve. If the side of the shift fork drags on the edge of the synchronizer sleeve's groove, it will cause a high-pitched buzzing noise and wear on the fork. Some cars (including some BMW models) are notorious for buzzing shifters, and there is not much that can be done.

VIBRATING AND DRUMMING

Sometimes, particularly at steady high speeds, the whole car will appear to vibrate from the area around the transmission with a low-frequency, cyclic vibration. This happens most often with rear-wheel-drive powertrains, and it is usually caused by a driveshaft problem. The front-wheel-drive equivalent is a vibration or shake that is felt in the steering wheel.

In the rear-wheel-drive drivetrain, there are three or four broad causes of this kind of trouble—an out-of-balance driveshaft, worn U-joint(s) or flexible coupling, or worn output yoke bushing. An out-of-balance driveshaft can be tested by adding a flexible hose clamp or two to the final drive end of the driveshaft and rotating the clamping portion until the vibration goes away (remove the rear wheels first and put the car on jack stands). Use a chalk mark to identify the starting position of the clamp.

Front-wheel-drive driveshaft vibration problems are often caused by worn inner CV or tripod joints; the inner CV joints on a front-wheel-drive driveshaft do not bend as much as the outer joints and the contact points do not move. All of the torque is transferred through a few small areas, which wear more quickly than the surrounding metal. As they wear, play develops that allows the driveshaft to twist back and forth on a steady road and cause vibration that is felt in the steering wheel.

To rule out inner CV joints, accelerate gently and confirm that the vibration occurs under light throttle applications. Let off the throttle and feel for the vibration—if it goes away when the car is not accelerating, the joints are suspect. Make sure that the test is done at the same speed—many other conditions (like an out-of-balance tire or bent wheel) are speed-related. Rotate the tires and run the test again to help rule out tire problems.

BANGING AND CLUNKING

Banging and clunking felt in the shift lever and heard under the car usually indicates a broken or loose motor mount. Generally, the noise will be loudest when letting out the clutch when taking off from a stop. If the rear transmission mount is bad in a rear-wheel-drive car, the most noise will occur when letting out the clutch in reverse as the tail shaft of the transmission rises up and slams back down. Broken

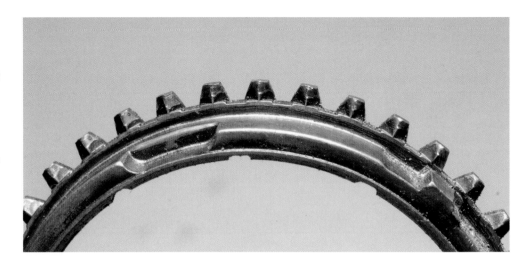

This blocking ring is completely worn out. The front surface of each tooth should be sharp and pointed—the dull, rounded edges of this blocking ring show the signs of many miles of grinding and crunching. These rings are designed to be softer than the surrounding steel parts and wear faster. If you replace them at the first signs of "crunchy" shifts, you will save yourself a lot of money later.

mounts may also result in a clunking noise when accelerating and decelerating gently. A failed mount will tend to increase overall vibrations from the drivetrain and can cause the shift linkage to bind.

Another frequent sign of a bad motor mount is clutch chatter. Contrary to popular opinion, clutch chatter is almost never caused by the clutch disc or flywheel. Usually, it is the result of overly flexible motor mounts, whether by design or wear. The mounts are rubber and absorb some of the movement that results as the clutch begins to transmit torque from the engine to the drivetrain. As the drivetrain takes some of the engine's torque, the pressure on the mounts eases and they spring back. This oscillation continues and the engine and transmission rock back and forth. As soon as the clutch stops slipping, the mounts return to their neutral position and the oscillation goes away.

Excessive backlash in the final drive gears in a rear-wheel-drive car can also give the same symptoms. A rhythmic knocking or chattering noise while using the engine to decelerate may be from the driveshaft U-joints in a rear-wheel-drive car. To check them, give the driveshaft a good shake and check for play in the joints. Check the rear suspension bushings and differential mounts at the same time—a loose mount or bushings will allow the differential to rock back and forth and produce symptoms similar to a broken transmission or motor mount.

SHIFTING TROUBLE

Shifting troubles rank right behind noise as a frequent transmission complaint. In an ideal world, every shift of a synchronized transmission would be smooth, free of crunching, and fast. In practice, parts wear, become damaged, and a once-smooth transmission can start grinding,

shifting hard, and jumping out of gear. Some of these problems can be caused by wear, but others are due to problems with the clutch and shift linkage. Always take the time to diagnose these external parts before assuming that the transmission has to be removed.

Issues with the clutch not releasing completely are the cause of most shifting difficulties. The clutch is an important part of the shift and synchronization process, and a clutch that hangs up will cause all kinds of shifting problems. A simple test should always be performed to check for a dragging clutch. With the engine running and the parking brake set, disengage the clutch and put the transmission in gear. Keeping the clutch pedal down, pull the lever out of gear, and then immediately push it back into the same gear. If it grinds on the second attempt to shift into gear, the clutch is probably not releasing completely. Also, if the problem occurs in all gears, it is very likely to be related to the clutch.

With the clutch disengaged, the synchronizer on the selected gear should stop the input shaft from spinning as it couples a gear to the mainshaft. The shafts will remain stopped for a moment, so the second shift does not require the synchronizers to do any work and the transmission should drop right into gear. If the clutch is dragging when the transmission is shifted out of gear, the input shaft will begin turning again and the synchronizer will be forced to stop the gear train and clutch disc once again.

A clutch that fails the drag test could have one of several problems, but the most likely are a worn or badly adjusted linkage, sticking input shaft splines, or failed pilot bearing. If the clutch passes the drag test with no problems, the issue is within the transmission or linkage. The topics below cover the major sources of shifting aggravation and should help to pinpoint the source of the problem.

A frequent, hard-to-diagnose source of shifting problems is worn or broken bushings in the shift linkage. Manufacturers like to use large, soft bushings in the linkage to prevent gear noise and vibration from traveling into the passenger compartment. This works great until they break, after which shifting can become difficult, sloppy, and imprecise. This, in turn, can lead to blocking ring and synchronizer damage.

CRUNCHING

The most common shifting complaint is grinding or "crunching" when shifting into gear. Usually felt as much as heard, it is probably the most annoying manual transmission failure mode. The noise is caused by the ends of the synchronizer sleeve internal splines banging against the external dog teeth splines because the gear and sleeve are turning at different speeds. This, of course, only happens if something goes wrong with the synchronization process.

Bad synchronizer performance can be caused by a problem in the transmission or a clutch issue. Cone-type synchronizers are simple and reliable, but, like any part that relies on friction to function (brakes and clutches), the blocking rings degrade with time. They are also easily damaged by "speed shifting" without using the clutch, a clutch that does not release completely, and incompatible lubricants. If the clutch does not fully disengage, the synchronizers will not be able to do their job—they cannot speed up or slow down the input shaft enough to allow a smooth shift, so it is important to check the clutch first.

Using the method above, first rule out the clutch by checking that the transmission shifts in and out of gear smoothly while the clutch is disengaged. If the grinding is present on the first shift into a gear but not the second, the synchronizer blocking ring on that gear is worn out. Check all of the gears in turn. If only one or two of them grind, the synchronizer rings on those gears are probably worn.

If the clutch appears to be the culprit, the problem may actually be the pilot bearing in the end of the crankshaft. This small plain bronze or needle roller bearing has a very important job to do—it supports the outer end of the input shaft and prevents it (and the input gear) from wobbling.

If this happens, the gears will eventually become damaged and take the rest of the transmission with them. In the meantime, the worn bearing will drag on the input shaft and cause bad shifting. If the bearing is a needle roller type, it can seize on the input shaft and cause severe damage to its surface.

It may sound repetitive, but check the transmission oil, too. Each transmission's synchronizers are designed to work best with a particular combination of oil viscosity and performance-enhancing additives. Lubricant that is too thick will impede synchronizer performance, and so will the EP additives in API GL-5 oil if it is used in a transmission designed for GL-4. Some transmissions are very sensitive to lubricant choice, and running the wrong type can cause the synchronizers to wear much more quickly than they otherwise would.

Even if the problem appears to stem from a sticky or badly adjusted clutch or incorrect oil, the synchronizer assemblies may be damaged from the missed shifts and grinding. Synchronizer blocking rings wear badly when the clutch doesn't fully disengage because they are forced to act against higher speed differences than they are designed for. The longer the grinding has been going on, and the worse it is, the less likely it will go away after the clutch is repaired. The transmission may still require disassembly and replacement of at least the blocking rings.

The grinding and banging will also dull the sharp ends of the synchronizer sleeve splines and the gear dog teeth—wear here contributes to bad synchronizer performance and hard shifting. As the ends of the internal splines and dog teeth become rounded off, they do not mesh cleanly on each shift. The ends of the splines bang into each other, preventing

If the blocking rings become worn and the gears start to "crunch" on each shift, the gear dog teeth will eventually look like this. This gear should be tossed. The round sides of each tooth make it more difficult for the sleeve to find its way into engagement with the gear and it will shift very hard.

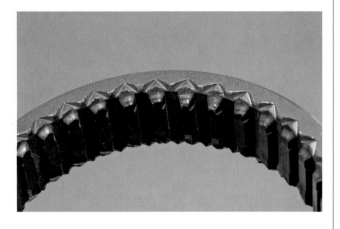

This is the flip side of the worn gear pictured above. This synchronizer sleeve is about as bad as it gets. These teeth are supposed to have points on the ends. The duller they are, the harder the transmission will shift as the dull ends of the sleeve and gear splines contact one another head-on instead of sliding past to one side or the other.

a shift even when the blocking rings do their job. The only cure for this problem is new synchronizer sleeves and possibly speed gears.

HARD SHIFTING OR WON'T GO INTO GEAR

"Hard shifting" is a somewhat vague term that covers several different problems that can be related to issues with the clutch, synchronizers, or shift linkage. Most, if not all, hard-shifting problems are related to the clutch, so check the usual suspects of clutch release and proper fluid. Of course, "hard" is a subjective term, and some transmissions are naturally more difficult to shift than others. If the problem does not develop suddenly, it might just be a characteristic of the transmission in question.

The most common types of hard shifting can have different causes, so take the time to determine which is the most likely based on the following descriptions. The first is stiff movement of the lever in one or more directions, the textbook definition of hard shifting. In this case, the problem is usually somewhere in the linkage, including the external linkage (if there is one), the shift rails inside the transmission, the shift forks, or the detents and interlock.

If the problem occurs in all gears, it is more likely to be related to external linkage. If it is an issue with only one pair of gears (such as first and second), the problem is probably internal. To diagnose external problems, first adjust the shift linkage according to the service manual. If that doesn't help, replace any bushings or bearings in the linkage. Most front-wheel-drive and some rear-wheel-drive cars have rubber bushings in the linkage between shifter and transmission, and they degrade over time. As the bushings wear, they prevent the linkage from moving smoothly and make the transmission hard to shift.

A very common internal cause of hard shifting is a bent shift fork—most transmissions have solid mechanical stops inside the case that block the shift linkage at both ends of its allowable travel to prevent the fork from overshifting. Some do not, and it is these transmissions that have the most trouble with bent forks.

If the linkage does not have a positive (internal or external) stop, the driver is able to force the lever and put pressure on the shift fork even when the synchronizer sleeve is bottomed out against the face of the selected gear. The shift fork can bend if it is forced hard enough, or the faces of the shift fork can be burned by their constant contact with the groove in the synchronizer sleeve. A really hard shift can even bend the internal shift rails and jam the interlock. A bent shift rail will not move smoothly in its bore, resulting in hard shifting. Bent shift forks also cause hard shifting, as well as missed shifts and jumping out of gear.

Transmissions with side or top covers, like older American designs, are easiest to check for bent rails or forks. Simply pull the side cover and inspect the linkage and detents for damage. If the shift rails and forks are fine, the problem is with the sleeve or gear. Full disassembly is the only option, and it is the only choice for transmissions without a removable side cover.

Look closely at the edges of the teeth on this reverse idler gear. It's been shifted with the car still moving too many times. The side of each tooth should be pointed and sharp, like the ends of synchronizer sleeve splines. If they look like this, the transmission will be difficult to get into reverse and might pop out of reverse under power.

The second type of hard shifting is the issue of notchiness. Sometimes a transmission will go into gear but it requires an unusual amount of force to shift past the detents. This can be a problem with either the synchronizers or the linkage. The external shift linkage is unlikely to cause notchiness, but it is possible. More likely are internal problems such as burrs on the synchronizer hub or sleeve splines or worn dog teeth. Internal linkage problems like damaged detent balls and springs or bent shift rails will also result in notchy or uneven shifter action.

In some transmissions, worn detent balls and springs are the culprit whenever hard shifting and notchiness appear. BMW ZF transmissions, in particular, are known for difficulty getting into fifth gear when the transmission (and oil) is cold. Sometimes this can be fixed from outside the transmission with new detents, although in most cases it requires total disassembly.

The third common type of hard shifting is more accurately described as "slow shifting." The transmission will not shift into gear immediately, but requires two or three tries to shift. It may crunch on one or two of the attempts, but inconsistently. This is usually a problem with the synchronizers, although it could be a linkage issue. The synchronizers are simply not doing their job correctly, either due to wear or improper fluid.

An extreme case of hard shifting is a transmission that will not go into one or more gears at all. The causes of this are the same as most shifting troubles—clutch, linkage, or synchronizers. It is somewhat more likely to be caused by a problem with the external linkage or forks than the synchronizers, however. If the linkage incorporates stops, they may be misadjusted, which prevents the transmission from reaching a particular gear.

To test for a linkage problem, try shifting into the gear with the engine off and the car stationary. If the transmission will not shift while the engine is running, but drops into gear when the engine is stopped, the problem is likely with the synchronizer assembly. If it does not shift in either case, the linkage is more likely to be the culprit.

If the transmission has external shift linkage, disconnect it and try to shift the transmission with a screwdriver or other suitable tool at the transmission end of the shift linkage. If the transmission shifts into gear with the external linkage disconnected, the problem is with the linkage. The synchronizer assemblies or shift rails and forks are probably the cause if the linkage checks out OK. Bent forks, rails, and detents are all frequent causes of an inability to get into gear.

The opposite problem of hard selection is getting stuck in gear and being unable to disengage to shift into neutral or another gear. The causes are the same as hard shifting—linkage

If the transcription won't drive in any gear, first check the driveshaft(s) and CV joints if it is a front-wheel-drive car. If they appear to be good, chances are that the drive pinion and ring gear (in a front-wheel-drive transaxle) or input shaft gears (in a rear-wheel-drive transmission) are stripped. Pinion gears usually go first because their teeth are smaller than those on the ring gear.

or synchronizer sleeves and gear dog teeth. Check the external linkage by disconnecting it first, to rule out an external cause like a broken cable or damaged rods.

The cause is probably in the shift selection mechanism inside the transmission if the external linkage checks out fine. Bent and damaged shift detents and rails can cause the transmission to stick in gear, as can a jammed interlock. Most of these problems can be solved only with disassembly, unless the transmission happens to have a removable side or top cover.

JUMPING OUT OF GEAR OR STUCK IN GEAR

Jumping out of gear can be caused by any of a number of internal and external problems like those described above. End play or preload problems with individual gears on the mainshaft are two of the most common, although linkage issues, worn bearings, and worn synchronizers can also cause jumping out of gear in some situations. As with other shift problems, start with external causes because they are the easiest to diagnose and repair.

One possible cause of jumping out of gear is bent, broken, loose, or binding shift linkage that causes the transmission to engage each gear incompletely. If a gear is not fully engaged by the internal or external linkage, the synchronizer

If your rear-wheel-drive transmission doesn't transmit power to the wheels, look at this pair of gears for a clue. The input gears are generally pretty strong, but they do fail. Usually the cause is abuse, especially low oil and drag racing.

sleep can slip back to neutral if power is applied. Check the operation of any linkage first, and make sure that there is not excessive free play in the shift lever.

It may sound obvious, but make sure that the gear shift lever is not hitting anything in the interior of the car, like the center console or armrest, that can prevent it from moving completely into gear. Other common and aggravating external problems that can cause a transmission to jump out of gear include loose engine-to-bellhousing or transmission-to-bellhousing bolts and broken motor mounts.

If the problem goes away after tightening mounting bolts or adjusting the shift linkage, the transmission is probably fine, but sometimes these problems may already have caused internal damage. Misadjusted linkage that allows the shift rails and forks to travel too far can bend shift forks and rails and damage the synchronizer sleeves (see note above about bent shifter forks and rails). If the problems persist even after repairing external related parts, the transmission is probably damaged internally and will have to be removed and disassembled to find the source of the problem.

The most likely internal causes of jumping out of gear are worn or damaged input and mainshaft bearings, worn gear dog teeth or synchronizer hub splines, loose shift forks or rails, broken or missing interlock pins, balls, or springs, or excessive end play or runout in the gears on the output shaft or countershaft. Unfortunately, most of these problems require removing the transmission. If other symptoms, such as noise, are present, diagnose the source and use that as a guide to the possible issues when you disassemble the transmission.

CRW1 CRWA1

These cutaways (courtesy of Chicago Rawhide) show the internal construction of rubber lip seals. The seal on the right has an additional dirt shield. This is similar to the seals used on the inner CV joint shafts of a front-wheel-drive transaxle. Like bearings, lip seals wear most when subjected to dirt, and the cleaner the seal the longer the seal's life.

If the transmission pops out of reverse only, the problem may be worn or chipped teeth on the reverse idler gear or on the mainshaft reverse teeth if the transmission has a sliding reverse idler gear. The reverse idler gear has a small internal bushing that also wears, causing the gear to run crookedly and the transmission to jump out of gear. If the transmission has a constant-mesh reverse idler gear, the reverse brake or synchronizer may be the problem.

TOTAL FAILURE

Total failure is the ultimate transmission problem, of course, but it is rare in a stock drivetrain. Much more likely is gradual wear that makes the transmission noisy and hard

Most modern transmissions require rebuilders to use RTV (Room Temperature Vulcanizing) silicone rubber gasket material. Apply a thin layer, as shown here, and allow it to "skin over" before assembling the parts. Torque all case bolts to the recommended value— overtightening can cause the silicone to squeeze out and leaks to develop.

Most transmissions have a reverse light switch located somewhere on the case. Failures are pretty rare, and never critical. These switches have been known to leak, however, so if you have a slow leak under the car, check them out. Install switches with a touch of RTV on the threads to prevent weepage (which can occur even with a new switch).

to shift, although there are a few common failure modes that will result in no drive reaching the wheels. Most total failures are the result of abuse or neglect, so they are avoidable.

If the engine cannot drive the wheels in any gear, start by checking the clutch. If the clutch appears to be engaging, a driveshaft, CV joint, or U-joint may be broken. If both the driveshaft and the clutch appear to be working in a rear-wheel-drive vehicle, the input shaft gear or countergear is probably stripped. Less likely is a failed mainshaft, or twisted-off input shaft splines.

A front-wheel-drive transaxle that does not transmit power is probably due to a stripped pinion gear or ring gear in the final drive, or broken differential gears. Occasionally, the shift linkage can fail in such a way that no gear can be selected, but the shifter will definitely feel wrong—there will likely be no detents, or, at best, very weak ones for each gear.

Transmissions are usually just strong enough for a stock application without being excessively strong or weak, because engineers are able to very accurately match a transmission design to a particular application. They calculate the power level and traction of the chassis and then choose a transmission (or in rare cases, design a transmission) to meet these requirements, as well as the demands of cost, size, and weight.

Production transmissions used for racing or behind a modified engine are another matter entirely. Racing is hard on all drivetrain components, not just transmissions. Problems are almost always the result of too much power and too much traction, or too much heat. Putting a stock T-5 between a small-block Ford making 400 lb/ft of torque and

a 4.11:1 rear-end gear with 22-inch drag slicks is just asking for trouble, for example.

Dump the clutch off the line, or "speed shift" by banging through the gears without using the clutch, and the teeth will peel right off the gears. Third gear is often the weakest, but every transmission has a gear that will fail first. First and second gear are less likely to break because the engine's power will probably overpower the rear wheels before the shock loads in the transmission get high enough to cause problems. Front-wheel-drive transmissions often exhibit stripped final drives from such treatment—the fragile pinion teeth are the first to go when the engine's torque and the tires' traction are too much for the gearbox to handle.

When one gear goes, it is just a matter of time before the rest are destroyed; pieces of broken gear teeth from one gear migrate very quickly to other parts of the transmission and destroy everything along the way. A small chip of steel from a failed gear (or bearing) can get stuck between two other gears and cause them to strip as well.

Another failure mode for transmissions used for racing or behind modified engines is case failure. As described in the section on helical gears, every pair of helical gears produces forces that tend to pull the gears apart in two directions. At low temperatures, most cases have no problems withstanding these forces. As soon as the temperature increases, however, the case material becomes more flexible, until it allows the gears to move apart slightly.

As soon as this happens, the case begins to stretch and bend. If the forces become too strong, the transmission case will stretch permanently or crack. A few cracks can quickly propagate (travel) through the metal of the transmission case and cause it to split apart suddenly. This is a problem inherent in helical gears in production transmissions that are used for racing.

LEAKS

There are a few other common problems that are often associated with manual transmissions, the most common of which are leaks. Oil leaks might seem like minor irritations, but there are a few good reasons for minimizing them. The first is environmental. All the oil leaking out of your transmission has to go somewhere, and poisoning the environment around you is the most likely result. Do your part to keep the car hobby safe from overzealous environmental laws by acknowledging the problem and reducing your own impact on water and ground pollution.

The second issue is that of a falling oil level and subsequent lubrication problems. Unless leaks are caught very early on, they can lead to bigger problems. The danger is that enough oil will leak out to cause problems without you knowing about it. Since most transmissions do not provide an easy way to check the oil level (like a dip stick or oil-pressure gauge), most people ignore it. This is not a good policy. Your transmission will last much longer if you check the level every year or 10,000 miles or so if you have no leaks and more often if you suspect a problem.

Several different types of seals do the work of keeping dirt out and lubricant inside a transmission case. Rubber lip seals stop oil from leaking out around rotating shafts and bearings. Generally, such seals consist of a pressed steel circular form molded into a rubber seal with a narrow inner lip that rides on the shaft. The lip is held in contact with the shaft by a narrow, light spring that encircles the inner lip. The outer edge of a lip seals against a tight-fitting machined bore in the transmission case or bearing retainer.

Shift shafts and linkages are sealed in the case by tight clearances between the shaft and bore, and by rubber O-rings and light-duty lip seals, generally without the metal core. Rubber O-rings are also used on speedometer drive housings, bearing housings, and similar round parts.

Lip seals work very well, but as they age the rubber hardens and the narrow lip wears. O-rings also tend to harden and leak over time, making them a common source of annoying leaks. Manufacturers are aware of this tendency, however, and the newer the seal, the better the rubber compound and the longer it is likely to last. The job of replacing them is still a pain, but at least it has become less frequent.

Most modern transmissions use very few gaskets. The main castings usually have silicone sealant between them instead of paper or cork gaskets, for several reasons. First, silicone seals require almost no space to seal, so bearing fits, clearances, and preload do not change after assembly. Second, silicone is more forgiving of slight imperfections in the surfaces in contact, so leaks are less likely than with gaskets. Third, silicone tends to stay pliable for a very long time, unlike paper and cork gaskets that harden, shrink, and leak.

Tracking down the source of an oil leak can be more difficult than it should be. As a car goes down the road, the air flowing under it blows any leaking oil backward, which can disguise the location of the leaking seal. The only way to find the source is to clean the underside of the car with pressure-washing or large quantities of solvent—it must be absolutely, perfectly clean or any leak detection will be much harder.

Once the underside of the car is clean, run it on stands or ramps until the oil begins to leak. The most common leaks are from the seals on the input and output shafts of a rear-wheel-drive transmission, or the input and axle shafts of a front-wheel-drive transaxle. Incidentally, before assuming that a leak in the bell housing area is coming from the input shaft, check the engine's rear main seal. A leak from either seal requires pulling the transmission, so always replace both the rear main seal and input shaft seal whenever you drop the transmission. It's a small price to pay to make sure the transmission won't have to come back out right away to fix an annoying leak.

ELECTRICAL AND ELECTRONIC PROBLEMS

With the exception of computer-controlled automatic transmissions, most transmissions and transaxles are free of extensive electronic controls, and failures are rare. When they do occur, the most common electrical problems don't require transmission disassembly. Electrically controlled transmission parts include reverse light switches, clutch-start and neutral-start switches, and speed sensors.

With a few exceptions, these parts can all be replaced outside the transmission. The most common exceptions are speed-sensor switches in front-wheel-drive transaxles. Speed sensors are located at the back of the transmission housing near the final drive—the sensors read the teeth on the ring gear to determine road speed. In some transmissions (transverse-engined Saabs are the best-known examples), the speed sensor cannot be replaced without removing and disassembling the transmission. Unfortunately, the same cars require a speed sensor signal for the engine to run properly—the ECU will get "confused" and drivability problems are the result.

CHAPTER 4
REBUILDING A TRANSMISSION

BEFORE YOU START

If there is one thing that should be perfectly clear from the previous chapters, it is that manual transmissions are pretty simple devices. There is nothing exceptionally complicated about rebuilding one, either. In many ways it is easier to disassemble, inspect, and reassemble a transmission than an engine. With the exception of seals, blocking rings, and bearings, most of a transmission's internal parts are not wear items, and the parts that do wear are more often replaced than repaired through expensive machine work.

The addition of computer modeling and design tools makes new transmission design straightforward and incremental, rather than revolutionary. Newer transmissions shift better, last longer, and make less noise than older designs, but they make use of the same basic technology. Blocking-ring synchronizers, for example, are used in almost all transmissions built in the past 40 years or so.

The internal parts of all transmissions are remarkably similar, so most of the tips and techniques detailed below will apply to any gearbox. Gears, synchronizers, bearings, and shafts wear in the same ways no matter what kind of transmission they are installed in. Although transmissions are very similar in overall design, the steps given in this chapter are necessarily very general, and some of them do not apply in all cases.

Always start your rebuild project by carefully reading through the manufacturer's rebuild manual. Once you understand the layout and assembly sequence for your unit, use the information in this chapter to clarify the manufacturer's instructions and make judgments on the condition of various parts.

By this point (assuming you've gone through the diagnosis steps outlined in Chapter 3), you should have a good idea of what ails your transmission. Some of these problems can be repaired with a partial disassembly rather than a complete rebuild, but others can only be repaired by total disassembly, replacement of worn or damaged parts, and reassembly. In general, problems with the shift linkage, mounts, and driveshaft(s) can be taken care of with the transmission in place, but most other issues require removal. Check your car's service manual if you aren't sure—some manuals separately detail repair procedures that don't involve removal of the unit.

Getting to the transmission in a front-wheel-drive car can be more difficult than actually removing it and rebuilding it. There is a transmission under this mass of wires and hoses. Take your time, follow the manual, and mark anything you remove so that you can put everything back together quickly and accurately.

While you've got the car apart and the transmission out, it would be foolish not to take the opportunity to check on the condition of the clutch pressure plate, disc, and throwout bearing. Clutch kits aren't all that expensive, and having a new one will save you having to pull the transmission for at least a while.

REBUILDING A TRANSMISSION

If your transmission has a bearing, gear, or synchronizer problem like those detailed in the previous chapter, it will have to come out. The service manual comes in handy for this, too—getting the transmission out of the car can be more difficult than the rebuild itself and it helps to know how the factory thinks it should be done. Ask a Porsche 944 owner if you think your transmission is hard to remove. Use the right tools, including good sturdy jack stands, and try not to damage any linkage or wiring.

Take a good look at the external linkage (if there is any) while you pull the transmission. This is a good time to rebuild it or replace any worn bushings or bent rods. When removing the transmission, avoid hanging the input shaft on the clutch disc splines. Doing so can bend the disc and cause clutch release problems later. It can also damage the disc hub springs and splines.

It's not a bad idea to pull and inspect the clutch at the same time as the transmission, and replace it if it looks even a little worn. A new clutch disc, pressure plate, and throwout bearing are not particularly expensive, and starting out with new parts is a good insurance policy against removing the transmission a second time. In addition, a new clutch makes troubleshooting the rebuilt transmission easier—it reduces the chance that a clutch problem will result in shifting trouble.

At the very least, remove the clutch pressure plate and inspect the disc and both drive friction surfaces (on the flywheel and pressure plate). This is a good opportunity to make sure the flywheel bolts are torqued to the proper specification and installed with Loctite. Check the input shaft pilot bearing's condition—make sure it is lubricated with fresh grease, and check the clutch release bearing for roughness or burn marks. If your bell housing, transmission, and engine block did not come off the assembly line together, this is a good time to check the bell housing concentricity relative to the crankshaft with a dial indicator.

Once the transmission is clear of the vehicle, clean the outside of the case before doing any work on it. Nobody likes to work on dirty parts, because it makes disassembly a lot messier and harder than it might otherwise be. Even worse, dirt from the outside of the transmission can get into the case during reassembly and cause bearing and gear damage later.

For a first quick wash, take the assembled transmission to a coin-operated car wash and hose it down in one of the stalls. Use a wire brush and canned engine cleaner to get all of the hardened grime and road dirt off the outside of the case. You can't make it too clean at this point, since the cleaner the case, the easier it will be to work on later. Don't let the transmission sit around after cleaning. Disassemble and clean the internal parts right away,

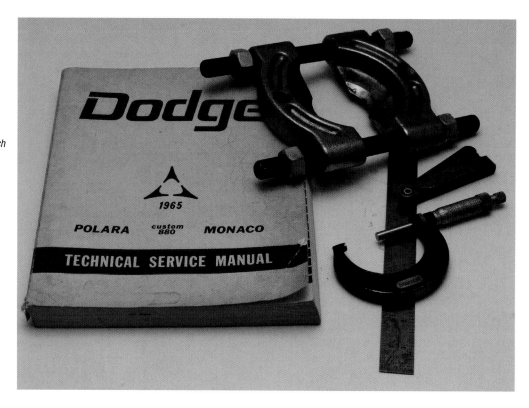

These are a few of the tools necessary to do a proper transmission rebuild: you may already have the shop manual and feeler gauges in your toolbox. The micrometer (1 to 2 inches is shown here, but it would be nice to have 0 to 1 inch also), bearing splitter, and 12-inch machinists' rule will all come in handy during a rebuild. All of these tools will make transmission work go much smoother.

because the moisture that gets into the case can cause the gears to rust and pit.

TOOLS AND TECHNIQUES
Workspace
The ideal transmission rebuilding station is a sturdy workbench with a dedicated shelf to store subassemblies and parts. Lots of light is a necessity, and so is a bench vice with aluminum jaw liners to protect soft parts. A stash of ¾-inch-to 1-inch-wide wood scraps are handy to level the empty case while you assemble the transmission.

Service Manual
Most of the tools to rebuild a transmission are probably already in your toolbox.

The most important tool in a transmission rebuilder's arsenal is a copy of the factory rebuild manual for the transmission or the vehicle in question. Without a manual, it will be very difficult to know the important clearances inside the transmission. TREMEC and several other manufacturers make their manuals available for free online, but most require you to buy a copy. They can be quite expensive, but, unfortunately, there really is no alternative. Generic aftermarket service manuals can give some guidance, but most are not nearly comprehensive enough for a total transmission rebuild.

Snap Rings and C-Clips
There are (at least) two tools that are absolutely required for any manual transmission work—two good pairs of snap ring pliers and good pair of C-clip pliers. The retaining rings that hold the transmission gears and synchronizer assemblies on the shaft fall into two categories: internal and external. Internal and external retaining rings with holes in the ends are known as snap rings, while those without are called C-clips.

Snap ring pliers come in two types, both of which have small pins on the tips that fit into the ends of the snap rings. The tips of internal snap ring pliers come together as the handles are squeezed, while those designed to remove external snap rings open as the handles are squeezed. There are "convertible" pliers that have a movable pivot pin to allow both types of action. Avoid these if you can—the pivots are usually weak and can allow the pliers to separate slightly, which makes them very difficult to use. Do try to find pliers with replaceable tips—the tips are delicate and break often.

C-clip pliers are designed only for the removal of external retaining rings, and the (flat) jaws open as the handles are squeezed. Internal C-clips and retaining rings are easier to remove with needle-nose pliers, an awl, or a small screwdriver. There are also tools that clamp the external C-clip in an open position so that it can be maneuvered onto a shaft more easily. These are nice to have but not really necessary. Good C-clip pliers have serrated jaws that grip the ends of the C-clip tightly.

C-clips and snap rings should not be reused. The steel that they are made from stretches slightly when opened, and they may not return to exactly the same shape as before. In addition, each time a retaining ring is opened, the metal fatigues slightly and becomes weaker. The consequences of a broken retaining ring (destroyed bearings and gears from the small pieces of steel, or damaged shafts from loose gears) are great enough, and retaining rings cheap enough, that new ones are a small price to pay for reliability.

A good pair of safety glasses should be a part of your retaining ring toolkit as well. Retaining rings can sometimes break or spring loose, and the small metal pieces have a better than sporting chance of pinging off your eye. Safety glasses keep this from being more than a nuisance.

Measuring Tools

A few machinists' measuring tools are absolutely necessary, and a few are nice to have. In the former category are feeler gauges. These are used to set gear and shaft end float, main shaft preload, and several other clearances inside the transmission. One set of gauges will work if necessary, but two are needed for accurate measurement of gear side clearance—put on opposing sides, two gauges prevent inaccurate measurements due to the gear cocking sideways on the shaft.

A good dial caliper and 12-inch machinist's steel rule are two more "must have" tools. Calipers are used for setting roller bearing preload and clearance inside the transmission and final drive, and the rule will be useful for checking part flatness and for rough measurements.

A pair of 1-inch and 2-inch micrometers will be more accurate and versatile than the caliper, but probably not

worth the expense just for transmission work (unless you're planning on doing a full "blueprint" rebuild). Bore gauges fall into the same category—nice to have but not necessary for most rebuild jobs.

A dial indicator with 1-inch travel is a good thing to have on hand, but not required unless you suspect a bent shaft or out-of-round synchronizer sleeve. A dial indicator and stand are needed for checking bell housing concentricity in a rear-wheel-drive drivetrain, however.

Torque Wrench

Fastener torque is just as important for manual transmissions as it is in engine work. Improperly torqued fasteners can cause all kinds of problems down the line, including leaks, bad shifting, and gear and bearing damage from shaft movement. Try to get into the habit of checking the torque of all fasteners. If the manufacturer does not specify the proper torque for a particular fastener, use the applicable chart below for the minimum permissible torque:

ISO Metric grade 6.6 (coarse thread, dry)

Size	Torque (ft-lbs)
M6	5
M8	15
M10	25
M12	40

Standard SAE grade 5 (coarse thread, dry)

Size	Torque (ft-lbs)
1/4-20	8
5/16-18	17
3/8-16	30
1/2-13	75
9/16-12	110

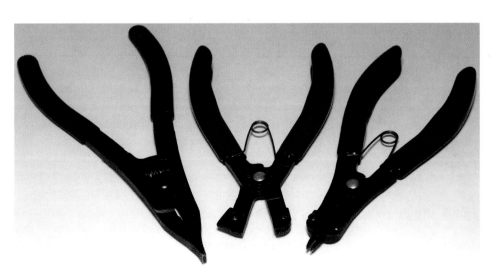

These three retaining ring pliers are the bare minimum necessary for a successful transmission rebuild. The duck-billed pliers on the left, with serrations on the outside of the jaws, are for external C-clips. The other two are snap ring pliers, one internal and one external. The fixed pivot pliers like these are better than the reversible ones—replaceable pins are a nice feature too.

A hydraulic press like this one is not really a necessity for most transmission work. There are a few jobs that are difficult, but not impossible, without it—removing and replacing the inner bearing race on a rear-wheel-drive input shaft is one example. Without a press, you will have to get creative with deadblow hammers, various tubular mandrels, and a sturdy bench vise.

A small torque wrench that measures down to 1 or 2 inch pounds is a good thing to have around, especially if you are planning on setting up hypoid gear sets. The small torque wrenches are used to determine optimal bearing preload for the pinion and differential side gears. Turning torque is a good measurement of bearing preload, and many manufacturers specify it instead of direct measurement of bearing clearance.

Pulling, Pressing, and Driving Tools

Removing and installing bearings that are pressed into their housings or onto a shaft can be a problem. More often than not, the press fits of each bearing are so tight that they cannot

be removed with gentle force and a few good taps with a brass hammer. The quickest and easiest way to remove these bearings is with a bearing splitter and a large hydraulic press. A small arbor press can be used for some of these jobs if a large one is not available, but there is no substitute for the pressure that a hydraulic press can bring to bear on recalcitrant parts.

Bearing splitters have two opposing bolts to clamp them together. They fit between the side of the bearing and its locating collar or gear, and allow force to be applied to the bearing's outer edge. A single 2- or 3-inch splitter should be plenty for most transmission work, but other sizes may come in handy. Many have threaded holes that can be used with two bolts and a steel strap if a hydraulic press is not available.

For lighter-duty pulling, including removing tapered roller bearing races from blind recesses, a two- or three-jaw puller with a central bolt is useful. Most of these pullers have short jaws, however, so they cannot be used to remove bearings that are pressed deep onto a shaft or far into a housing. Seals and small bearings are easily installed with a few good taps from a brass hammer, but be sure to use a round arbor of some kind to ensure that the parts are installed square and even. Large sockets make very good arbors, as do short sections of thick-walled steel tubing.

Making Tools

In the transmission rebuilder's arsenal of parts are a number of homemade tools. The most important of these are sections of steel pipe to drive bearings and gears onto shafts and into housings. The most-needed sizes will be in the 1- to 2-inch inside-diameter range with thick walls to withstand the pounding and pressing forces they are needed for. Don't spend a lot of money on these—just check your local scrap metal dealer for short sections of these diameters. Cut them off with an angle grinder or power hacksaw. Other scraps of brass and steel can come in handy during assembly for driving seals or bearings onto shafts, or for aligning stacks of parts.

A few transmissions and hypoid final drives are easier to set up properly with special "test" bearings. In some cases, bearings may have to be pressed on and off of a shaft repeatedly to calculate the shims or spacers needed for the right preload. It helps to have a bearing that has been modified to give a light push fit rather than the original press fit. The easiest way to do this is with a good used bearing and a brake hone. Hone the center bore until the bearing can be slid on the shaft with hand pressure. Bearing races are manufactured with very tight tolerances, so one bearing is very close in size to another, and the setting measured with a test bearing will be the same as that with the new bearing.

These short pieces of thick-walled steel tube are used to press bearings and synchronizers onto shafts. The ones pictured here are designed with splined ends to locate them for quick production work, but the home rebuilder doesn't need this feature. A selection of lengths and diameters will be needed.

CHECKLIST OF NEEDED TOOLS

General:
Set of standard or metric socket wrenches
Set of standard or metric open- and box-end wrenches
Assorted pliers and screwdrivers
Large hex driver bits (for fill and drain plugs on some transmissions)
Torx bits (used on GM and some others)
⅜-inch drive torque wrench
Large ball-peen hammer
Gasket scraper
Several small-diameter punches
Two sets of feeler gauges

Special:
Hydraulic press (nice to have)
Medium bearing splitter
Snap ring pliers (internal and external)
C-clip pliers
Brass-faced and shot-filled plastic hammer
Long brass draft
Inch-pound torque wrench
Large flat-blade screwdriver or seal puller
Scribe
Micrometer or calipers
Dial indicator and base
Selection of thick-walled steel tubing pieces from 1-inch to 3-inch inside diameter. Length around 10 to 12 inches.
Selection of 1-inch by 6-inch steel straps or blocks made from ¼- to ½-inch-thick material

Disassembly

Disassembly is one area where the shop manual is necessary, unless you have some prior experience with the transmission. There is usually a set order of disassembly; sometimes hidden clips or roll pins prevent the case halves from being split until they are removed. For this reason, never force anything during disassembly. Keep a rubber or plastic mallet on hand to persuade tight parts, but do not use a steel hammer or pry on the case with a screwdriver.

The first step in disassembly is splitting the transmission case. Once the two halves (or main case and extension housing) are separated, the shafts can be removed as an assembly and taken apart. Transmission shafts are assembled from both ends as a stack of parts. The order and direction of each part is important, so take good notes or follow the manual closely during the disassembly process.

There are a few inspection steps that should be performed during disassembly, including gear end float and bearing clearance. Check the mainshaft end float during disassembly of each section. Pay particular attention to the end float and shift fork wear when disassembling a transmission with gear pop-out problems.

Check that the bearings are located properly; make sure there are no missing circlips, and that all present circlips are correctly seated in their grooves. Make note of any that are missing or bent so that you can replace them. Check

During disassembly, do a quick check of the end float of each gear on the shafts if you can. Use two feeler gauges as shown here, so that a crooked or cocked gear doesn't give a false reading. It's easier to check during disassembly than reassembly—otherwise you will have to partially assemble each shaft and then disassemble it.

Check that all retaining rings (this one is a C-clip) are located and situated tightly in their grooves. A loose or missing clip could be an indicator of a worse problem, like a worn shaft or collapsed thrust bearing. Don't reuse these clips for reassembly—they don't return to their original shape after being removed.

approximate bearing preload during disassembly, too—note whether the shafts are hard or easy to turn; the approximate tightness will be a good guide during reassembly.

Disassembly of some transmissions is possible without a press, particularly if the parts that are disassembled will be replaced—bearings can be heated to remove them, or tapped off with a hammer. If they are not a tight press fit, the bearings on the ends of the mainshaft are quite easy to remove

with inertia. After removing the retaining ring(s), tap the end of the shaft gently on the bench a few times. Usually the weight of the gears and synchronizer assemblies (assuming they are not pressed on) will knock the bearing free.

To remove a tapered roller bearing outer race from a blind recessed housing, normally you would use a two- or three-jaw puller with the jaws facing outward. Another method, useful only when you are discarding the bearing, is to quickly weld

A quick and easy home-shop method for disassembling loaded gear shafts is to drop them lightly on a floor. The inertia of the gear stack will knock the retaining bearing race or spacer off the end of the shaft. Do this only on a wood or metal floor—concrete can chip. Don't drop the shaft from any higher than necessary.

Keep all of the parts of each synchronizer together during disassembly. It helps to mark the hub and sleeve with a scribe so that you can be sure of reassembling them properly. Keeping the synchronizer together makes inspection easier, since you can quickly determine which assembly is faulty and why.

a bead around the inside bearing surface of the race with a MIG welder. As the weld bead cools and shrinks, it will pull the race inward and the race will drop out of its bore.

Keep the synchronizer assemblies together as you remove them from the shafts, and disassemble them on the bench. Mark the hub and sleeve with a scribe before separating so that they can be reassembled in the same relative position. Sometimes they do not fit together more than one way, but even if they can be assembled in any position, rotating them can cause shifting problems. The two parts wear together and it's best if their long-term relationship does not change. Mark them on one side only to keep the parts' axial relationship constant. The fork groove is often offset to one side or another in relation to the hub.

Clean all of the internal and external parts thoroughly with solvent. The cleaner the parts, the easier the inspection will be. If you have a dishwasher and an understanding domestic partner, consider running all of the parts through two or three dishwasher cycles (with detergent) after the solvent bath. This will get them very clean—transmission shops in environmentally sensitive areas use a similar industrial system. Dry the parts as soon as possible so that no rust film can form.

If the transmission will not be assembled for some time, give the parts a quick coating of oil or WD-40 to prevent rust. Then store them carefully so that they don't bang against one another or other parts during storage. Small dings, chips, or cracks could cause more problems down the line. Be extra careful with gears and synchronizer parts.

INSPECTION
Shift Forks, Rails, and Detents

If the transmission has a removable side or top cover, pull it and check the interlocks, shift rails, and selector system before completely disassembling it. Check the shift stops at the same time (if the transmission has them). Run each shift rail to both ends of its travel, putting the synchronizer

Check the shift forks for wear at the ends. This one is quite badly worn— unless the manufacturer specifies a wear limit, discard forks with more than .010 inch of wear on the tips. Any more than this and the shift lever travel will be excessive and the transmission may not stay in gear.

Check the other end of the shift rails too. The fingers on the end may be attached with roll pins or small bolts. Whatever the attachment method, make sure that it holds tightly. Check that the holes have not been enlarged and that the fingers are not bent from a jammed synchronizer or bent shift rail.

sleeve into gear, and check that there is sufficient clearance between the sides of the shift fork and the groove.

Check carefully for bent shift forks. This is a particularly common problem in transmissions with no external stops in the shift linkage. Bent forks are not always obvious, so check them against a straightedge rather than eyeball them. Look for cracks on the unsupported ends of the forks and near the mounting screws or pins. Check for wear on those

areas of each shift fork that contact the synchronizer sleeve. If the wear is excessive, replace the forks or wear pads, if so equipped.

Check that the shift forks and levers are securely attached to the shift rails before disassembly—some transmissions use roll pins, which can work loose. Others use bolts or setscrews. After removing the forks, detent balls, and interlocks, check that the shift rails slide easily in and out of their bores in the transmission case. Inspect the bores, making sure that they are clean and not jammed with dirt or metal chips. Check that they are not worn out, and that they still have a tight fit on the shift rails.

Make sure that the rails are not bent by rolling them on the edge of a flat bench or table.

Check that notches for the interlocks and detent balls are in the right place and not worn, and look for scoring, particularly in the areas where the detent balls ride. Make sure the shift selector fingers are firmly attached to the ends of the rails: most of the time these are not removable, and if they are loose the rail must be replaced.

During disassembly, make sure that the interlock plungers, detent balls, and springs are present and undamaged. These small parts are durable, but springs can collapse with time. Check that the detent balls and any interlock plungers move freely in their bores and that the bores are clear and not scored. Make sure all detent springs are present and not collapsed or broken—usually there are two or three of the same type that you can compare with each other.

Synchronizers

After removing and disassembling the main shafts, inspect the synchronizers as assemblies first. Check that the sleeve

Check all shift rails for straightness. The easiest way to do this is to roll the rail along a flat surface, such as the edge of a bench. A precisely machined flat surface like this table saw surface will make this inspection more accurate. Any bowing or bending is cause for rejection—don't try to straighten a bent rail.

Inspect the synchronizer hub splines for wear. It is difficult to see in this photo, but the shiny areas on the sides of the splines are where the sleeve has worn grooves into the spline. These grooves cause hard shifting. For best performance, reject any hub with more than a few thousandths of wear.

Check the condition of the inserts after disassembling the synchronizer assembly. The insert pictured here is worn, but not excessively so. Make sure that the projection on the top of the insert is still prominent—some transmissions have sharp, narrow projections that tend to wear down over time. Worn inserts may allow the transmission to pop out of gear.

fits on the hub and can slide back and forth without trouble. Note the position of any springs holding the inserts in the hub. After disassembly, inspect the inserts for damage, scoring, and wear. The center raised portion should be distinct and sharp-edged. Make sure that the insert springs are not broken, bent, or otherwise damaged.

Check for general damage to the hub and sleeve. Look for evidence of thrust wear on the sides of the hubs. Check for wear on the faces of synchronizer hub splines which cause looseness in drive. Examine the internal splines on the sleeve for similar wear. If theses splines become too worn, the transmission will jump out of gear.

The edges of the sleeve's internal splines must be absolutely sharp and free from wear for perfect operation. The more wear seen on the ends of these splines, the harder the transmission will be to shift. A little wear is acceptable, but if the edges of the splines become worn down and rounded, they are more likely to run into the external teeth on the synchronizer rings and gear faces.

Check the condition of the fork grooves in the synchronizer sleeve. The finish should be smooth and flat with no nicks, burrs, scratches, or burned areas. Some transmissions have wear specifications for the width of the groove. If the

Check the synchronizer sleeve internal splines. This sleeve is worn to the point that it would cause hard shifting and bad synchronizer action. The grooves seen on either side of each spline in this picture are not wear—these are "backcut" grooves designed to keep the sleeve engaged with the gear under power and deceleration. Any more than .030 inch of rounding on the tip of each spline is unacceptable.

The fork groove in this sleeve appears to be in good shape. Some manufacturers give a width specification, others do not. Reject the sleeve if the groove is scored more than a few thousandths of an inch or discolored from heat.

groove is wider than the limit, replace it. Some manufacturers do not supply the synchronizer sleeves and hubs separately. In these transmissions, replace the complete synchronizer assembly if either the sleeve or hub is damaged.

Check the runout of the groove as well. There are two ways to do this. If the transmission allows access through a top or side cover, use a dial indicator to check the total runout of the shift fork grooves in the synchronizer sleeves. Test with the sleeve in neutral as well as engaged with each gear in turn. Repeat the measurement several times to be sure of repeatability, and alternate the engaged dog teeth. Runout should not exceed .020 inch or so.

If the transmission does not allow access to the synchronizer sleeves, runout can be measured less accurately after the synchronizer assemblies have been taken apart. Place the separated ring on a machined flat surface or piece of glass. Measure the distance from the surface to the edge of the groove in at least four places around its circumference.

Turn the sleeve over and measure the same dimension on the other side. The measurements should not vary by more than .010 inch per side. Of course each side may be different—the important variance is between the measurements on the same side.

Check for wear of the blocking rings. Inspect their inside surfaces first—if the "threads" cut into the brass are dull or missing, reject them. With paper or carbon fiber blocking rings, check that the inside surface is not glazed, shiny, or heavily scored. A dull, flat conical surface is ideal. Next, place them on the proper gear. Push the blocking ring gently onto the gear's synchronizer cone. It should grip the cone tightly when turned under hand pressure; the tighter the better. If it does not grip the gear cone, try a new blocking ring on that gear. If neither ring grips the gear, replace the gear.

Inspect the dog teeth on each ring. They should be sharp on all sides, with even wear on both sides of the teeth. Any

Above left: The first step in inspecting a blocking ring is checking the inside surface of the ring. The "threads," or machined-in grooves, should be sharp-edged and distinct. If they are flattened, the ring is probably worn out and should be discarded. Above right: Check the blocking ring teeth next. They should be as close to sharp as possible. The teeth on this ring are worn slightly. It could be reused for fourth or a higher gear as long as it passes the other tests, but with the transmission already apart it wouldn't hurt to replace it.

Above left: Check that the blocking rings grip their gear cone tightly. If not, check a new blocking ring against the same gear. If the new ring grips the gear tightly, toss the old ring. If not, the gear should be replaced. Above right: Some manufacturers give a clearance specification for checking blocking rings. If the ring grips the gear cone tightly, measure the clearance between the gear dog teeth and the inner surface of the blocking ring. If the clearance is less than the specification, discard the blocking ring.

dulling and uneven wear is cause for rejection. Check the insert slots on the synchronizer side of each blocking rings for any damage, scratches, or wear. Replace rings that are worn in this area.

If any gears are rejected, replace the synchronizer blocking ring for that gear so that the two parts can wear in together. Generally speaking, the synchronizer blocking rings should always be replaced in a rebuild, unless you are absolutely sure that they are not worn. The rings are relatively inexpensive, but they require a lot of time to reach and replace.

Reverse Gear

The first step in inspecting reverse is to check the operation of the reverse idler gear and linkage. Make sure that it can be fully engaged with both the mainshaft and countershaft gears with the reverse fork and detent in their proper positions. Do this before disassembly, if possible, so that you can see all of the reverse gear parts in their usual locations.

Remove the idler gear and check the bearing bore for wear. Make sure that the bearing is present and in good condition, and that the clearance between it and the idler shaft is not excessive. Some manufacturers give a specification for this clearance, but many do not. Most do not supply the center bearing separately. When in doubt, discard the gear or bushing with more than .010 inch of clearance between it and the shaft. Excessive clearance will cause noise and possibly allow the reverse gear to pop out of engagement. Check the tapered front edge of the reverse teeth for damage— these are fragile and can be rounded off by grinding against the mating gears. Replace the gear if it fails these tests.

Before moving on, check the reverse gear's mating components on the mainshaft and countershaft. In most transmissions, at least one of these gears is incorporated into a synchronizer sleeve, so check the operation of that synchronizer assembly first. Examine the edge of the reverse drive teeth for wear and rounding. These teeth are not as critical as the dog teeth of a speed gear, but heavily worn gears will make a transmission more difficult to shift into and out of reverse. Make sure that the synchronizer sleeve is otherwise in good condition.

Pay special attention to all of the reverse-related parts closely when diagnosing a reverse pop-out problem, particularly the reverse synchronizer/brake if the transmission has one. In general, the reverse synchronizer is not nearly as sensitive to wear as the others, but difficult reverse engagement can be caused by wear of these parts.

Drive Gears

Gear teeth tend to wear much more slowly than other parts, with the possible exception of the shafts, but several important

A reverse idler shaft that shows this much wear should be replaced. Too much clearance between the idler gear and its shaft will result in a reverse gear that is difficult to engage, jumps out of engagement, and could potentially damage the teeth on the countershaft and mainshaft synchro sleeve.

The sharper the front edge of the reverse idler teeth, the easier reverse will be to engage. This gear is pretty well worn, but some quick work with a die grinder or file will revive it to a serviceable level. Don't try this trick with gear dog teeth—they are much too precise to modify by hand.

Shown here are the mating teeth on the countershaft. These are moderately worn as well, but since the reverse idler teeth are not particularly important for transmission performance, they can probably be left as is. If they bother you, give them a dressing with a file or die grinder. Only when the teeth become completely rounded should the countershaft be discarded.

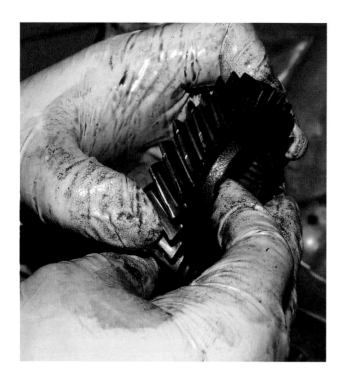

Above left: *Check the tooth surface of each gear. Look for any chips, deep gouges, discoloration, or other damage. The teeth of a used gear should look like these— shiny, flat on top, and smooth. Small chips on the edge of the teeth are nothing to worry about, but chips that encroach on the contact area of each tooth (the shiny area) are more dangerous. Discard gears with more than one or two chips, or chips on the contact area.* Above right: *Inspect the hub of each gear for deep scoring, wear marks, or discoloration from heat. This gear looks fine—the surface is smooth, almost polished, and any marks are not deep enough to feel with a fingernail. If the manufacturer gives a bore specification, measure it with an internal expanding bore gauge and micrometer.*

gear surfaces can and do wear out. Wear affects mainly the hub bore, the thrust surfaces, and the synchronizer cone and dog teeth, but the drive teeth are vulnerable to damage from lack of lubrication and abuse. Gear noise is almost always the result of damage or wear on the faces of the gear teeth.

If gear whine and noise were the reasons for disassembly, inspect the sides of the gear teeth very closely. Check the drive side of the teeth if the noise occurred only under acceleration, and check the coast side if the transmission whined on deceleration. Pay particular attention to any scoring, chipping, or pitting of the gear teeth. Also look at the shape of the worn-down contact area. It should be shiny and evenly distributed on the center of the gear tooth. Any deviation from a smooth gear tooth finish with an evenly centered wear pattern is a reason to discard the gear.

Check for dings, dents, or chips if the gears are known to make knocking or clicking noises. Small uneven areas of the tooth cause these kinds of sounds. Most of these areas can be filed out or ground down by hand if they are small and do not intrude onto the contact area of the tooth. If these marks affect the contact area, discard the gear. Any pitting on the contact area is also a good reason to reject the gear.

The gear's center bearing bore must be smooth with minimal or no scratches, and no deep scoring or discoloration. The same goes for the thrust surfaces on either side of the gear. Check both sides for grooving and excessive wear—polishing or wear marks from running against the synchronizer hub or locating collar are fine, but deep grooves and burning are not. Some manufacturers give a wear limit for gear width—if the gear is narrower than this limit, it may not be possible to set up the gears with the proper end float.

Carefully look over the synchronizer cone on each gear. It should have a smooth, lightly polished finish with no wear marks, grooves, or burned areas. Inspect the dog teeth for wear at the same time. They should be sharp and pointed on the ends. Different transmission manufacturers have their own standards, but in general up to .020 inch of the point from the outside edge of each tooth can be worn off with no detrimental effect on the transmission's shifting performance. Inspect all dog teeth for bends, chips, or worn-down sides. The sides of the dog tooth behind the point should be straight and even—if they appear very rounded or worn, reject the gear.

Above left: *Look carefully at the thrust surface of each gear. If the transmission is starved for oil, these narrow strips of high-speed contact are among the first to show signs of damage. This gear should probably be rejected—the marks are deep and show clear signs of metal displacement. Some manufacturers give a gear-width specification that should be used to reject worn thrust surfaces too.* Above right: *The synchronizer cone should be silver and mirror polished. This darkened cone shows clear signs of overheating. In this case, an improperly assembled fourth-gear synchronizer caused the blocking ring to drag against the input shaft cone until the blocking ring burned up. The resulting carnage destroyed the input shaft bearing and the third/fourth synchronizer assembly.*

The gear dog teeth are very important for good synchronizer performance. These dog teeth are worn beyond the point of salvage. As with the sleeve's internal splines, reject any gear with more than .020 inch or so of wear on the tips of the dog teeth. The sharper these teeth, the better the transmission will shift.

Bearings

All bearings are first inspected for roughness and "sticky spots." The smallest piece of grit will make a bearing rough, so it is important to make sure they are clean before testing. If the bearing races can be separated, like a tapered roller bearing, visually inspect the outer race and the surface of the rollers. Very faint scratches are probably OK, but any deep scratches, pitting, dents, or blue areas are cause for instant rejection.

For the most part, transmission bearings are wear items and, along with synchronizer rings and oil seals, are usually replaced while a transmission is apart for any reason. It helps that most bearings are relatively inexpensive. A $12 bearing requires four hours to replace, so it rarely pays to keep even a good one.

To save some money, buy new bearings and seals at a specialty bearing supply store. Look in the phone book under "Bearings" or "Industrial Supplies" for a list. Bearings from industrial retailers are normally much cheaper than from the dealer—the bearing houses do not have as high a markup as the manufacturer's suppliers do.

Bring the old bearing or races and make sure that the replacement is an exact one. Also, make sure to request

Inspect both parts of bearings with separate races. The rollers should be lightly polished with no visible marks, discoloring, or chips. Reuse bearings only if there is minimal to no wear, since they are heavily loaded and quite inexpensive. The scoring on the rollers of this countershaft bearing consigns it to the scrap-metal pile.

high-quality bearings. Some bearing houses are used to the demands of industrial customers who want cheap bearings. Bearings are precision components, and it pays to buy the best ones you can find. Incidentally, the bearings you buy at a car dealership or auto parts store are usually not better quality, and can be worse, than the ones you can buy at a bearing supply house.

Another word of warning concerning tapered roller bearings—although they are all theoretically designed with the same angles, don't mix and match inner and outer races if you can help it. If the angle varies even slightly, one end of all the rollers will become overloaded and will fail much sooner than otherwise. Use races and bearings from the same manufacturer and series whenever you have the chance.

Warning:
Never spin a tapered roller bearing on your finger with compressed air. The windows in the bearing cage act like turbine blades and can accelerate the bearing to 10,000 rpm or higher. At such high speeds, the bearing cage and rollers are subjected to very high forces that can cause them to blow apart. The resulting small pieces can cause serious injury.

Shafts and Splines
The main shafts in the transmission are unlikely to be damaged through simple use, but they should be inspected for any signs of abuse or excessive wear. Check the splined areas at both input and output shafts for evidence of twisting—hard clutches and high traction can cause the shaft to twist. In splined areas this is easy to see, since the splines can be quickly inspected for any deviation from parallel. Check the shaft for straightness by sighting down it, or using a dial indicator and V-blocks. More than .010 inch of total runout is unacceptable and the shaft should be replaced.

Take a good look at the bearing areas of each shaft, especially where bearings run directly on the surface. The bearing area under each speed gear should be looked at the most closely since these bearings are poorly lubricated. Also

A good bearing race should look like the one on the left. The inner surface is uniformly dull in the central load-bearing area and lightly polished on either side of that area. There are no cracks, scoring, or other damage. The bearing race on the right, however, is junk. The inner surface is pitted and shows signs of corrosion damage. The light "peppering" of dents on the surface is another sign of water in the oil.

REBUILDING A TRANSMISSION

Inspect the end of the input shaft for any damage. Make sure the splines are straight and not worn from the movement of the clutch disc. Check that the clutch pilot bearing surface is polished, straight, and clean. This shaft should probably be rejected because of the scoring on the pilot bearing surface, but it could be reused in a nonperformance application.

Check the internal bearing surfaces of each shaft for scoring, dents, burning, or other damage. The questionable area on this shaft is the bearing surface for the third speed gear. It is scored and damaged, so this shaft should not be saved. Any damage to the bearing surface under each gear will cause the needle bearings to wear quickly.

Long transmission life requires perfect gear mesh, which requires perfectly straight shafts. This Mopar mainshaft is mounted in two V-blocks on a bench to check its straightness with a dial indicator. Any performance rebuild should not skip this step, since straight shafts are the foundation of a good transmission. Reject any shaft with more than .010 inch total runout for a stock rebuild.

check the pilot bearing area on the front end of the mainshaft in a rear-wheel-drive transmission. Some run directly on the bearing rollers and damage is likely. Look for chips, scoring, or other damage on the rest of the shaft.

Main Case

Check the main case for cracks, warping, or other damage. Look closely at any threaded holes, such as drain and fill plugs, and repair them if they are damaged. Use a straight-edge to check the flatness of gasket surfaces. If any of the bearing bores in the case appear to be scored or damaged from a spun bearing, discard the case or have it repaired.

In a rear-wheel-drive transmission, take a close look at the extension housing and make sure that it is not cracked near the driveshaft yoke bushing. An out-of-balance driveshaft can cause cracks. Install a new bushing any time you disassemble the transmission—they are inexpensive to replace but do tend to wear quickly.

Check all of the machined surfaces of the case for damage. This case has some damage to the casting's internal strengthening ribs, which could be a problem. Make sure that there are no stripped threads, warped mounting surfaces, or cracks.

REASSEMBLY
Cleanliness and Lubrication

The most important thing to keep in mind when rebuilding a transmission is cleanliness. Before starting the process of reassembly, clean the work area thoroughly and prepare all of the internal parts on a clean surface. Make sure to have a good supply of clean rags or paper shop towels on hand.

Check the driveshaft yoke bushing during any rear-wheel-drive transmission rebuild. A worn bushing will cause vibration and possible cracking of the extension housing. They are easiest to replace while the transmission is apart, so it's probably a good idea to replace it regardless of its condition.

Remove all dirt and metal filings from inside the transmission case before starting. If a bearing or gear failed completely, be very careful to eliminate all foreign material—a small chip of steel or brass can cause extensive damage after the transmission is rebuilt. Sometimes this means that unrelated parts (such as the countershaft) have to be removed to gain access to awkwardly located areas of the case, even if the transmission is not being completely rebuilt.

Assembly lube is not strictly necessary when rebuilding a transmission, but it helps to protect parts during storage and makes assembly easier. There is no need for special assembly lube when doing transmission work—unlike engines, the low temperature and surface pressures on startup mean that there is plenty of time for lubrication to reach all the critical parts of a transmission. Many professional shops use Vaseline because it dissolves in transmission oil and does not contain any harmful friction additives that can affect synchronizer performance. Other shops use low-temperature chassis grease in moderation.

At the minimum, fill an oil can with the manufacturer's recommended lubricant and use it liberally during assembly. This will ensure that critical parts of the gear train are not dry (and cannot rust) during storage and assembly.

Small Parts

During any rebuild, always replace circlips, loose needle bearings, thrust washers, roll pins, rubber O-rings, and gaskets that are removed or disturbed. Rubber lip seals may be able to withstand being removed and replaced, but it is a good practice to replace them with new ones. Of course you

Lay out all of the new and clean used parts that you intend to use before starting your rebuild. There is nothing more frustrating than digging through boxes of dirty parts in the middle of reassembly. The rags laid out on the bench are a nice touch and prevent the parts from picking up small bits of grit and dirt from the bench. At this stage, the cleaner your work area the better.

Keep an oil can full of your transmission's recommended lubricant on hand during the rebuild process. Apply it liberally to aid in reassembly and prevent damage to dry parts while you put things together. If you want to use an assembly lube to keep parts together, use a light grease or Vaseline since they are sticky but will wash out of bearings quickly as oil reaches them.

REPAIRING UNAVAILABLE PARTS

If you are working on an old transmission for which parts are not available, or for which parts are very expensive, there are some options for fixing otherwise hopeless cases. A good machine shop with an experienced welder and centerless grinding machine operator are the minimum requirements. The work can be done by any shop that can work with the required precision—a few thousandths of an inch of error can result in gears that don't mesh properly or shafts that bind. In both cases, the errors can cause bad shifting, noise, and possibly broken parts. A good shop won't be cheap, because accurate machine setup takes time.

If a shaft support bearing lets go, it can take out part of the transmission case at the same time from the shaft's flailing around. If your transmission is cheap and easy to find a replacement case for, fine, but if not, some machine work will be in order. A good machine shop can bore the case oversize, press in an aluminum bushing, and align-bore the whole thing. The work must be done with absolute accuracy or the transmission will be worse off than before the repair.

Shafts with worn bearing journal areas, such as the tip of the input shaft, or the mainshaft pilot bearing, can be welded up and ground back down to repair the damage. Splines are harder to repair, particularly since they require very specialized equipment to cut. If the shaft is sufficiently rare, a good machinist can turn or grind a replacement area and weld it onto the shaft. Transmission input shafts are often repaired this way: the shaft is cut, and a new splined shaft is located accurately and welded on. If the welding is done properly, the resulting shaft will be nearly as strong as the original.

Minor seal damage on a shaft does not usually require machine work. Rubber lip seals eventually wear grooves onto the surface of the shafts they seal against. This wear damage can be repaired with thin steel sleeves that are tapped into place over the shaft. The most popular brand is called "Speedi-Sleeves," manufactured by Chicago Rawhide. A good parts store or bearing house can supply them in almost any diameter.

Gear teeth wear more slowly than the rest of the gear, particularly the inner bearing bore, the synchronizer cone, and dog teeth. If the gear's inner bore is burned or scored, a machinist can bore it out to a larger diameter and press in a bronze bearing insert similar to those used in camshafts. If the bearing originally ran on needle bearing, a hardened steel sleeve can be installed instead of the bearing insert.

Gear dog teeth and synchronizer cones can also be repaired with some careful machine work and a donor gear with good dog teeth. The good dog teeth are removed from the donor gear on a lathe, creating a ring with teeth around its circumference. The worn teeth are then machined off the bad gear, leaving a stub onto which the good teeth from the donor gear are welded. Most transmissions use the same dog teeth and cone on more than one gear, so gears that are used less, such as fourth and fifth, wear the least and make good donors. A shop can machine the good teeth off of a fourth or fifth gear and weld them onto worn gears. The center of the gear will have to be honed out to remove the extra weld metal and any distortion. This can be combined with the bushing or sleeve installation described above.

For some popular transmissions, such drastic measures are not necessary. Recently, reproduction gears and shafts for classic transmissions like the Ford "Toploader" four-speed, Borg-Warner's T10, and Chevrolet Muncie transmission have become available. These gears can give new life to otherwise unsalvageable transmissions, but be warned—many are "close ratio" gear sets and cannot be mixed and matched with OEM gears.

Worn forks, shift rails, and cases can all be rebuilt with similar techniques. Worn forks can be built up by welding or brazing and machined back down, and shift rails can be welded up and reground. Damaged cases are easiest to repair if they are aluminum—a good welder can work wonders on cracks and damaged sealing surfaces. Always check for warping if the case has been welded on. Spun bearings are a common occurrence and relatively easy to fix. A machine shop can bore the case oversize and press in an aluminum bushing to repair the surface of the bore.

Almost anything is possible with enough setup time and experience. Bring your worn parts to your machinist and discuss your needs before giving up on an "NLA" component. You might not like the prices you are quoted, but it allows you to salvage parts that would otherwise be discarded.

Transmission bearings and seals are another matter entirely. Most roller and ball bearings are standard designs and sizes that are available from industrial bearing supply houses. A few bearings can be difficult to find, and some of the more unusual thrust washers, etc., will likely have to come from the manufacturer.

Most bearings and seals are marked with their size. The numbers etched or molded into the outside edge of these parts can be used to cross-reference them to industry-standard parts. If the original parts are missing, the shaft and housing diameters and depth will be necessary to find a replacement.

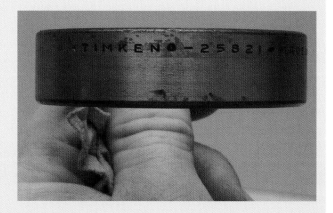

All ball and roller bearings are marked somewhere on the inner or outer race. The marking will give the brand of the bearing, a part number, and sometimes a fit class or subtype. If you buy replacement bearings at an industrial bearing supply house, bring your old bearing, or as much of it as you have, so that they can find an exact match.

should replace any silicone sealant that is disturbed. All of these parts are inexpensive, but they are difficult to get to and critical to good transmission performance. There is nothing more frustrating than pausing in the middle of a rebuild to track down a particular special clip, but the consequences of a broken retainer are even more frustrating.

When replacing a shaft in a housing that contains a rubber lip seal, watch out for splines that can tear or nick the fragile lip. Some mechanics wrap all splines with masking tape, and if you are naturally clumsy it can't hurt.

Gear Shaft Assembly

As you assemble the gear stacks, check parts frequently for proper fit. Make sure that the gears are free to turn when assembled and that the synchronizer hubs are tight on their shaft splines. Some clearance specifications may be given by the shop manual, including end play (or end float). This refers to the axial space between the rotating gears on a shaft.

End play is important because excessive end play can result in popping out of gear as the gears move axially on the shafts and disengage from their synchronizer sleeve under engine power or engine braking. This is especially critical in setting up a rebuilt transmission with used parts because end play increases as the gears wear. A gear shaft that is too loose right after a rebuild starts out with a disadvantage, and it will not be able to withstand as much wear before shifting problems pop up.

Gear end play is usually controlled during transmission assembly through variable-thickness snap rings or thrust washers. Some transmissions do not provide a way to change end play; in these gearboxes the only way to reduce end play is replacement of worn parts. Check it anyway—excessive end play is one of the most common causes of jumping out of gear and poor shifting performance.

Backlash, the gap between teeth of adjacent gears, is the other important parameter related to gear tooth contact. Backlash is determined by gear tooth size and shape, as well as the center distance of the gear shafts, none of which are easily adjustable. Backlash varies somewhat between transmissions—the larger the gear teeth, the more backlash is required for maximum efficiency and gear tooth life.

Manufacturing errors in or damage to the case or gears can result in a gear pair that binds or has tight spots, however. For this reason it is a good idea to always check that each pair of gears in an assembled transmission has at least some backlash before buttoning up the transmission. Simply rock the mounted pair back and forth, making sure there is at least some clearance. A few transmission manufacturers measure gear wear with backlash specifications—if the backlash clearance is greater than specified, the gears should be rejected.

These pictures show the proper way to install synchronizer insert springs. In most transmissions (check your shop manual to be sure) the springs spiral backward in relation to the shaft's rotation. This means that viewed from the front (picture 1), the spring should wrap counterclockwise. From the other side of the hub (picture 2), the spring should wrap clockwise. Both springs start and end at the same insert in this case.

During the reassembly process, also check any new parts before using them. Make sure that new gears, synchronizers, and shafts are free from problems such as rounded dog teeth, pits, chips, dings, and machining marks. Inspect gear teeth particularly carefully—a chip or ding on a single tooth will make noise when assembled into a transmission. Check that all parts fit during reassembly, too. It sounds obvious, but don't force anything. Stop what you're doing and check your parts carefully before forcing and possibly breaking something.

Synchronizer Reassembly

Reassemble each hub and sleeve in the same relationship they were disassembled in—check the scribe marks you made during disassembly. Make sure that the sleeve slides easily yet without play on the hub. Check the assembled synchronizer against the shop manual to make sure that it is oriented correctly in radial and axial directions.

Install the inserts and detent springs per the service manual—some can only be installed in one direction. If the synchronizer uses circular insert springs, install them so that they end at the same insert and that they are positioned in opposite directions (the same direction when looking at the assembly from either side).

Place the blocking rings (or blocking ring assemblies) in place on the inserts and splines. Make sure that any notches or drive pins on the blocking rings mesh properly with the gear and synchronizer. After mounting the synchronizer assembly on the shaft, check that it can be shifted into either gear. Make sure that it is mounted the right way—the groove may be offset to one side or another.

Bearing Assembly

Installing bearings onto shafts and into housings is done with a hydraulic press. Although it can be done without one, it's more difficult. A hammer and suitable arbors (thick-walled steel pipe) can be used, but the slightest slip can cause expensive damage to the hardened gears and bearing races.

Bearings that are pressed onto a shaft can be heated in a home oven to 300 degrees F. and then quickly slipped onto the (cold) shaft. The success of this method depends on the relative temperature of the two parts and the tightness of the press fit—a very tight fit will make it harder to assemble the parts. Placing the shaft in a freezer or refrigerator will help. In any case, make sure to have the workspace and tools set up to install the bearing as quickly as possible. If the bearing makes it only partway onto the shaft before it cools down, it will be much harder to remove.

Whenever you use force to install a bearing, whether from a press or hammer, make sure you apply the force to the race with a press fit. In this example, the bearing is going into a press-fit bore in the case, so the rebuilder is tapping only on the outer race. A bearing being pressed onto a shaft should have all force applied to the inner race. Failure to do this could result in bearing trouble down the line.

Whenever a bearing must be pressed onto a shaft or into a housing, be very careful to press or tap on the press-fit race, whether inner or outer. If the bearing is driven onto a shaft, apply pressure only to the inner race, and if into a housing, press only on the outer race. Pressing on the wrong race will dent the races and balls or rollers and cause the bearing to make noise and fail sooner. Rolling-element bearings are not designed to take heavy axial loads when the bearing is not turning. Don't worry about this during disassembly since the bearings will be discarded anyway.

Once the shafts are assembled and placed in the transmission case, the most important aspect of transmission bearing assembly is the axial clearance (or preload, if pressure is applied) between the main shaft ball or tapered roller bearings. Bearing preload or clearance is usually determined by shims or thick retaining rings placed between either the inner or outer races of opposing bearings. Since shafts, cases, and bearings all vary somewhat, the shims or rings will probably need to be replaced whenever the transmission is rebuilt.

Bearing preload or clearance is measured one of two ways: by direct measurement or by turning torque. With direct measurement, the position of the installed bearing race is measured relative to the transmission case or shaft. Shims are added until the measurement matches that recommended in the service manual. With the turning torque method, a low-range torque wrench is attached to the splined end of the shaft, and the torque required to turn the shaft is noted. If the torque is too high, the preload is too high, and if the torque is too low, the preload is also too low.

Always check preload, even if all the same parts are being used with no new parts—a large error in either direction will significantly reduce bearing lifespan and increase transmission noise. In general, use the manufacturer's recommended

Setting bearing preload or clearance is an important part of the rebuild process. Most transmissions use shims of various carefully controlled thicknesses to set preload. Before you can determine what shim you need for a given setting, you must use a micrometer to accurately measure the shims you have now. The more accurately this is done, the more accurate the final setting will be.

preload setting, but there are some situations where you might want more or less than suggested. See the chapter on modifications for a more detailed explanation of the consequences of changing bearing preload.

Shift Fork Alignment

An often-overlooked but important aspect of careful transmission assembly is the alignment of the shift forks in relation to the synchronizers. The shift forks should not be biased toward either side of the groove in the synchronizer sleeve in neutral. If the forks are dragging on the side of the groove, this can cause burning or scoring on the groove and fork.

If the bias is bad enough, it will force the synchronizer blocking ring to be in constant light contact with the gear cone. The blocking ring will wear out, and the gear can even be damaged by the friction and heat that develops against the ring. In addition, when the transmission is shifted into gear, the fork may bottom against the groove and bend or break off. This goes for reverse as well— reverse fork misalignment can cause the reverse idler gear to be damaged by running into the reverse drive gears on the mainshaft and countershaft.

When a gearbox is assembled at the factory, rails and forks are chosen to result in proper alignment with the case

and gear stack of each box. If all of the original parts are retained during the rebuild, the shift fork alignment should be fine. There is enough clearance that small variations are not critical for most uses.

Some transmission service manuals give specifications for shift fork alignment and clearance that should be checked during the rebuild. Many, however, do not. Those that do, have alternative shift forks that are biased to one direction or another in relation to the attachment point. In either case, at least verify that the shift forks do not appear to be dragging on the synchronizer sleeve in neutral. If the transmission manufacturer does not make alternative parts, it will take some creative fabrication work to change the fork's relationship to the shift rail. The modifications chapter explores this in more detail.

When installing new forks, make sure they are mounted correctly on the shift rails. Use new roll pins if required, or properly torque the mounting fasteners. Check the operation of the interlock and detents before finally closing the transmission—run the linkage through each gear and check for any shifting problems. Make doubly sure that the linkage cannot select more than one gear (or reverse and any other gear) at the same time.

CHAPTER 5
THE TREMEC/ BORGWARNER T-5

The T-5 transmission is a simple, lightweight five-speed transmission produced by the hundreds of thousands since introduced in 1982. It was a gradual evolutionary step from a family of lightweight four-speed transmissions built by Borg-Warner's automotive division. All of these transmissions were designed to handle reduced power levels of smog-era U.S.-built engines like the various small four- and six-cylinder engines from AMC, Chevrolet, and Ford.

The T-5 shares shaft center distance, synchronizer design, aluminum case, and overall layout with the Borg-Warner SR-4 four-speed, introduced in 1974 and used by Ford, AMC, and Jeep. The T-4, also introduced in 1982, was an improved version of the SR-4, with tapered roller bearings instead of ball bearings on the input shaft and mainshaft, and caged roller countershaft bearings instead of needle roller bearings. The T-4 was used by the same manufacturers (Ford, AMC, and Jeep) as well as GM, where it soldiered on long after the design should have been obsolete—until 1987 in some applications.

The T-5, envisioned as a "fuel economy" transmission, added an overdrive fifth gear in the extension housing of the T-4, behind the mainshaft bearing support. Like its predecessors, the first T-5 had brass blocking ring synchronizers and no rolling-element bearings between the gear hubs and mainshaft. The first applications were GM S-series trucks, AMC cars, Jeep trucks, and the Nissan 280ZX turbo.

By 1983 the T-5 could be found in all of these, as well as the Ford Mustang and GM F-body (Camaro and Firebird). It was these two applications—particularly the 5.0-liter V-8 Mustang—that did the most to promote the T-5 as a performance transmission. Ford has installed it behind V-8s, V-6s, and 4-cylinders (both NA and turbocharged) in the Fox, SN95, and DEW98 chassis Mustangs ever since, making them some of the most common rear-wheel-drive manual transmissions ever produced. While the original use was envisioned as a fuel-economy move, the performance aspects of the T-5 behind some of the more powerful Mustangs soon became apparent.

Through the 1990s, the T-5 was also used in the Isuzu Rodeo and Honda Passport twins, and the Ford Mustang, as well as the GM S-series/Astro van and F-body. Both Ford and GM eventually dropped the T-5 from V-8 service—in 1993 for GM and 1994 for Ford—but the long-serving T-5 continues to give Ford a manual transmission for the V-6 Mustang with the release of the face-lifted 2005 model, the last production use of the T-5 in the United States. In other markets, Ford used the T-5 in the Sierra Cosworth in the United Kingdom and continues to use it in various performance Falcons in Australia. U.K. sportscar manufacturer TVR has used the gearbox in several vehicles, as has Korean/Chinese light-truck manufacturer Ssangyong.

PRODUCTION CHANGES

Borg-Warner made many incremental improvements to the T-5 over its production lifespan, including improved synchronizers and bearings, improved steel alloys for the main gears, a synchronizer/brake for the reverse idler, and dozens of gear ratios. Several of these changes stemmed from development work carried out by Ford of UK for the Sierra RS Cosworth in 1983 to 1984. Engineers improved the T-5 to cope with the demands of the high-revving, powerful turbo engine. The improved version of the T-5 that came out of this work, called the "World Class" T-5 (often shortened to WC), differed in many minor ways from the earlier T-5.

The WC T-5 added tapered roller bearings to the countershaft; needle roller bearings between the first, second, and third gear hubs and mainshaft; fiber-lined third and fourth gear synchronizer blocking rings; and improved three-piece first and second gear synchronizer assemblies. The new fiber-lined blocking rings improved shift quality greatly over the earlier units, and the gear hub needle bearings made the transmission less sensitive to lubrication failure and more tolerant of high-rpm use.

The first T-5 design became popularly known as the "Non–World Class" or "NWC" T-5, although it had no official name. Ford replaced it with the WC T-5 worldwide from 1985 on, but GM switched to the WC T-5 only later, in the F-body cars from 1988 and the S-series trucks from 1992. Although the changes from the NWC to WC T-5 were drastic, they were not the end of Borg-Warner and Ford's gradual improvements.

The first NWC T-5s used in Ford and GM V-8 applications are stronger than other NWC T-5s because of their higher gearing—these had a 2.95 first gear and .63 or .73 overdrive, and are rated for 265 lb-ft. The tapered counter-gear bearings of the WC transmission improved shaft stiffness and gear train strength, which allowed Ford to use a lower, 3.35 first gear with a similar overdrive ratio (.68) behind the 5.0-liter V-8. Even with the lower first gear, Borg-Warner did not change the transmission's torque rating.

In addition to their muscle-car V-8 applications, Ford and GM used the T-5 behind 4-cylinder and small V-6 engines for many years. The most common of these are the ubiquitous Mustang and GM gearboxes with 3.76, 3.97, 4.03, and 4.30 gear ratios. While these transmissions are externally very similar to the V-8 transmission, they are much weaker and have poor ratios. Even the WC versions, used in four-cylinder Mustangs, Cougars, and T-birds with turbo and nonturbo engines from 1985 to 1993, are not as strong as the V-8 T-5s. The late Mustang SVO (1986 only) box with its 3.50 first gear is stronger than the other four-cylinder T-5s.

A reduced-ID bearing or different clutch disc can be used to adapt one of these transmissions to a V-8 engine, but it is not a good idea. Despite their larger input shaft bearing, the low first gear multiplies engine torque too much for the T-5's tight shaft centers, giving it more of a mechanical advantage over the gearbox internals. While the early V-8 T-5s are rated at 265 lb-ft of torque, the four-cylinder gearboxes can only handle 240. In addition, the extremely low first gear is essentially unusable unless the final drive gearing is increased to compensate. Even then, the large gap between first and second gear means that the engine rpm will drop significantly between gears, not a particularly good situation for a performance engine with a narrow power band.

In 1990, the V-8 WC T-5 was improved again, this time by machining the input shaft, and second and third driven gears from a high-nickel-content steel alloy. The second and third gear were lowered from 1.93 and 1.29 to 1.99 and 1.33, respectively. Both changes increased the transmission's overall strength, and BW gave the improved gear set a higher, 300 ft-lb rating. Third and fourth gear synchronizer blocking rings were also upgraded slightly, with carbon fiber in place of organic fiber linings, and the shift linkage was modified to reduce shifting effort (although it increased throw slightly). A concurrent detail change was a new speedometer drive gear, with seven teeth instead of eight.

In 1993, the ultimate production T-5 was released for use in the Mustang Cobra. In production until 1996, the "Cobra Spec" WC T-5 was the only production unit to use a tapered roller bearing between the input shaft and mainshaft. This small change (replacing loose rollers and a needle thrust bearing) enabled the transmission to be built with greater preload than previous versions, which improved shaft stiffness and overall strength. The gears, including the 3.35 first gear and

.68 overdrive, remained the same as the basic WC T-5 used behind other V-8 Mustangs, although the changes resulted in an increased torque rating—to 310 lb-ft.

The Cobra gearbox also incorporated a steel input bearing retainer, replacing the troublesome aluminum version used on all other Ford T-5s. The Cobra transmission was the first to incorporate another gradual T-5 improvement—a reverse gear brake (synchronizer) to reduce reverse gear crunching.

Also in 1993, Ford began selling an aftermarket version known as the "Z-spec" T-5. It shares all of the Cobra's enhancements, including the stronger gear steel and improved bearings, with the further benefit of higher, closer gear ratios, and a short-throw shifter. First gear in the Z-spec T-5 was 2.95, with a .63 overdrive. Borg-Warner conservatively rated the transmission for 330 lb-ft of torque. Racers' personal experience has shown that the Z-spec T-5 will withstand nearly 400 lb-ft for street use, road racing, and street tire drag racing.

For 1993, GM dropped the T-5 behind V-8 engines, turning to the larger, stronger T-56 six-speed previously used in the Dodge Viper. The remaining F-body T-5s were installed behind the V-6 and shared much with the Ford WC T-5. This basic design was used until the end of F-body V-6 production, in 2002.

Ford continued to use the non-Cobra T-5 behind the 5.0 V-8 engine for two more years—1994 and 1995. The T-5 used in these Mustangs was redesigned to accommodate the stretched "SN95" platform. Deeper bell housings were used to move the transmission back in the chassis, which required the use of a longer input shaft (7.85 inches). These transmissions also have no neutral safety switch (since a switch was added to the clutch pedal). The 1994 and 1995 Cobra used a long-input-shaft variant of the upgraded transmission, while the new V-6 models used a variant of the 3.35 first gear standard V-8 transmission, but with a .72 overdrive rather than .68.

In 1998, Borg-Warner sold the T-5 design and all tooling to Transmission Technologies Corporation, or TREMEC, a Mexico-based transmission manufacturer. TREMEC continues to produce the T-5 for OEM and aftermarket users in the United States and worldwide. The TREMEC-built T-5 is essentially the same as the final Borg-Warner production transmission with minor differences, primarily the casting stamp on the side of the transmission case.

Ford again changed minor details of the T-5 used in the V-6 Mustang in 1999, reverting to the V-8 overdrive ratio of .68 and eliminating the speedometer cable drive gear from the mainshaft. In its place was an electronic trigger that produces square wave pulses for a digital speedometer. This and all following versions of the T-5 also eliminated the troublesome aluminum front bearing retainer. With the release of the updated 2005 Mustang V-6, Ford tweaked the T-5's gear ratios once again. First gear is now 3.76, with a .72 overdrive, but the transmission is otherwise similar to previous versions. The torque rating remains 300 lb-ft.

PARTS SWAPPING

The T-5 transmission was produced for many years in many different configurations. According to TREMEC, altogether nearly 260 different T-5 transmissions have been produced. The T-5's modular case and gear set design means that there are nearly unlimited options available for building a custom transmission. There were at least two different front case bolt patterns, at least three different shifter locations, three different transfer case bolt patterns, a dozen gear ratio combinations, and multiple fifth-gear pairs.

The first step in modifying, rebuilding, or assembling a custom T-5 is proper identification of the transmission you are starting with. Because there are so many visually similar T-5s out there, the transmission can be hard to identify. Even if you remove the transmission yourself or know exactly the year and model car that it came from, it may not be what you think it is. Twenty or more years of parts swapping and repairs mean that not all cars in the junkyard have the same equipment they rolled down the assembly line with.

The surest way to identify an unknown T-5 is the number stamped on the aluminum tag hanging from one of the extension housing bolts. The list of tag numbers given in the appendix covers the most popular variants of the T-5 and their gear ratios, where known. Unfortunately, the casting numbers on the case or extension housing will not help to identify the transmission.

T-5 parts are most easily swapped between similar transmission families (that is, WC and NWC) with a few exceptions. WC and NWC main cases are different and cannot be swapped. The gear set and mainshaft from the matching class must also be used. All T-5 extension housings can be used on any T-5 with a similar-length mainshaft, although transmissions with a reverse brake must use an extension housing with this feature.

In addition to several different front bearing diameters, there are two common T-5 bell housing bolt patterns: Ford and GM. The Ford bolt pattern is similar to that used for the old Toploader four-speed, although it is narrower. The two top bolts are 7.875 inches from center to center. All Ford T-5s use this bolt pattern. The GM pattern is the same as the Muncie, T-10, and other "standard" GM transmissions used in the 1960s and 1970s. The two top bolts are 8.125 inches apart, and the mounting bolts are in distinctive "ears" that stick out from the sides of the case.

GM NWC transmissions and WC transmissions used behind the GM V-8 use the GM bolt pattern, while the Chevette T-5 and later GM V-6 WC transmissions use the Ford bolt pattern. AMC, Isuzu, and Nissan T-5 transmissions use the Ford pattern as well. In the Camaro/Firebird, the transmission is installed canted over at a 15-degree angle counterclockwise. The bell housing bolt pattern is therefore slightly off square, as is the transmission mount pad at the end of the extension housing.

The most common input shaft diameters and spline counts are those used on the Ford and GM T-5s. All Ford T-5s have a 1.0625-inch-diameter shaft with 10 splines. The input shaft on V-8 transmissions from 1983 to 1993 is 7.18 inches long with a .668-inch-diameter tip for the pilot bearing. The Ford four-cylinder boxes use a longer shaft (7.41 inches) and a smaller-diameter pilot bearing (.590 inch) than the V-8 version.

The input shaft on transmissions used behind Ford V-8 and V-6 engines from 1994 to 2005 is 7.85 inches long with the V-8 pilot diameter. The very latest Ford V-6 transmissions are internally the same as previous V-8 transmissions with the exception of the longer input shaft. A new, short input shaft can be used to bolt them to the early V-8 bell housing, although there is no way to use a mechanical speedometer.

All T-5s used behind GM engines have a .590-inch-input-bearing diameter. V-8 engines use a 1.125-inch-diameter shaft with 26 splines, while four-cylinder and V-6 transmissions have a 1-inch, 14-spline shaft. Both are 7.18 inches long. Late V-6 transmissions used in Camaros and Firebirds (with the standard Ford bell housing bolt pattern) have a slightly shorter (7.14-inch) input shaft with the V-8 diameter and spline count.

The input bearing retainer can be swapped between classes, as long as the input bearing and shaft are the same size (that is, not between four-cylinder and V-8, or GM and Ford). The latest steel bearing retainer is a definite improvement over the aluminum unit used on early Ford T-5s. All GM T-5s used a steel input bearing retainer.

Gear sets (including input shaft) can only be swapped within the same class. WC gears must be used with a WC mainshaft and case, and NWC gears with a NWC mainshaft and case. The countershaft bearing bores in the case can be rebushed to use WC gears in a NWC case, but it does not make economic sense since used WC cases are so cheap and plentiful.

With a few exceptions (some of the speed gears in four-cylinder and V-8 transmissions and overdrive gear pairs), the individual gears are not mixable. The entire gear set, including input shaft, must match. The input shaft can be

THE TREMEC/BORGWARNER T-5

exchanged only for one with the same number of teeth on the gear. If you are building a T-5 for performance use behind a V-8 or other powerful engine, the only gear sets worth considering are the 3.35 and 2.95 first-gear WC gear sets. The rest can be used, but are hardly high performance. They are all generally weaker than the close-ratio gear sets.

All of the parts needed to convert any WC T-5 to the latest, close-ratio gear set with the Cobra mainshaft pilot bearing are available new from TREMEC (Z-spec gears). The mainshaft can be modified by a centerless grinder for the Cobra tapered bearing if the new shaft (Ford only) will not work, although this still requires use of the Ford input shaft and a 2.95 first-gear set. The late-model 3.35 first-gear set with improved steel gears is available and can be used to upgrade earlier transmissions (although without the tapered mainshaft support bearing). Complete new transmissions with both gear sets are available new from TREMEC.

The overdrive gear pair is commonly swapped to increase or decrease the gear ratio in top gear. For racing, overdrive can be lowered to reduce the gap between fourth and fifth, or to make fifth gear usable on long straights. For street/drag use with an extremely low rear axle ratio, the opposite is required—a higher overdrive ratio will lower engine rpm at the same speed and compensate for acceleration-optimized gearing in first through fourth.

There are a few common and a few uncommon overdrive gear sets for the T-5. The important thing to remember about overdriven gears is that they depend on the ratio between the input gear and countershaft drive gear. In the T-5, the lower the first-gear ratio, the greater the difference between the input and countershaft teeth. This lowers the overdrive gearing as well, so the same pair of gears will produce a different ratio in the 3.35 and 2.95 first-gear ("wide" and "close") ratio boxes. The following chart shows the commonly available overdrive gear pairs and the ratio that results from using them with the two strongest gear sets.

The 53/33-tooth gear pair is the rarest of the four. It was used on only aftermarket applications in the United States, although it is the standard gear pair for the U.K. Ford Cosworth Sierra. It is available now through Ford Motorsport in the United States (but only with the Ford mainshaft

spline). The 55/31 gear pair is available for both GM and Ford applications. There are a few other overdrive ratios from the GM and Ford four-cylinder and V-6 transmissions, but the four listed below are the most readily available.

Overdrive gears, for the most part, must match the class of the remaining gears. In addition, the driven (mainshaft) overdrive gear must match the manufacturer—GM and Ford T-5s use different splines for the fifth driven gear. Some GM gears used a .125-inch spacer between the gear and snap ring on the countershaft—make sure that the spacer is not missing.

All Ford T-5s have a 27-spline output on the mainshaft, while GM transmissions have 28 splines with the same diameter. While lengths vary somewhat, there are many combinations of extension housing and mainshaft that can be used to vary shifter position. Make sure to use the yoke and extension housing bushing that matches the output splines—Ford with Ford and GM with GM.

GM WC T-5s (and NWC after 1988) do not have speedometer drive gears on the mainshaft, and neither do 1994-and-newer Ford T5s. To use these transmissions with a mechanical speedometer, an early extension housing and mainshaft must be used with the proper speedometer drive gear and adapter. In all cases, the mainshaft must match the class—WC mainshaft, gears, and case cannot be mixed with NWC shaft, gears, and case.

Early NWC and WC T-5s have a 7-tooth speedometer drive gear. The 1990-and-up Ford T-5 has an 8-tooth gear. The 7-tooth speedometer drive gear allows easier speedometer calibration for lower final drive ratios, since the speedometer driven gear is limited to 21 teeth. Generally, the limit is a 3.55 final drive ratio—go lower than this and the 7/21-tooth combination will not be enough. Some four-cylinder T-5s had a 6-tooth drive gear, and these are available from TREMEC if necessary.

MODIFICATIONS

The T-5's popularity and widespread use in the 1980s and 1990s, as well as its OEM modularity, make it an attractive target for the aftermarket. At present there are at least half a dozen alternative shifters, three gear sets, an alternative case and mainshaft, strengthened front bearing retainers, several

5th gear teeth (countershaft/ mainshaft)	53/33	55/31	51/25	59/27
2.95 first gear (24-tooth input, 31-tooth counter)	0.8	0.73	0.63	0.59
3.35 first gear (23-tooth input, 34-tooth counter)	0.92	0.83	0.72	0.68

Fifth gear ratios depend on the ratio of the input shaft gears. As this chart shows, the higher the input ratio, the higher the 5th gear ratio.

$$\text{Driven Gear Teeth} = \frac{\text{Drive Gear Teeth x Axle Ratio x Tire Revolutions Per Mile}}{1,000}$$

For Ford speedometers (100 revs per mile), this formula gives the correct driven gear for a given final drive ratio, tire size, and drive gear tooth: Tire Revolutions Per Mile can usually be estimated from the tire's effective radius (distance from axle center to ground) or the tire manufacturer's published specifications.

overdrive gear ratios, and improved countershaft bearing supports. The only TREMEC parts needed to build a complete transmission are the extension housing and shift linkage.

The most common and necessary aftermarket modification is the shifter mechanism. The stock T-5 shifter has long, vague throws, and the stock linkage is not known for durability. The shifter geometry and rubber isolator conspire to make shifts feel rubbery and light. There are no internal stops for the shift rail or forks, so overtravel and bent or broken shift forks are a constant problem with hard-driven T-5s—the most common failure is breakage of the thin areas of the shift fork, which results in the loss of two adjacent gears (usually the third/fourth fork breaks first).

Aftermarket shifters address both of these problems. Most slightly reduce the distance the lever must travel between gears, but, more important, they have stops that prevent linkage overtravel and shift fork damage. In addition, aftermarket shifters eliminate the rubber isolators between the lever and shift linkage. Both Gearboxman in the United Kingdom and G-force in the United States make stronger shift forks, but these are no substitute for a shifter with stops.

Gearsets are somewhat less common—only G-force and Quaife produce aftermarket gear sets for the T-5 transmission. Both manufacturers make use of stronger steels, wider gear teeth, and lower tooth pitch to strengthen the lightweight T-5. The Quaife sets, marketed by Gearboxman, are synchronized and come in two different ratios—standard 2.95 first gear and close 2.53 first. Both sets use the Cosworth Sierra's 23-spline, 1-inch input shaft with a .590-inch pilot diameter, which can be a problem for U.S. applications. The gear set also requires modifications to the transmission case and front bearing retainer because of the large-diameter input gear teeth.

G-force makes five gear sets, including a synchronized helical gear set, a nonsynchronized helical gear set, and three different straight-cut dog ring gear sets. The helical sets have gearing similar to the T-5 Z-spec transmission, but the straight-cut gears are available in a lower, 3.22 first-gear set or an ultraclose 2.46 first-gear set. All are available with a .59 or .73 overdrive ratio. The dog ring gear sets are also available with a road-racing-suitable .90 overdrive. The G-force gear sets are designed with the demands of drag racing in mind, and even the helical set can withstand several hundred

Don't confuse the large female Torx bolt for a drain or fill plug. Removing it will do very bad things to the reverse shift linkage and ruin your day.

more lb-ft than the factory sets—G-force says approximately 500 lb-ft with their mainshaft. G-force uses a GM 1-inch, 26-spline input shaft for their gear set, which will require a smaller input bearing and different clutch disc to use in a Ford application.

G-force makes a few other trick parts for the T-5, including a sand-cast aluminum transmission case with the Ford bolt pattern. The original T-5 case is die cast from an aluminum alloy chosen for its appearance and easy casting properties, rather than strength. The G-force case is cast from a strong alloy with increased section thicknesses in critical areas. Together with one of the G-force gear sets and mainshaft, the case will provide the foundation of a nearly unbreakable T-5—quite an evolutionary step from the humble roots of this lightweight "economy car transmission."

If an aftermarket gear set sounds too drastic, Liberty's Gears offers a "pro-shift" service for the T-5 that involves machining the synchronizer cone and dog teeth from the gear and welding on a stronger dog ring. The modified gears have the benefit of not being synchronized, although they are no stronger than stock T-5 gears.

The final aftermarket T-5 modification is a larger, heavier bearing retainer and support for the rear countershaft bearing race. The stock T-5 part is stamped from thin sheet metal, and under heavy stress the rear countershaft bearing can move around in the case. This puts undue stress on the case and will eventually cause fatigue damage and case stretching—the result will be stripped teeth on the overdrive gears at a minimum, or damage to the other gears at the worst. The aftermarket bearing retainer (available through G-force, Mediatronics, and others) is machined from thick, heavy steel and will hold the countershaft bearing steady. Countershaft preload can be increased with the heavier retainer, and overall gear train strength will be increased.

INSTALLING AND USING THE T-5

The T-5 is an excellent transmission for swapping into many rear-wheel-drive chassis—it is relatively small, light (75 pounds), and fairly sturdy for its size. It also comes with a mind-boggling array of input shaft diameters, spline counts and lengths, gearing, bolt patterns, and shifter locations that make it uniquely adaptable to other uses. It makes an excellent street transmission, but its adaptability also makes it a good basis for a drag- and road-racing transmission.

The T-5 has been swapped into both imported and domestic cars as varied as early Datsun 240Zs, 1932 Fords, 1950s Chevy pickups, Volvo 240 turbos, rear-wheel-drive Mopars, Ford Falcons and early Mustangs, Merkur XR4Tis, Triumph TR-6s, and many others. It can be bolted to many Ford, GM, AMC, and Nissan engines from the 1950s to present with nothing more elaborate than one of the production bell housings from these manufacturers. For other engines, the engine's factory bell housing may be able to be modified, or an adapter plate can be used to mount the transmission to the original bell housing.

Adapters for the Mazda Rotary, Ford Flathead, Mopar rear-wheel-drive engines, Volvo four-cylinders, GM six-cylinders, vintage Ford V-8s, and several others are available from the aftermarket. In addition, the GM T-5 case bolt pattern makes it easy to use a T-5 in place of many classic GM three- and four-speed transmissions used since the mid-1950s. If the case bolt pattern and shifter position (see the chart below) don't match the input spline and gearing you need, it's a simple matter to mix and match parts to get the layout you need.

The most common change is the shifter position. Of the commonly available T-5s, the most forward shifter position is the S-10 transmission, followed by the GM F-body. The Mustang has the most rearward shifter. To change shifter location, use the required extension housing with the matching mainshaft, overdrive driven gear, shift rail, and shifter (since Ford and GM shifters do not share the same bolt pattern).

Some mixing and matching of mainshaft and extension housing will work, but always use the yoke and extension housing bushing that match the brand of the mainshaft: GM with GM and Ford with Ford. The biggest problem occurs when the position of the speedometer gear along the mainshaft does not match the extension housing's cast-in boss. Since the gear is not highly stressed, you can use steel shim stock to increase the mainshaft diameter in the gear location, although you will still have to drill a hole through the shaft for the locating pin. Later extension housings do not have the boss for a speedometer gear, which makes them unsuitable for swapping into older cars (unless an electronic speedometer or expensive adapter is used).

In general, if you are looking to use a T-5 in a mostly street car, try to get the newest version you can find. The later T-5s have better torque capacity and are more reliable, although the early NWC T-5 is still a decent lightweight transmission. The transmission's maintenance history and condition are more important for strength than its torque rating. If the transmission is used, at a minimum pull the input shaft and check the condition of the input shaft bearing and blocking ring. If the dog teeth or blocking ring look worn out, disassemble and rebuild the transmission.

Despite its reputation as fragile and hard-shifting, the stock T-5 stands up well to light drag racing (even with slicks) as long as the engine makes less than about 300 ft-lb

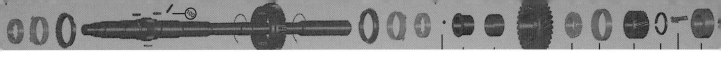

of torque. It can withstand even more power if its weaknesses (lack of countershaft bearing support in fifth, no shift travel stops, and weak gears) are addressed with aftermarket parts like those mentioned above. The T-5 also makes an excellent road-racing transmission as long as the synchronizers are up to snuff—use the latest blocking rings and synchronizer assemblies at a minimum, or upgrade to a dog ring gear set like the G-force gears.

The transmission's light weight, small size, and low rotating mass (small gear size) actually give it an advantage over more traditional drag-racing manual transmissions like the Jerico or Richmond transmissions, especially in horsepower- or tire-limited drag-racing classes. A T-5 with all the tricks will spin up faster and allow more engine power to go into accelerating the car, rather than the gears. A fully built T-5 also tends to be a little cheaper than most aftermarket racing transmissions, since many of the parts can be recycled from production car cores.

CARE AND FEEDING

Getting the most out of the T-5 requires at least three things: the right oil, careful setup, and a good aftermarket shifter. The WC T-5 in particular is very sensitive to fluid type and viscosity. The brass blocking rings in the NWC T-5, on the other hand, are fine with 70w GL-4 gear oil, but GL-5 oil will reduce shifting performance somewhat. The WC T-5 requires Dexron III-Mercon automatic transmission fluid (ATF). Do not use heavy gear oil in the WC T-5—the needle bearings in the hub of each gear hub will fail, and so will the fiber blocking rings. Some people have reported success with lightweight synthetic gear oil such as Redline MTL, but TREMEC recommends only ATF.

Many WC T-5s have been ruined by well-meaning quick oil-change shops that dump in a load of 85w90 gear oil. The symptoms of this treatment are bad shifting in general, particularly in fourth gear. If you have any reason to suspect that your WC T-5 has suffered a similar fate, drain out all of the bad fluid as soon as possible, remove the input bearing retainer and shaft, and inspect the fourth blocking ring. Replace the blocking ring if it looks burned. If the transmission grinds badly in all gears, it will have to be stripped apart and rebuilt, but most can be salvaged with just a quick swap of the fourth-gear blocking ring.

Whatever oil you use, change it at least yearly for the longest gear and bearing life. The easiest way to fill a newly installed T-5 is through the shifter mounting pad on the top of the transmission—install it without a shifter and fill before assembling the console. Note that both the drain and fill plug are on the right side of the case. The large hex (NWC) or Torx (WC) bolt on the left side of the case is the

TRANSMISSION
TECHNOLOGIES
Corporation

INSTALLATION DIMENSIONS
TREMEC T5

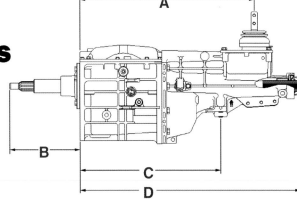

APPLICATION	MODEL #	A	B	C	D
1985-86 Jeep CJ 4x4	1352-000-077	329.4	182.8	332.5	383.0
1989 Chevy S-10 4x4	1352-000-191	298.3	181.9	468.9	686.6
1992 Mustang	1352-000-208	495.7	182.6	367.2	628.6
1993 Chevy S-10 2.8L	1352-000-234	298.2	182.1	406.7	635.3
Mustang 3.8L	1352-000-238	495.8	199.9	367.6	628.2
1996 Camaro V6	1352-000-247	538.3	182.1	406.5	635.3
1993 & Prior Mustang	1352-000-251	495.8	182.6	367.6	628.2
1996 Isuzu Rodeo	1352-000-258	455.0	181.3	483.2	635.3
1999 3.8L V6 Mustang	1352-000-260	495.8	199.9	400.8	628.2
Semi-Remote Gas SYM	1352-000-261	599.7	195.1	454.7	477.4
Semi-Remote Diesel SYM	1352-000-262	599.7	166.6	454.7	477.4

T-5
3 April 2005

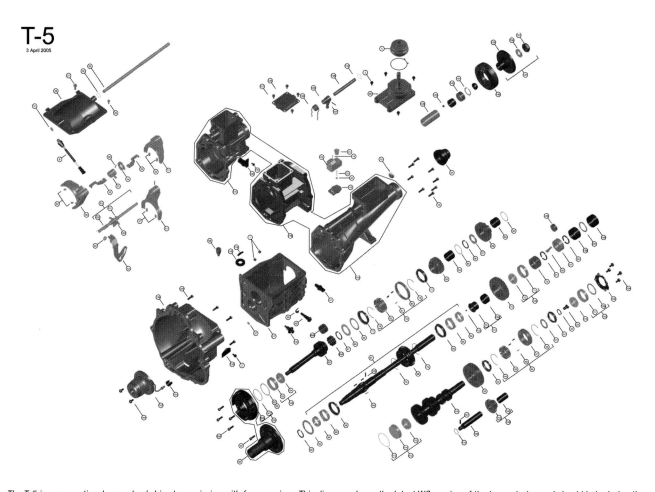

The T-5 is a conventional rear-wheel-drive transmission with few surprises. This diagram shows the latest WC version of the transmission and should help during the rebuild.

pivot pin for the fifth/reverse shift lever. If you remove it, the transmission has to be disassembled and the linkage reset. All T-5 variants require 3 quarts of oil.

In any T-5 used for racing or street performance, the mainshaft bearing preload should be increased. For non-Cobra T-5s with needle thrust bearings, do not increase the preload beyond .001-inch negative. With the tapered roller input bearing, the preload can be more, as much as .005 inch. The countershaft in both types should be set up with .001 inch to .004 inch of preload. Preload can be increased beyond this point, but bearing life will be reduced. Check and reset the preload on both shafts after every few weekends if the transmission is used for racing. The increased preload will help the shafts resist spreading and gear damage.

To avoid shift fork and linkage failure, use an aftermarket shifter with adjustable stops. The Pro 5.0 shifter is one of the best and is recommended by many T-5 shops for its robust construction and accurate throw. Set it up according to the manufacturer's instructions and enjoy the vastly improved shift quality.

EXAMPLE: T-5 REBUILD

The transmission shown in the example rebuild below is a Ford Mustang WC T-5 expertly stripped and rebuilt by Monte from Anaheim Gear. While he can disassemble a T-5 in less than 30 minutes, the average backyard mechanic will probably require double that amount of time. Reassembly should take another two hours at least. If you've never rebuilt a transmission before, reread Chapter 4. Take your time and lots of detailed notes or digital photos—a cheap digital camera that you don't mind getting greasy is excellent for this. Don't even think of rebuilding a T-5 without the TREMEC service manual (you can download it from the TREMEC website)—the exploded diagrams and service specifications will complement the information given here.

DISASSEMBLY

Above left: *Remove the shifter by removing the four bolts holding it to the extension housing. In some applications, it helps to remove the shifter before dropping the transmission. Next, disassemble the remote shift linkage—tap out the roll pin holding the shift finger to the shift rail. Do not lose the detent ball and spring under the shift finger. Also, keep track of the plastic socket in the shift finger—it comes out with gentle pressure.* Above right: *Remove the bolts holding the extension housing to the main case and remove the extension housing. Tap the housing with a rubber hammer to break the RTV bond.*

Remove the neutral safety switch and its actuating pin—don't lose the small pin. Remove the bolts holding the top cover and shift linkage to the case, and remove the top cover. Tap gently to break the RTV bond. You will have to move the cover slightly sideways to remove it. Keep the top cover bolts separate—note that some of them have a tall shoulder to locate the cover on the case. Keep the linkage together unless the fork or interlock appears damaged. In general, the interlock is hard to reassemble and most of the parts are nonwearing. If you do need to disassemble the linkage and replace a fork, the shift rail must be removed.

Remove the snap ring holding the fifth gear synchronizer onto the countershaft, but leave it on for now. Drive out the roll pin in the fifth shift fork (shown in this close-up), being sure to support the shift fork to avoid bending the rail, and remove the fork by tapping gently. Remove the fork and fifth gear synchronizer assembly together. Keep the parts together until inspection.

Remove the bolts holding the input shaft bearing retainer to the case and remove the retainer, input shaft, and mainshaft pilot bearing rollers and cage. Remove the needle thrust bearing and washer (unless the transmission has a tapered roller mainshaft pilot).

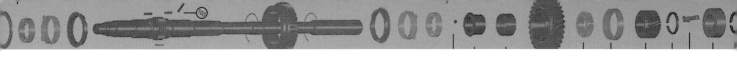

Remove the mainshaft by first loosening the rear mainshaft bearing and removing its outer race. The overdrive driven gear and speedometer drive gear may be removed at this point, but this is not necessary. Lift the front of the mainshaft to remove it from the case—twist it free of the fifth/reverse shift linkage on the left side of the case as you pull it out.

Disassemble the mainshaft on the bench—this is easiest if the shaft is clamped in a vise with soft jaws, front end up. Start by removing the fourth blocking ring, then pry under third gear to slide third gear and the third/fourth synchronizer assembly off the shaft together. Some transmissions are tighter than others and will require a hydraulic press (apply pressure to the shaft while supporting third gear), but most come apart easily. Remove the third-gear hub needle bearing and thin spacer.

THE TREMEC/BORGWARNER T-5

Remove the second-gear C-clip and thrust washer. Remove second gear, its hub bearing, and spacer. If the transmission has three-piece synchronizer assemblies, remove the damper and antirattle spiral thrust washer by twisting it out of the groove in the mainshaft. Remove the inner and outer cones and blocking ring. Disassemble the first/second synchronizer assembly by removing the synchronizer sleeve, inserts, and spring on the third-gear side. Mark the sleeve and hub so that they can be reassembled in the same relationship. Note that the synchronizer hub is integral with the mainshaft.

Turn the mainshaft over and clamp it in a vise with soft jaws. Tap out the clip holding the speedometer drive gear on the shaft and slide the gear up the shaft.

Remove the C-clip behind the fifth driven gear and remove the gear (and spacer, if there is one).

If the gear is tight on the shaft, remove it by prying under the bearing or with a press (support first gear and press the shaft). Remove first gear and its hub bearing.

Remove the first-gear bearing race—watch out for the small steel ball that prevents the race from rotating. Some versions have a pin instead of the ball. Remove the remaining spring from the synchronizer hub.

Begin disassembly of the transmission case by unbolting the rear countershaft bearing retainer (bend back the locking tabs first). Keep track of the shims and remove the rear countershaft bearing outer race.

Push the countershaft as far to the back of the case as possible.

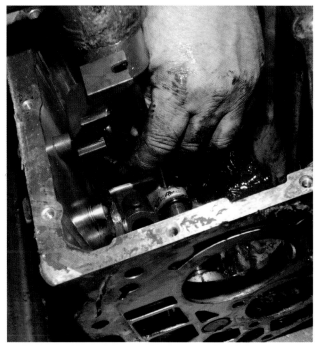

Above left: *Using a long drift inserted from the top of the case through the rear mainshaft bearing bore, tap the rear countershaft bearing off the end of the countershaft. Remove the countershaft and press off the front bearing. Warning: If you remove the front countershaft outer race, be prepared for leaks. Do not replace it unless it is worn beyond salvage. A rubber O-ring seals the original race to the case. If disturbed, it is very difficult to get the O-ring to seal again. A common amateur's mistake is to use silicone to seal the race—if you do, the O-ring will be displaced and is even less likely to seal properly.*   Above right: *Use a narrow punch to remove the roll pin holding the reverse idler shaft in place.*

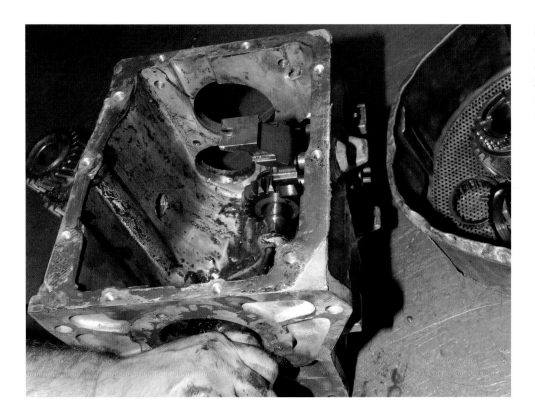

Push the reverse idler shaft out of the case with a punch. It is not usually necessary to remove the pivot bolt for the fifth/reverse shift linkage from the side of the case.

INSPECTON

The T-5 is fairly standard in design, and the inspection tips in Chapter 4 apply. If the transmission was used behind a V-8, check the input shaft splines for twist or cracks. Disassemble the third/fourth and fifth synchronizer assemblies, making sure to mark the relationship of the sleeve and hub. Check that the first/second synchronizer hub is firmly attached to the shaft—any looseness and the shaft must be discarded. The same goes for wear, unfortunately. If the hub is worn excessively, the mainshaft must be replaced.

REASSEMBLY

Above left: *Press the front countershaft bearing onto the countershaft. Push the bearing all the way flush with the shoulder on the countershaft, or the countershaft bearing preload will be difficult to set.* Above right: *Install the reverse idler gear and shaft, making sure that the O-ring is properly located on the shaft between the gear and case. Tap in the roll pin.*

Grease the countershaft front outer race and install the countershaft.

Above left: *Install the rear countershaft bearing with a steel pipe and a few blows from a hammer.* Above right: *Install the outer race and retainer, setting the preload using old or new shims (use instructions in the TREMEC manual).*

Bend up new tabs (don't use previously bent and flattened tabs) on the bearing retainer.

Install the reverse fork and spring. Make sure the fork engages the groove in the reverse idler gear. Install the fifth/reverse shift rail.

Reassemble the mainshaft, starting with the first/second gear synchronizer. Install the sleeve, aligning the marks made during disassembly and making sure that the inserts align with the sleeve's detent grooves (seen here to the left of the shaft).

Install the inserts and springs. Make sure that the springs start in the same insert and rotate in the same direction relative to the shaft's rotation.

Install the first-gear blocking ring assembly and lubricate thoroughly with automatic transmission fluid.

Install the first-gear inner race and its locating steel ball. Make sure that the groove matches the ball and the race seats properly against the synchronizer inner metal cone.

Add the first-gear needle roller bearing (the largest of the three) and gear.

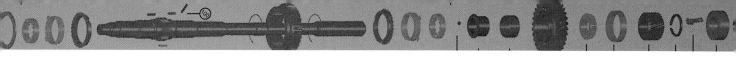

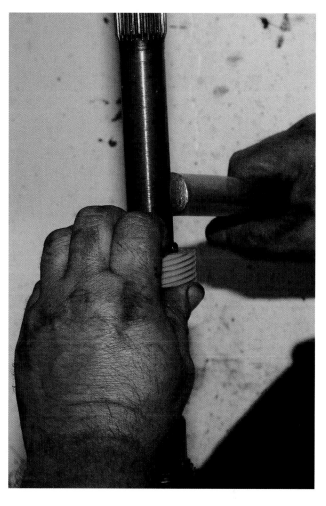

Above left: *Tap the rear mainshaft bearing inner race onto the shaft. Install the fifth driven gear and C-clip. Make sure the C-clip is properly engaged with its groove.*
Above right: *Install the speedometer drive gear and clip.*

Flip the shaft over and begin assembly of the front half by installing the second-gear blocking ring assembly (be sure to lubricate with transmission fluid). Install an antirattle washer and spiral retaining ring. Make sure the ring is located completely in its groove.

Install the thin needle roller bearing thrust washer and second gear needle bearing. Install second gear, the second-gear thrust washer, and the C-clip. Check the operation of the first/second synchronizer—shift into each gear in turn.

Above left: *Install the thin needle bearing thrust washer and third-gear needle bearing. Install third gear and the third-gear blocking ring. Reassemble the third/fourth gear synchronizer, following the directions above. Make sure the hub and sleeve are reassembled in their original relationship, and that the springs begin and end in the same insert.* Above right: *Install the synchronizer assembly on the mainshaft next. Tap it into place with a short piece of steel pipe or ½-inch drive socket. Install the hardened thrust washer with grease to hold it in place, followed by the needle thrust bearing.*

Drop the mainshaft into the case, output end first. Prepare the input shaft by pressing a new input bearing onto it.

Above left: *Pack the mainshaft pilot bearing bore inside the input gear with grease and install the rollers.* Above right: *Install the input shaft, making sure the bearing rollers are not knocked out of place.*

Install the rear mainshaft outer race.

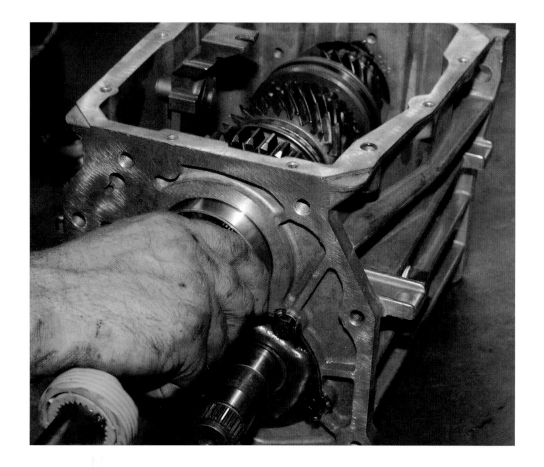

Press a new oil seal into the input shaft bearing retainer—tap it carefully with a socket and hammer if you don't have a press. Install the retainer temporarily (without a shim or RTV) to hold the internals together. Grease the fifth-gear journal on the countershaft and install the fifth drive gear.

Reassemble the fifth-gear synchronizer assembly with its blocking ring. Install the synchronizer assembly together with the shift fork (tap onto the countershaft splines if necessary), then install the sheet-metal synchronizer retainer and snap ring.

Install the roll pin holding the fifth shift fork to the rail—support the shift fork to prevent damage to the rail. Install the oiling funnel in the end of the countershaft.

Replace the wear pads on the first/second and third/fourth shift forks in the top cover. The old pads are easily pried off with a small screwdriver; new pads simply pop onto the ends of the shift forks.

Apply a bead of RTV to the top of the transmission case.

Install the top cover with a sideways movement so that the shift forks engage the synchronizer sleeves. Install the top cover bolts, making sure to replace the shouldered bolts in the correct places. Use caution when tightening these bolts; they are small and break easily.

Prepare the extension housing by installing a new bushing. Tap out the old one with a screwdriver and break it apart. Tap the new one in using a socket as a mandrel. Install a new oil seal.

Make sure the vent tube at the top of the extension housing has not been displaced. Apply a bead of RTV to the extension housing. Install a new O-ring on the shift rail boss on the rear of the top cover and coat the boss with RTV.

Install the extension housing, making sure that the fifth-gear funnel, shift fork, and reverse brake, if one is present, are not hanging up on the inside of the casting. Both must be in their proper position or the extension housing will not go together. Bolt the extension housing to the case.

Install the steel ball into the detent plate, and the detent spring into the bottom of the shift finger. Slide the finger onto the shift rail. Align the roll pin bore as shown here.

Drive in the roll pin and install the plastic bushing with plenty of grease.

Install the neutral safety switch and its actuating pin. Use teflon or silicone sealant to prevent leaks.

Right: *Remove the input bearing retainer and set the mainshaft bearing preload according to the shop manual and the measurements you took before. Reinstall the input bearing retainer with plenty of RTV.*

Below: *Make sure the marks you made during disassembly are lined up. If you are installing a new retainer or do not have marks, note that the retainer is installed with the wider groove on the bottom and the narrow groove on top. Install the shifter after replacing the transmission in the car and filling it with three quarts of ATF.*

THE TREMEC/BORGWARNER T-5

CHAPTER 6
THE HONDA B-SERIES TRANSAXLE

From 1989 to 2001, the B-series was Honda's top engine, installed in Integras, Civics, and Del Sols for the United States, as well as the CRX in other markets. Today, B-series engines are popular because of their low cost, light weight, high specific power outputs, and easy installation into U.S.-market Hondas. Produced in capacities from 1,600 cc to 2,000 cc, and with horsepower ratings from 140 to nearly 200, the B-series is a versatile, powerful engine that can shrug off abuse that would kill lesser motors.

Keeping the B-series popular for engine swaps in the United States is a ready supply of cheap, lightly used Japanese imported engines and transmissions. Because of this popularity, several aftermarket manufacturers produce kits to make swapping these engines into a U.S.-market Honda product a bolt-in proposition. OEM parts can be used for most chassis, but using an aftermarket swap kit can be easier and cheaper than tracking down elusive imported parts.

The five-speed transaxles used with these engines are essentially the same as most Honda transaxles in overall design, and they resemble other manufacturers' front-wheel-drive transaxles. They have two shafts, and the final drive unit is incorporated into the transmission case. Most of these transaxles have an open differential, but many were available with a very nice Quaife-licensed helical limited-slip differential.

There are two groups of B-series transaxles, classified according to their method of clutch actuation (cable or hydraulic), although the internal and external differences are greater than just linkage. In general, the cable-clutch transmissions are older than hydraulic-clutch transmissions, although both were used in the early 1990s and some models have interchangeable internals.

You can use any B-series transmission (cable or hydraulic) with any B-series block as long as you make sure that you use the correct clutch and flywheel. The clutch splines vary somewhat between models of the transmission, and the matching disc will be necessary. In some cases, the clutch diameter is different, which requires a different pressure plate and thus flywheel bolt pattern.

Racing Hondas like this clean Civic driven by Ali Arsham in the U.S. Touring Car Championship have shown many skeptics that the Honda B-series engine and transmission make a potent on-track combination. The transmission's light weight and simple design are certainly factors in the success of the powertrain.

This is an S80 transmission from a U.S.-market Acura Integra GSR. It is readily identifiable as being a hydraulic transmission—notice the clutch fluid line bracket above the clutch fork hole. This is a common B-series transmission and a good one for street-driven engine swaps. The gearing is moderate, with a low first gear and high second and final drive.

While there are detail differences between the hydraulic and cable transmissions, and their gear ratios vary, the overall torque capacity is about the same. Despite the transmission lore, the power-handling ability of a cable-clutch transmission is as good as a hydraulic-clutch transmission with a few exceptions. In general, the newer the gearbox, the stronger, since Honda made many detail improvements to the transmission design over the years. As with any transmission, mileage, maintenance, setup, and driving technique have more of an effect on reliability than the transmission model.

All versions of the transaxle are designed for use with equal-length axles. Front-wheel-drive cars often exhibit an undesirable handling characteristic known as "torque steer" when the two drive axles react differently to acceleration torque. Front-wheel-drive installations with unequal-length driveshafts have inherent torque steer, which is made worse by a limited-slip differential. Honda avoided this problem by using a large-diameter external intermediate shaft to run from the differential on the right side to a support bearing bolted to the engine. The outer end of the intermediate shaft is splined to the inner CV joint of the right axle, which allows two equal-length axles to be used and reduces torque steer.

Because the two B-series transaxle types were installed in different models, some of the external mounting points differ. This is easily remedied by kits produced by Hasport (and other noted swap experts) that make it easy to use either transmission in just about any Honda chassis. In addition to mounts, the left axle and intermediate shaft may also have to be changed to swap transmissions and engines—the intermediate shaft and inner CV joint splines are not all the same. There are a few different types, and the axles must match. So-called "hybrid" axles may be necessary to match some chassis/transaxle combinations that were never dreamed of by engineers back in Japan—or at least never imported here. These are readily available from the aftermarket for just about any combination of engine, transaxle, uprights, and chassis.

TRANSAXLE IDENTIFICATION

B-series transaxles are stamped with an alphanumeric code that identifies their original application. This two- or three-digit code is located near the fill plug of the transmission case, and although it gives some indication of the original application and gearing, it is far from exact. All U.S.-market pre-1993 Acura Integra transaxles, for example, are marked YS1, whether they are the high-geared LS type or the low-geared GSR version. This makes identification somewhat difficult. If the transmission is not bolted to an engine or installed in a chassis or imported front clip, the task of deciphering the application can be impossible unless you disassemble the transaxle and count the number of teeth on each gear pair.

Because prices for each transaxle can vary significantly, it pays to investigate the source of a particular transaxle for yourself. At a minimum, check that the transaxle code matches the alleged engine and car combination. If necessary, be prepared to split the case and count gear teeth.

Limited-slip models can be identified quickly by looking for a stamp marked "LSD" somewhere on the case. Failing that, a quick look down the inner CV joint splines should reveal either a clear view to the other side of the room (with LSD) or the differential cross shaft (without LSD).

If you find an S80 transaxle and want to know what final drive ratio is installed, check the code stamped on the transmission housing. A "4jhd" means the transaxle is filled with a 4.40 final drive gear set, and an "ne3" means it has a 4.785 final drive. The chart on page 116 lists the transmissions used with various B-series engines in the United States and abroad. USDM is short for "U.S. Domestic Market," and JDM stands for "Japanese Domestic Market."

If you find a transmission with a number not listed below, check that it is not a D-series Civic transmission. Those have a casting number of P20. If the following serial number has a serial prefix of A, it indicates that the gearing was originally for DX/CX/VX; a serial prefix of B was for EX/Si.

DESIGN

The Honda transaxle has two shafts: an input shaft (also called mainshaft) and an output shaft (also called countershaft), as well as an internal final drive gear set. The input shaft has a pilot bearing area that rides in a clutch pilot bearing, unlike some front-wheel-drive designs, and is partially splined for gears and synchronizers. The output shaft is machined integral with the final drive pinion gear, and it is also splined for gears and synchronizers.

The first and second drive gears are located on the mainshaft and are machined integral with it. The driven members of each pair are located on the output shaft, along with their synchronizer. This reduces the speed differential between the gears and shaft, which is a concern with front-wheel-drive transaxle design. The third/fourth and fifth/reverse synchronizers are splined to the mainshaft, and the driven gears for all three are splined to the output shaft.

The mainshaft is supported at both ends by ball bearings (which tend to be more vibration-resistant than tapered roller bearings). The outer bearing is a large angular-contact ball bearing designed to take the thrust loads generated by the helical gears, while the inner bearing is a smaller, radial-contact ball bearing. The inner bearing is press-fit into the transmission case, while the outer bearing is pressed onto the end of the mainshaft.

The countershaft is supported at the first-gear end with two back-to-back ball bearings: one radial and one angular contact, and at the pinion end by a drawn-cup roller bearing that rides directly on a hardened and ground section of the shaft. The two ball bearings are held onto the shaft by a press fit and a large nut. The helical final drive pinion drives a mating ring gear bolted and tightly pressed onto the differential housing.

The differential/final drive assembly rotates on two large shielded ball bearings that press onto the differential and fit tightly into the case halves. Some variants of the B-series transaxle (some Y80 and S80 transaxles) use tapered roller bearings instead of ball bearings to improve reliability. Later versions reverted to larger ball bearings to make factory assembly easier. All gears ride on needle roller bearings between third, fourth, and fifth drive gears and the mainshaft, and between first and second driven gears and the countershaft.

The gear train is splash-lubricated from oil thrown off of the ring gear. A sheet-metal scraper catches some of the oil as it comes off of the ring gear and directs it to a plastic funnel in the roller-bearing end of the countershaft and to a sheet-metal channel that runs to a similar funnel in the opposite end of the mainshaft. Both shafts are hollow and cross-drilled for lubrication.

In early versions of the transaxle, the second-through-fifth-gear synchronizers all use one-piece conical brass blocking rings. Later versions (after 1994) incorporated dual-cone blocking rings into second gear as well as first (because these synchronizers have the greatest rotating inertia to slow and wear the most quickly) with single-cone rings on the remaining gears. The Honda synchronizers do not have inserts. Instead, the spring wraps around the blocking ring, between the blocking ring's dog teeth and the gear's dog teeth. As the synchronizer sleeve meshes with the blocking ring, the sleeve's internal splines run over the spring wire and grip the blocking ring tightly. It is a simple, light, and effective design—the kind of thing that Honda really excels at.

Shift forks are steel on later transaxles, and aluminum on early versions. Each shift fork is pinned to an internal shift rail, which is actuated by a finger-style interlock. Steel detent balls are inserted from the outside of the case. The transmissions have a reverse brake to slow the mainshaft and make engaging reverse gear easier. The reverse idler gear is a standard piece. All versions of the B-series transaxle have a rod-style external shift linkage that is specific to each chassis and engine combination.

B-SERIES TRANSMISSION CODES

No.	Chassis Application	Engine	Stamped Code	Clutch	LSD	2nd-gear Synchro
1	JDM Integra Type R 98-01	B18C	S80	Hyd.	Yes	Dual
2	USDM Del Sol "DOHC VTEC" 95-99	B16A2/3	Y21/S21	Hyd.	No	Dual
	USDM Civic Si Coupe 99-00	B16A2			No	
3	USDM Integra Type R 96-01	B18C5	Y21/Y80	Hyd.	Yes	Single
	JDM Integra Type R 96-97	B18C	S80/S4C		Yes	Dual
	JDM Civic R 97-00	B16B			Yes	
	JDM Civic SiR 92-00	B16A			Optional	
4	USDM 94-01 Integra GSR	B18C1	S80/Y80	Hyd.	No (1)	Dual
	JDM 94-01SiR-G (GSR)	B18C			Optional	
5	USDM Integra LS/RS/GS/SE 94-01	B18B1	S80	Hyd.	No (1)	Dual
6	JDM CRX/Civic SiR 88-91	B16A	Y1	Cable	Optional	Single
7	USDM Integra GSR 92-93	B17A1	YS1	Cable	No	Single
	JDM Integra XSi 92-93	B16A			Optional	
8	JDM Integra XSi 90-91	B16A	S1/J1	Cable	No	Single
9	USDM Integra LS/RS/GS/SE 90-93	B18A1	S1/YS1 A1	Cable	No	Single

Type	First	Second	Third	Fourth	Fifth	Reverse	Final Drive
1	3.230	2.105	1.458	1.034	0.787	3.000	4.785
2	3.230	2.105	1.458	1.107	0.875	3.000	4.400
3	3.230	2.105	1.458	1.107	0.848	3.000	4.400
4	3.230	1.900	1.360	1.034	0.787	3.000	4.400
5	3.230	1.900	1.269	0.966	0.714	3.000	4.266
6	3.166	2.052	1.416	1.103	0.870	3.000	4.266
7	3.307	2.105	1.458	1.107	0.880	3.000	4.400
8	3.230	2.105	1.458	1.107	0.848	3.000	4.400
9	3.166	1.857	1.259	0.935	0.742	3.000	4.400

Notes: 1—These transaxles have a stronger open differential than similar transaxles.

PARTS SWAPPING

Internal parts can be swapped between all members of the same type—hydraulic with hydraulic and cable with cable. The entire gear set can be used to modify overall gearing, or just the third/fourth/fifth gear pairs or final drive from one transaxle can be used in another. The exception to this general rule is the YS1 stamped transaxles—internal parts from these models can be used in later hydraulic clutch transmissions as a whole, although there may be detail differences.

First and second gear must be swapped as a pair—since both drive gears are machined into the mainshaft, there is no way to separate them. The other gears can be mixed and matched (as a pair), although they must remain in the same position—fifth gears can only be swapped with other fifth gears, for example. The inner bearing bore of each gear varies, making them noninterchangeable. It should go without saying that drive and driven gear pairs should not be mixed.

The final drive gears can be swapped between transaxles, but there are a couple of things to be aware of. The first is that ring-gear diameter and bolt pattern varies between B16 and B18 transmissions. You can swap them as long as you also change the differential itself. In addition, the differential carrier bearings must match the transmission case—later models have larger bearings. Finally, the inner bore of the first driven gear (and countershaft bearing journal) is different between the OEM 4.40 final drive and 4.785 final drive. To use the Japanese-market Type R gear set requires a new first driven gear, thrust washer, and split needle roller bearing.

Since the drive pinion is integral with the countershaft, changing final drive ratios requires a full transmission rebuild and resetting the countershaft bearing preload. The mainshaft does not have to be disturbed, but this would be a good time to replace the blocking rings and possibly upgrade to a limited-slip differential as well.

The limited-slip differential used on the U.S.-market Integra Type R can be swapped into the other transaxles with a matching ring gear and carrier bearings. The unit is designed and manufactured by Quaife and is similar to that used by many front-wheel-drive racers. As with swapping final drives, changing the differential requires splitting the transmission case and gives a good opportunity to freshen up the rest of the internals.

MAINTENANCE AND UPKEEP

The B-series transmission is overall quite sturdy, but it does have a few weak points, not all of which have been addressed by Honda in production-line upgrades. The single most common issue with the transmission is worn second- and third-gear synchronizer blocking rings or sleeves. The shift quality degrades quickly on these transmissions as they are used, and they do not withstand poor shifting and abuse without significant blocking ring wear. If the problem appears on your transmission, take care of it as soon as possible to avoid having to replace the synchronizer sleeves, hubs, and gears.

The early single-cone brass blocking rings are the most fragile and tend to wear quickly. Later multipiece synchronizer assemblies are sturdier and last much longer between rebuilds. Rebuilders like Gearspeed, Inc., can replace the brass blocking rings with modern fiber-lined sintered metal rings that hold up better to quick shifts and hard use, and they can even convert some models to dual-cone synchronizers. When rebuilding these transaxles, always use the best-quality blocking rings you can get your hands on, and replace the sleeves and gears if they look worn.

The B-series transaxle does not withstand repeated drag-racing starts with slicks or higher-than-stock engine torque. The two most common abuse-related failures are stripped teeth on the ring and pinion gears, and broken differential side gears. Stripped pinion gears are almost always the result of clutch-dumping drag-strip starts—the fragile teeth on the pinion gear cannot handle high shock loads and will strip.

Broken differential side gears are almost guaranteed with a combination of high horsepower, an open differential, and limited front traction. The only cure is some form of LSD or spool. The small stock gears, their plain steel bearings, and minuscule pins are just not up to the demands of high-performance use. Do yourself a favor and cure this "Achilles' heel" of the B-series transaxle as soon as you can.

Stripped pinion gears are another common failure. In this case the problem is too much traction for the stock final drive gears—the pinion teeth are smaller and tend to be damaged first. There's really no good way to avoid this except by developing a gentle clutch foot. Use only OEM Honda or shot-peened aftermarket gears, and have them magnafluxed frequently if used in a racing gearbox.

A spool like this one locks both axles together, eliminating the differential and its troublesome side gears. Of course this makes the car nearly impossible to turn, and removes the possibility of driving it on the street.

The differential side gears, on the other hand, are most often damaged by burnouts—without a limited-slip differential or spool, only one wheel spins during most burnouts. The high relative motion between the two shafts causes lots of heat and friction between the nonbushed gears and their steel shafts. Eventually, they seize and break. In either case, the torn gear teeth and other small steel shavings will destroy the inside of the transmission case in a short time unless the engine is shut down immediately.

The best solution for the weak differential problem is a spool (for drag racing only), or a limited-slip differential if the car is to be used on the street or a road course. Both solutions eliminate the weak differential side gears and prevent differential failure. At the same time, don't be tempted by aftermarket "pseudo limited-slip differentials" that preload the side gears. The preload forces and the friction that develops during a burnout will destroy the side gears even faster than without the limited-slip differential.

Honda recommends engine oil for these transaxles, either 10w-30 or 10w-40, depending on the climate. While this works well for daily driving, engine oil does not have high levels of EP additives, and the gears inside these transaxles tend to wear faster than others. A good-quality, lightweight synthetic manual transmission gear oil in the 75w range will help shift quality and gear train lifespan. Something like Redline's MTL or Pennzoil Synchromesh would be a good starting point for experimentation.

MODIFICATIONS

The popularity of the B-series engine and transaxle means that there is a lot of aftermarket support for the combination, both in the United States and Japan. Currently in the United States there are two or three gear sets, dog ring conversions, bearing gussets, LSDs, and different final drive ratios.

ATS, Spoon of Japan, and Quaife of England produce synchronized gear sets. All three kits have helical gears and are suitable for both street and racing use. The Spoon and Quaife gear sets are extremely close ratio and are the more radical of the three. The chart on page 119 lists the gearing and ratio choices of these three gear sets.

The ATS gear set has quite close ratios compared to stock but it is the widest of the aftermarket gear sets and the least expensive. The ATS gear set differs from others on the market in the way the first gear ratio is changed—ATS has devised a way to change the first gear ratio without changing the mainshaft. By playing tricks with gear tooth shape, the replacement driven gear is designed to mesh with the transmission's original drive gear.

ATS recommends using their gear set with the B16A/Type-R mainshaft and second gear, since the GSR 1.90 second gear will be too close to the ATS 1.652 third gear. This means using the B16A mainshaft and second driven gear along with the ATS first, third, fourth, and fifth gears. The ATS gear set also works with the OEM final drive ratio, which can be an important consideration.

If a synchronized aftermarket gear set won't work for your application, Liberty's Gear offers a complete nonsynchro spur gear rotating assembly with custom ratios for each of the four low gears and final drive. Such a conversion won't be cheap, but it will allow the Honda gearboxes to withstand the most abuse without the slow shifting, heat, and stress associated with synchronized helical gears. Houseman Autosport makes a similar conversion. BPM sports and PPG of Australia also make nonsynchro dog ring gear sets for the Honda transaxles, but their products are not widely available in the United States.

The main bearings in the Honda transaxle are not accessible for reinforcement, but the area between the shafts can be strengthened in other ways. Phantom Grip has designed a trick way to support the shafts—a billet girdle and two large ball bearings replace both members of the fifth gear pair. The housing and bearings support the two shafts and prevent all of the separating forces from being absorbed by the transmission case. Since fifth gear is eliminated, this modification is best for transmissions used for drag racing, autocross, or rallycross—four gears may not be sufficient for road racing.

	First	Second	Third	Fourth	Fifth	Final Drive
Quaife	2.462	1.81	1.500	1.250	1.045	Special (1)
Spoon	2.53	1.94	1.591	1.280	1.03	Special (2)
ATS	3.08	2.10 (3)	1.65	1.31	1.033	OEM (4)

Notes:

1—The Quaife gear set requires a special countershaft and thus final drive gears. The following ratios are offered: 3.79, 4.15, 4.5, 3.79, and 4.75.

2—The Spoon gear set comes with one of two final drive ratios: 4.643 or 4.857.

3—ATS uses an OEM Honda second driven gear and mainshaft. The 2.10 second gear is preferred.

4—The ATS gear set can use any OEM final drive ratio and is offered with two different first gears for the different OEM countershaft bearing diameters. ATS also manufactures a 4.929 final drive.

DISASSEMBLY

The following rebuild of an Integra S80 transmission was performed by the Honda manual transmission experts at Gearspeed in Rancho, Cucamonga, California. In the following pictures, Jason Wishmeyer rebuilds an Integra hydraulic clutch unit. The disassembly process should take the home mechanic no more than an hour, once the transmission is out of the car and on the bench. Reassembly should take about twice that amount of time or more. Make sure you've read the chapter on rebuilding and take the time to assemble all the parts to rebuild the gearbox before proceeding with reassembly. Get a copy of the Honda factory service manual if at all possible. A manual covering the similar D-series transmission is available online through Honda of the United Kingdom.

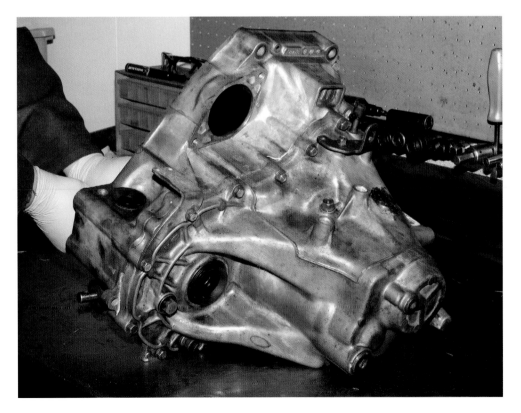

Start the disassembly process by removing the clutch fork and boot, as well as any external brackets that will make the case unwieldy. Turn the transaxle onto its bell housing face. Use a couple of blocks of wood to make the case sit level on the bench—the pilot bearing sticks out beyond the face.

Remove the 14-mm-headed bolt that attaches the reverse idler shaft to the inside of the case. It is located on the top side of the outer transmission case, near the two large-diameter studs for the transmission mount.

Remove the 12-mm-headed bolts holding the two halves of the transaxle case together.

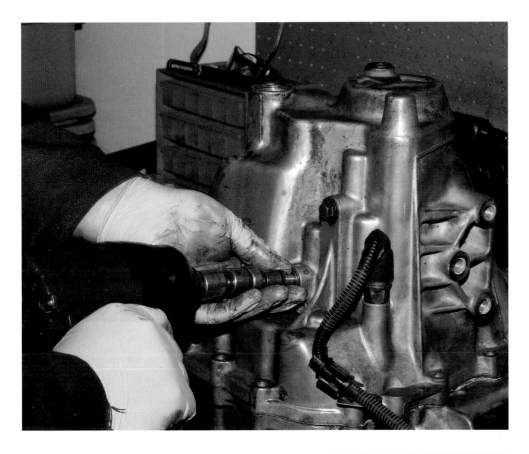

Remove the two 14-mm-headed detent spring plugs on the bottom side of the outer transmission case, near the reverse light switch. These are easily recognizable by their large flanged heads and aluminum sealing washers. Take care to keep track of the detent spring and ball under each plug—use a thin magnet or magnetized screwdriver to get them out of the bore. Remove the reverse light switch at this point too.

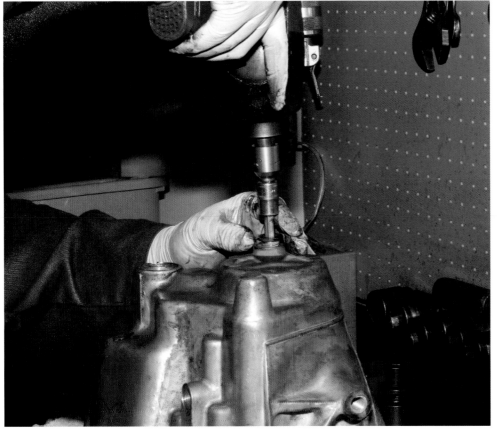

Remove the 32-mm-diameter plug near the end of the countershaft on the outer transmission case—the plug has a square broached hole that fits a 3/8 inch drive ratchet. Remove the Allen-headed plug near the same end of the mainshaft and the oil drain and fill plugs lower on the case.

Look into the threaded hole near the countershaft bearing and locate the two ends of the internal expanding snap ring. Use a pair of external (reverse opening) snap ring pliers to spread the two ends apart and allow the countershaft outer bearing to come free of the snap ring and case. Separate the case by pounding gently around the edge of the case with a soft-faced mallet while keeping the ring compressed. If the outer case half does not come free, check that all of the bolts have been removed and the snap ring is properly compressed.

Once the outer case half is free of the bell housing half, remove the shims and seal from the differential bearing bore, as well as the plastic mainshaft oil funnel, and oil catch baffle shown here (held into the oil fill plug threaded boss by a tight push fit).

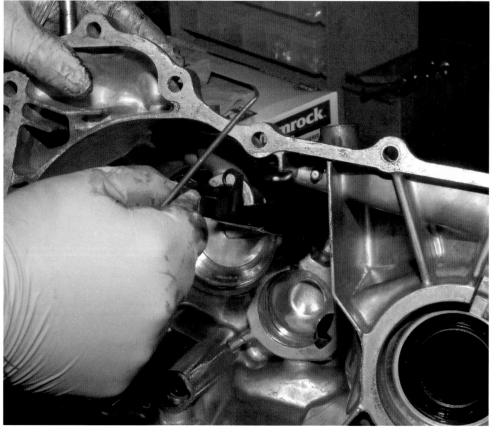

Pull the pivot out of the shift interlock/selector assembly and remove the cast-steel shift finger ("shift piece" in the Honda manual) and bent metal interlock. Remove the three 10-mm-headed bolts that hold the interlock/selector assembly to the case.

Remove the two 10-mm-headed bolts between the reverse shift fork pivot plate and case. Remove the reverse fork and pivot, as well as the reverse idler gear and shaft.

Remove the large nut from the end of the countershaft at this point to make the countershaft disassembly on the bench easier.

Remove the main shift rod detent plug (near the bottom of the case, between the two shafts), spring, and ball from the bottom of the case. Remove the bolt holding the selector finger to the end of the shift rod and remove the finger. Pull the shift rod out of the transmission case. Remove the magnet from the bottom of the case and check for large chips.

Grab the two shafts, shift rails, and forks as one unit with both hands; pull them straight up and out of the case. Set them aside.

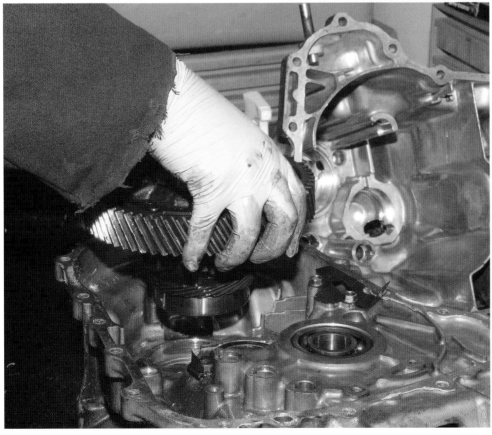

Lift the final drive ring gear and differential assembly from the case.

Bend back the locking tabs on the countershaft roller bearing retainer and remove the bolt and retainer. Remove the two 10-mm bolts holding the oil scraper to the case and remove it.

Remove the countershaft roller bearing with the internal bearing puller or slide hammer with a thin metal hook. Do the same for the mainshaft input bearing.

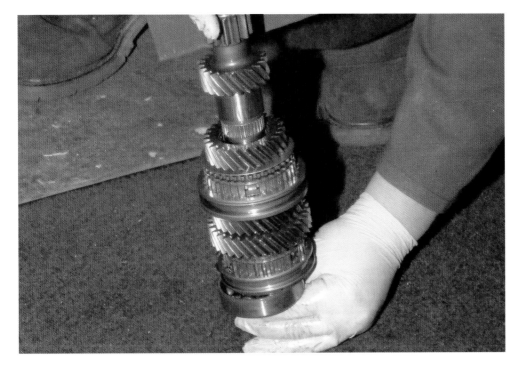

Left: *Returning to the two shafts, remove the shift forks and rails and separate the shafts. Drop the mainshaft on a wood or aluminum plate or the floor to loosen the ball bearing (use a deep socket as a spacer to apply force to the shaft and not the bearing race). If the bearing does not move easily, press or pull it from the shaft. Most are not very tight.*

Below: *Slide the gear stack from the mainshaft. Mark the relationship of the third/fourth synchronizer assembly and disassemble it for inspection and cleaning. Do the same for the fifth/reverse synchronizer.*

Drop the threaded end of the countershaft on the ground or a soft plate until the bearings drop from the shaft. Remove the gear stack from the countershaft and disassemble the first/second gear synchronizer. Remove the first gear split needle bearing and thrust washer from the shaft, and keep track of the small rubber/metal damper under both gears.

INSPECTION

Pay very close attention to the second- and third-gear synchronizer blocking rings, sleeves, and gear dog teeth; they are a known weak point of these transaxles and wear quickly. The steel spring surrounding each blocking ring (replacing the inserts that are used in most synchronizers) causes the ends of the sleeve splines to wear very quickly.

Also check the wear areas on the shift forks—the Honda forks do not have wear pads, so the fork must be replaced if there is much wear (more than .005 inch or so).

Honda gives good, detailed specifications for gear side clearance and width, as well as wear of the component parts of the interlock assembly. Take advantage of Honda's precision and check these while you have the transmission apart—not many manufacturers give such detailed specifications. Some of the translations in the factory shop manual could be improved on, but the measurements are generally understandable.

REASSEMBLY

Prepare the synchronizers and gears by laying the appropriate blocking ring on each gear. Install the synchronizer springs around the projections on each blocking ring. Also match each gear with its inner needle roller bearing— they are all different sizes and it is important not to mix them up. Assemble the synchronizer sleeves to the hubs—notice that most of them are "keyed" and cannot be assembled incorrectly. On the rings that are not keyed, match the long splines in the sleeves with the deeper-grooved hub splines. There are three sets of two splines each spaced evenly around the sleeve.

If the differential side bearings are to be replaced, press new ones on the differential before starting the rebuild.

Prepare the transmission case half first by installing the axle oil seal and the drain and fill plugs. The drain plug has a square recessed head, while the fill plug has a regular hex head.

Install the mainshaft oiling funnel and lubrication channel. Bend the outer end of the channel so it fits tightly into the threaded hole for the countershaft bearing retaining ring.

Prepare the bell housing case half next. Install the input shaft oil seal, shifter shaft oil seal, and axle oil seal. Install case magnets into their groove and the oiling funnel into the countershaft bearing recess.

Install the input shaft bearing and countershaft cupped roller bearing. These fit tightly into their bores, so tap only on the outer race—be careful not to cock them in the case. The countershaft roller bearing should be installed with the thicker race (if there is one) toward the blind end of the bore. Install the oil scraper with two 10-mm bolts.

Install the countershaft bearing retainer and bolt, and bend up the locking tabs.

Install the shift shaft and finger with the 10-mm bolt. Be careful not to nick or scrape the lip of the shaft oil seal when inserting the shaft. Install the detent ball, spring, and plug. Check that the shaft moves smoothly in and out of the case, and that the detents work positively.

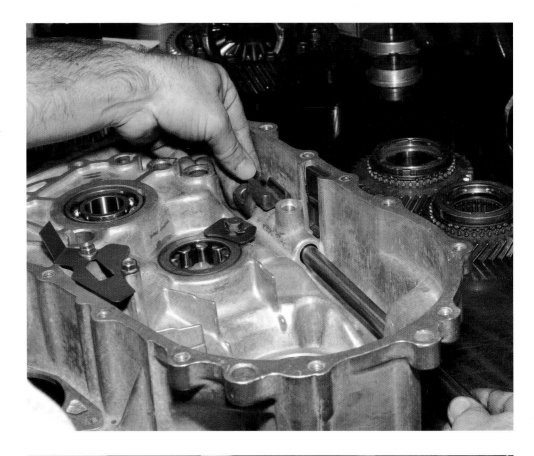

Drop the differential into place and tap the slide bearing home. Temporarily set the outer case half on the differential and check the side clearance of the differential bearing with a feeler gauge through the axle seal bore. Clearance should be as close to 0 inches as possible. Transmissions with tapered roller or angular contact ball bearings can be assembled with more preload.

Choose a washer that results in the necessary clearance—generally the original washer will be close enough, unless the differential housing or transmission case has been replaced. Install the washer in the outboard case half.

Temporarily install the countershaft into the case to make it easier to assemble the gear stack. Start assembling the countershaft gear stack by installing the first-gear thrust washer and split-race needle bearing (some transmission variants have an inner race for this bearing as well).

Install first gear, cone side up, and the first-gear synchronizer blocking ring. Install the friction damper inside the first-gear synchronizer hub with the lip facing up.

Drop the first-gear synchronizer hub onto the countershaft (be sure to align the blocking ring and friction damper projections with the cutouts in the hub), followed by the synchronizer sleeve. Install the hub with the thrust side up (as shown), and the sleeve with the reverse driven teeth on the bottom. Shift the synchronizer into first gear to give more clearance around the second-gear splines.

Install the second-gear assembly, starting with the needle bearing inner race. Then add the outer blocking ring and spring and friction damper with the lip facing down. If the transmission has a dual-cone second-gear synchronizer, add the inner friction cone and blocking ring.

Install second gear, making sure to align the projections on the inner cone and friction damper with cutouts in gear. Install the gear needle bearing.

Install third and fourth gears on the splined area of the shaft. Third gear should be installed with the projection facing up, and fourth with the projection facing down. They are a tight fit and may require some light persuasion from a hammer and steel tube. Install the fifth driven gear next, with the deeply grooved side facing up.

Install the inner bearing, being sure to press on only the inner race. Then install the outer angular contact ball bearing (making sure that the retaining-ring groove is on the upper side of the bearing). Both are a light press fit.

Install the spring washer and nut, with the dished side of the washer down. Torque the nut to 80 lb-ft. Peen over the edge of the nut into the groove in the shaft to prevent it from loosening.

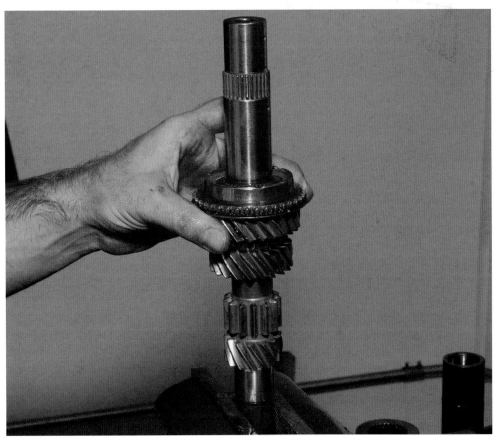

Next, begin to assemble the mainshaft, standing in a vise with soft jaws. Install third gear (cone side up) and its needle bearing. Install the blocking ring and spring.

Install the third/fourth synchronizer hub and sleeve. Make sure the blocking ring projections match the cutouts in the synchronizer hub. The hub is a tight fit on its splines, so use a short section of thick steel tubing to tap it on. The hub should be installed with its sleeve—the blocked spline should be at the top so the sleeve cannot be removed after the hub is assembled onto the shaft. The sleeve will then be situated such that the grooved shoulder is on the bottom.

Install the fourth-gear blocking ring and spring. Then install fourth gear and its needle bearing and the fourth/fifth bearing race. Note that the gear must be installed before the bearing and race—the shoulder on the bearing race is too large to pass through the gear.

Place the fifth needle bearing on the race, followed by fifth gear, cone up. Install the fifth-gear blocking ring and spring.

Install the fifth/reverse synchronizer hub, aligning the blocking ring projections with cutouts on the hub. The hub is installed with the shallow side facing up. Install the sleeve next, with the angled shoulder up and the square shoulder down. Install the reverse blocking ring.

Drop the reverse brake cone into the blocking ring, followed by the reverse brake needle bearing and race.

Install the reverse brake stop ring, being sure to engage the notches in the reverse brake cone with the projections in the stop ring.

Tap the rear countershaft bearing onto the shaft. Make sure that the narrow side of the outer race faces down, and the thicker side faces up.

Measure the mainshaft thrust clearance, following the instructions in the shop manual—this basically involves placing the assembled mainshaft into the outer transmission case without the outboard thrust washer and measuring the distance from the edge of the case to the front surface of the input bearing thrust washer. This measurement, plus the distance from the clutch-side case surface to the edge of the input bearing, is the total side clearance of the assembly. After subtracting .93 mm (.037 inches, or half of the clearance range of the spring washer

not measured in this step), the resulting number is the thickness of the outboard shim needed. In practice, as long as you are using the same shaft and cases, the shim thickness needed should not change. The Honda system of clearance control using a spring washer makes the actual setting fairly flexible, even if some parts are mixed up.

For racing, two solid washers can be used instead of the spring washer. Measure the distance with both washers stacked on the mainshaft and add .025 mm to .05 mm (.001 to .002 inch) to add some preload and stiffen the assembly.

Install the chosen washer into the outer case half.

Prepare the clutch-side case for assembly by setting the spring washer (dished side up) and input bearing thrust washer on the input bearing. Then space the bell housing face off the bench with a few blocks of wood.

Align the two shafts side by side with the gears meshing roughly and all of the synchronizers in neutral. Drop the shift forks and rails onto both shafts, making sure that the shift fingers at the end of the rails are aligned and kept together. Make sure the first/second shift fork is assembled with the detent grooves facing away from the bell housing.

Grab both shafts and all three shift forks as an assembly. Keep them together and drop them into the bell housing side of the transmission case on the bench. Make sure that the input bearing thrust washers are not dislocated. Engage the pinion gear with the ring gear, and make sure all three shift rails go into their respective bores.

Check that the shift fingers are aligned properly in neutral, and make sure that all three shafts (mainshaft, countershaft, and final drive) can turn freely.

Install the shift selector assembly, making sure that the selector arm properly engages the slots in the finger at the end of the main shift shaft.

Install the cast-steel shift finger and bent-metal interlock. Install the pivot pin through both parts and the selector mounting plate. Make sure the shift finger and interlock mesh properly, and check that the interlock's ball stud engages the slot in the top of the selector arm. The interlock and shift finger should both also engage the ends of the shift rails.

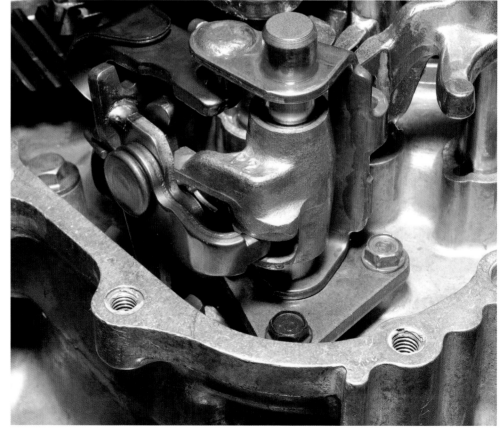

Install the reverse shift detent plate and fork—make sure that the pin on the fifth/reverse shift finger engages the end of the reverse fork.

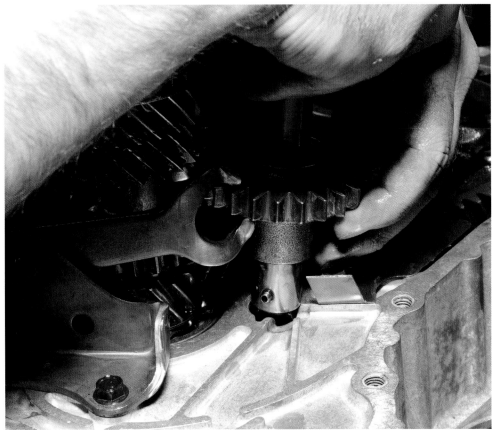

Engage the reverse idler gear in the fork and drop it into the case with the reverse idler shaft. Make sure the small roll pin in the end of the shaft aligns with the groove in the idler shaft bore.

Position the reverse brake stop ring so that its external tab will engage the recess inside the outer case half. Install the countershaft bearing snap ring into its recess in the outer case half.

Coat the case mating surface with RTV silicone.

Lower the outer case half onto the transmission internals. Make sure that the upper end of the shift rails and reverse idler shaft fit into their bores properly, and that the reverse brake tab engages its recess. Once everything is in place, the outer case should drop down until the retaining ring contacts the outer countershaft bearing.

Use a pair of external expanding pliers and open the retaining ring as you tap on the case. The two halves should drop together perfectly. If they do not, check that all of the items mentioned above are in their proper positions.

Before bolting the case halves together, check that the countershaft retaining ring is located properly through the threaded access hole. Make sure that it engages both the bearing and the case.

Install the case half bolts, and the clutch cable or hydraulic line bracket, which also attaches to the case through these bolts.

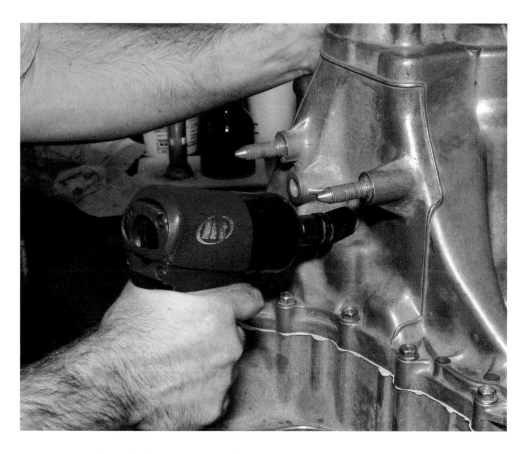

Install the reverse idler shaft bolt through the top of the case.

Install the first/second and third/fourth detent balls, springs, and threaded plugs in the bottom of the outer case.

Coat the threads of the two sealing plugs with RTV silicone and install them.

Install the hanger bracket on the top of the case.

Install the reverse light switch. Use teflon tape or silicone on the threads.

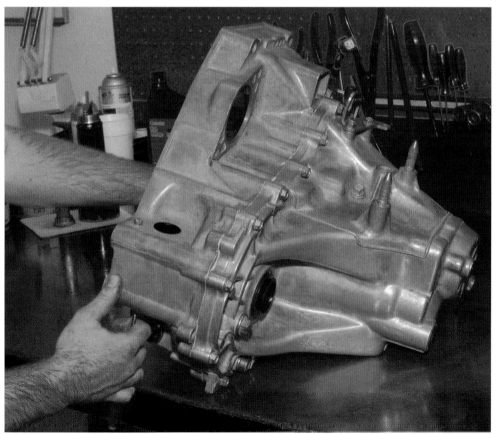

Turn the transaxle on its side and test the operation in each gear. Insert a screwdriver through the hole in the shift shaft and engage each gear in turn. Turn the input shaft and make sure that all five gears and reverse can be engaged. Place the rubber boot over the end of the shift shaft, and the transaxle is ready to be used.

CHAPTER 7
MODIFYING MANUAL TRANSMISSIONS

WHY?

Nearly every street car has a manual transmission that is strong enough for the car's factory weight, intended use, and engine torque. Motivated mainly by the desire to avoid warranty claims, manufacturers try to match drivetrain parts to a car's performance potential. With a few notable exceptions, manufacturers don't knowingly equip their cars with weak transmissions or drivetrain parts. Modern design tools allow engineers to analyze drivetrains very well and to choose parts that won't break under the expected engine torque, gearing, traction, and usage.

However, cost constraints often play a large part in design decisions. Even though a given part might be only marginally strong enough, engineers are often forced to use it because an alternative part is too expensive. In automotive design, a few dollars per part can make a vast difference over thousands and thousands of vehicles and may be enough to discourage its use.

An existing transmission design that can be used without any modifications to the rest of the car is usually the cheapest option. Since there are only a few different transmissions that a manufacturer has to choose from, but dozens of engine and chassis combinations, some cars leave the production line with less-than-optimal transmissions. Some of them may be only marginally strong enough.

A just-strong-enough transmission may be fine for hundreds of thousands of street miles, but it will not be able to cope with changes in the weight, power, or traction of the vehicle. If the vehicle weight increases significantly, as with a heavily loaded pickup or SUV, or engine torque increases through modifications, a weak transmission will be the first to show the signs of strain.

The final factor in transmission design—usage—is no less important than engine torque and vehicle weight. A transmission designed for a street car application where the engine speed is limited to under 7,000 rpm will not be able to cope with a race engine tuned for peak power above that point. Also, with very few exceptions, street car drivetrains are not designed with slicks and clutch-dumping drag-strip starts in mind. Unfortunately for production-based race car builders, stock transmissions are notoriously weak in their handling of shock loads and constant high revs. The easiest

way to make your transmission last as long as possible is to drive it like Grandma on a Sunday.

There are lots of ways to increase the strength of your drivetrain. Manual transmissions (as the first few chapters showed) are simple devices, and they can be strengthened through careful assembly and parts replacement. There are limits, of course, and in some cases the only alternative will be to replace the original transmission with something more suitable for the new power, traction, or use.

In addition to weakness, some transmissions aren't known for their smooth or fast shifting. Shifting in these transmissions can be improved by using modifications like short shifters and improved linkages. For racing use, the synchro rings and gear cones can be discarded, making the transmission shift fast and hard. For street use, the gears can be lightened, and in some cases, the synchros can be updated or backdated to make a "hybrid" transmission with better shifting.

Another reason for transmission modifications is the chance to select gearing that better matches the power output of a modified engine or different driving demands. As mentioned in the first chapter, gearing is important to make best use of a particular engine and chassis combination. By swapping either the final drive gears or one or more of the transmission speed gears, a transmission designed for road use can be adapted to different engine torque characteristics and speed or acceleration demands.

COMPROMISES AND SETTING REALISTIC GOALS

Any modification involves some compromise. With the exception of blueprinting and rebuilding with careful attention to detail, nearly any deviation from stock will have some kind of tradeoff. The same compromises that are made when a new car is designed also apply when you modify an existing car. It is up to the transmission builder to make sure that the compromise is worth it—if a small, light transmission can be rebuilt to handle significantly more power, you shouldn't be surprised if the transmission does not last as long as it might in a lower-powered application.

In the example above, the tradeoff is between weight and gear drag (a light, small transmission) and durability. In

152

other cases, the tradeoff may be comfort—a dog ring–shifted transmission would be a lousy choice for a street-driven vehicle because every shift must be made lightning fast. There is no way to shift gently in traffic. The same goes for straight spur, or reduced-angle helical gears. Sure, the transmission will be stronger, but you may be forced to wear earplugs on your commute to muffle the howling noise of these gears at steady speeds.

The final consideration—and a large one for many people—is cost. Assuming unlimited funds makes the rest of your plans much easier—if you want different ratios, or better synchronizers, just pay someone to make them for you. For the rest of us, however, all performance gains should be considered in the context of how much they will cost. There is no sense spending $5,000 on an ultratrick dog ring conversion if your engine will never make enough power to stress the stock gear set, for example, but it would be foolish not to spend that money to build a transmission to the full extent of the rules in a production-based racing class.

BLUEPRINTING

The least drastic modification to an existing manual transmission involves rebuilding the transmission with special care to internal clearances and measurements, often called "blueprinting." Blueprinting allows the builder to improve transmission reliability and strength by taking advantage of the manufacturer's original tolerances. Bearing preload, gear float, backlash, and even gear fatigue strength can all be juggled to make a transmission as strong as possible without using any aftermarket parts.

Blueprinting can be as simple as the very careful assembly of a transmission with parts already on hand, or as involved as measuring dozens of parts to find a set of "perfect" gears and shafts. In addition, blueprinting can sometimes include small modifications to "trick" synchronizers, or make gears stronger and absorb less power during racing use in stock classes where every advantage, no matter how marginally legal, is necessary to win.

While blueprinting has been perfected in these classes, since it is the only modification allowed, the techniques of basic blueprinting can be used to squeeze more durability out of a street transmission. A careful blueprint-style rebuild of any transmission or transaxle can pay off big in increased reliability, quieter running, and less wasted power. All of these are desirable attributes whether the gearbox in question is used in racing or on the street.

Blueprinting will take much more time than a simple rebuild because the transmission may have to be built and stripped down many times to check clearances at each stage of assembly. All clearances inside the transmission can (and should) be optimized during a blueprinting rebuild. If the blueprinting is being done outside of a machine shop, it will take longer than a stock rebuild: sometimes reassembly has to be paused repeatedly while parts are modified.

CASE AND SHAFT ALIGNMENT

The first step in blueprinting a transmission is to strip the gearbox down to the last bolt and inspect it like a standard rebuild. Only after this is done, and the baseline condition of the gearbox known, can the work of assembly begin.

Every part inside the transmission is located precisely by the cast-aluminum or iron case. Any deviation from perfectly centered and perfectly square will make a transmission that is less than ideal in some way—whether in durability, power loss, or noise. The distance between the center of the main shaft and countershaft or output shaft is especially critical.

Because it is so important, every machined face of the transmission case and extension housing should be measured for squareness. Every bearing bore should be measured for the proper bearing fit, and the center-to-center distance of every shaft should be checked and verified for accuracy. The shafts must be absolutely square and straight at both ends of the transmission case—no deviation can be allowed.

A good machinist can think of lots of ways to accurately check the bearing bores in both ends of the main housing, but the simplest way is to turn two tight-fitting steel bushings to fit into the bores. These steel bushings are then bored out to precisely fit over a shaft of gauge steel. If the shaft slides through both bushings with no drag, the bores are straight. If not, one of the bearing bores is not properly aligned.

The distance between the shafts should be exactly the same at both ends of the transmission case. No measurable variation is acceptable. Most production cases are spot-on from the factory, but it is important to double-check before wasting time and money on a transmission that will never perform well.

If you get a bum case there are a few ways to correct the deviation. The first is simply to find another case. Given enough cases, there is bound to be at least one that is accurate in all machined dimensions. If cost or availability prohibit checking through a big stack of transmission cases, a good machinist can modify one end or the other to locate the deviant shaft by modifying one of the original bearing bores to accept a large-diameter bushing. After accurately locating and boring the oversize hole, a turned steel bushing that accepts the original bearing's outer race is pressed into the case to support and locate the shaft in the new location.

The result is an accurate bearing bore and less friction and heat inside the transmission.

Once the case has been checked out and found to be perfectly square and in alignment, the shafts should also be inspected for straightness. Put each shaft between centers or on V-blocks, and set up a dial indicator. For a factory rebuild, the shafts can be off by as much as .005 inch total, but for a performance rebuild they should not deviate even .001 inch from straight.

The straightness of the shafts and housings is far more important than the other parts—bearings and gears usually have very tight tolerances, and gears and synchronizers can be shimmed to change their play or location.

GEAR END PLAY

From the standpoint of ideal gear mesh and shift quality in a high-performance transmission, there should be minimal end play between the gears and thrust washers. Unfortunately, a transmission assembled with no end play would not last very long at all, since some clearance is necessary for good lubrication. The sides of the gears act as plain thrust bearings, so there must be some minimal clearance to allow for an oil film to build up between the side of the gear and synchronizer hub. In addition, in some transmissions, the needle or plain bearings in the hub of each mainshaft gear are fed oil through the gaps on either side of the gear. The more clearance, the more oil can reach the bearings.

This is particularly important in transmissions with solid mainshafts. Too little clearance between the gears could starve the bearings for oil and cause them to gall or seize. For road transmissions with hollow shafts or pressure lubrication, end float should be kept very close to zero, because these transmissions do not need as much clearance between each gear. Select a locating snap ring that will result in the minimum allowable end play for the transmission in question. With a solid shaft, the best strategy is to aim for the loose side of the manufacturer's specifications.

Aftermarket gears and shafts can be very sensitive to gear end play. Most replacement shafts are not drilled like the originals, and the gear side clearance should be increased to compensate. Check with the manufacturer of the shaft for details, but generally treat the resulting gear train like a splash-lubricated system and increase end play to the maximum allowable, or a little more. In transmissions without gear needle roller bearings, the clearance between the center bore of the gear and the shaft can be increased by honing the bore of the gear.

BEARING PRELOAD

During blueprinting, the preload on the shaft bearings is carefully controlled to improve transmission reliability and shift quality at high heat and stress levels. Generally, the more preload between a pair of shaft bearings, the stiffer the resulting assembly will be, and the more shock loads will be able to be transferred through the bearings to the outer races and thus to the case. Because of this, a tightly preloaded shaft will be better supported and deflect less under power than a loosely installed shaft, all else being equal. A stiffer shaft will also allow for more positive shifts since the shafts and bearings will not be able to move in relation to one another as easily.

The more abuse the transmission will be expected to withstand, the more preload should be used on the bearings. This is because most cases are machined from aluminum castings, while shafts, gears, and bearings are generally steel. As they heat up, these metals expand at different rates, and this causes problems with initial preload. As the aluminum case heats up, it expands more than the steel shafts.

The bearing outer races are held in the aluminum case, and therefore move farther apart, while the inner races (mounted to the steel shaft) stay relatively stable. This causes the initial preload to become looser as the transmission gets hotter. On the street this is rarely an issue, but a racing transmission can see significant changes in overall preload with increasing oil temperature due to differential expansion. To overcome this problem, racing transmissions are set up with more preload than street transmissions.

The tradeoff inherent in juggling bearing clearances outside the manufacturer's recommendations is more friction and slightly faster bearing wear at low temperatures and loads. Heavily preloaded bearings will require more force to rotate (which absorbs power), and they will wear out faster than lightly preloaded bearings. If the transmission is run at higher temperatures, however, the running preload will be much less than the starting preload and bearing life will actually be increased over a lightly preloaded bearing.

For maximum bearing life and shaft stiffness in a blueprinted transmission, most builders use the tightest of the factory-recommended preload settings a little tighter. The higher quality the bearings, the more preload they will be able to withstand, but the optimal preload varies by the type of bearing and the other bearing(s) on the shaft.

Tapered roller bearings are usually preloaded several thousandths more than recommended, particularly in shafts with two opposing bearings. Shafts running with two standard ball bearings should be set up with a very slight preload. Ball bearings do not like high levels of preload like tapered bearings, although radial contact ball bearings can withstand more than radial bearings. If the shaft has a ball bearing on one end and a (nontapered) roller bearing on the other, it should, in general, be set up with no end play and no preload. These shafts are designed with thrust control at one end only, and plain roller bearings are not designed to cope with much preload pressure.

SHIFT LINKAGE ALIGNMENT AND OPTIMIZATION

As pointed out in previous chapters, the axial alignment of the shift forks with the sleeves and gears on the mainshaft is very important. Many novice transmission builders ignore the issue, and it comes back to haunt them. The ultimate cause of the problem is the stack-up of all the manufacturing tolerances for the forks, rails, synchronizers, and gears. Problems arise when parts from several different sources (including the aftermarket) are assembled together into a complete transmission. Some combinations of these parts can result in misalignment, which will cause poor shifting as well as gear, synchronizer, and fork damage.

In a transmission without synchronizers, the alignment is even more important. There are no synchronizer hub inserts in a dog ring transmission, so the shift forks, detents, and interlock provide all of the force that holds each hub in neutral. If the forks become bent or broken from bottoming against the slider groove, the "neutral" detent position may no longer correspond to true neutral at the slider. The edges of the gear dogs can be damaged if there is not enough clearance in neutral; in the worst case, the transmission could lock into two gears at once.

When building a transmission for high-performance use, always check the shift fork travel and make absolutely sure that no bottoming out is occurring. If the rail overtravels, the fork may become bent, while too little clearance can result in a transmission that pops out of gear. Check that there is sufficient clearance in neutral as well. Many transmissions do not address the issue of fork alignment in their service manual, and this means that the builder will have to do their own research to find the optimal setup. Stops will have to be added to prevent fork overtravel, or machine work may be required.

For even better shifting performance, some builders like to polish the shift rails and their bores in the case. The smoother the action between these two parts, the quicker the transmission can be shifted by the driver. At the same time, the detent recesses in the rails can be polished and radiused to provide a softer, easier detent position. This will reduce shift effort as well.

UPGRADED BEARINGS

At the same time that the transmission is being rebuilt, and the clearances optimized, some of the internal parts can be upgraded. Bearings are the easiest to upgrade because of their standardized dimensions. As a matter of course, many professionals replace the standard bearings with heavier-duty versions. Bearing manufacturers usually produce several different grades of bearing in a particular size.

The standard bearings, and the ones included in most rebuild kits, are fine for standard rebuilds, but stronger bearings in the same size are more suited to performance use. Because they are so standardized, heavy-duty versions are no farther away than your local bearing shop. A good bearing dealer will have no problem cross-referencing a given bearing size to a heavier-duty precision version if one exists. In general, the more balls in a caged ball bearing, the more support the bearings give to the shaft and the longer the bearing will last.

GEAR STRENGTHENING

The gears inside a manual transmission are often the strongest parts of the assembly. With very few exceptions, problems with manual transmissions start with the bearings or synchronizer assemblies. However, gear trouble is not unheard of—the ubiquitous T-5, for example, is known for its weak third gear. In some transmissions used for racing, the gear teeth are simply not strong enough for extreme torque and shock loads.

There are few ways to strengthen steel once it has been manufactured into a finished part. Assuming the gears are properly heat-treated and machined from the factory, the ultimate strength of each tooth will be relatively constant, and it will reflect the properties of the steel alloy and the hardening process used. The overall strength of each gear can only be increased incrementally, if at all.

What can be improved on, however, is the fatigue strength of each gear. Without getting into the messy metallurgical details, gear teeth break because of the way steel behaves when it is repeatedly flexed. As each tooth in a gear rotates into contact with its mate, the gear flexes slightly. This tiny amount of flex causes tension, or pulling stress, to build up in that tooth. Like any metal subjected to constant high alternating stresses, steel will eventually crack if the stresses are high enough and continue long enough. When this occurs, it is only a matter of time before the tooth breaks off and migrates to another gear pair or bearing.

Small imperfections in the gear tooth surface (like those left from machining, or created by wear) can make this problem worse because they interrupt the flow of stress through the material and concentrate it in a few small points. These "stress raisers" can encourage cracking by acting as wedges that split the steel surface of the gear. Stress raisers can be reduced by carefully polishing the surface of the gear and deburring the edges of each gear tooth with emery cloth or a very fine stone.

During a performance rebuild, avoid using cracked or pitted gears and shafts if possible; unfortunately, many of the small stress cracks that develop in used gears are invisible to the naked eye. To find them, take the parts to a reputable machine shop for crack-checking using a Magnaflux machine or other crack-detection method. If you want to check them yourself, get a Zyglo kit from your local aircraft parts supplier. The kit consists of a cleaner and a special penetrating dye and developer. After cleaning the part and spraying on the dye and developer, any cracks will glow under a black light. It takes experience to use Zyglo effectively, so it might not hurt to pay someone else to check your gears.

The constant small tension stresses that affect the fatigue life of gear teeth can be reduced significantly by treating the surface of the steel gear. The most popular and proven stress-relief method is called shot peening. In this process, small beads of hard steel shot are blown at the surface of the gear with high air pressure. The shot pelts the gear surface and compresses the outer layer of steel a microns deep. The compressed outer layer then acts as a buffer that absorbs some of the constant tension stress before it can affect the gear steel. Shot peening works so well that most manufacturers of high-performance and racing transmissions shot peen their gears before assembly.

If your transmission gears are not shot peened, they will definitely benefit from the process. Don't expect miracles, though, since it only increases fatigue strength. The ultimate strength of each tooth is not much higher after treatment, and severe shock loads can still cause damage. Shot peening may increase gear noise since the surface of the treated gears is slightly rough, but the rough surface can also increase the stability of the oil film since it gives the oil small pores in which to accumulate.

In the past few years, racers have started to increase their use of chemical surface treatments for transmission gears. The proprietary chemical polishing process from REM chemicals, called "isotropic finishing," is the most popular of the commercially available treatments. Parts are pickled in a chemical solution that softens the microscopic "peaks" of the gear surface, allowing them to be polished away by ceramic media in a vibrating tub. The valleys remain unaffected by the process. The result is a gear or other part with an extremely polished surface; unlike traditional polishing, however, the gear tooth shape has not been changed and gear mesh is not affected.

The REM process reduces friction between the teeth of each gear, and this lowers oil and gearbox temperatures and power lost to friction. In addition, the polished surface increases gear fatigue strength because it leaves a finished radius on edges and removes surface asperities that create microscopic stress raisers. Since the EHL film is a constant thickness, a fine surface finish reduces micropitting and stress crack propagation. The cost of the REM process is not exorbitant, certainly within the budget of a production-based racing team, and the results are very good.

Another, somewhat controversial, method of steel treatment is called "cryotreating." In this process, the steel parts (gears and shafts) are frozen to approximately 300 degrees below zero Fahrenheit. According to the companies offering this service, cryotreating rearranges internal stresses in the part and provides a benefit similar to shot peening. The jury is, unfortunately, still out on this process, but it appears to work in some applications, including transmission gears. The hard evidence for its positive effects is a little hard to find, in part because many of the processes are proprietary. In some tightly controlled racing classes, cryotreating has become a required step during engine preparation, but even here it may be as useful for its psychological benefit on one's opponents as anything else.

Yet another option for the racer looking for an edge is a variety of modern engineered coatings that are sprayed or otherwise applied to the surface of gears. These coatings can reduce friction for a while, but many are eventually worn off the gears, limiting their benefit to only a short time. While they are widely used on engine piston skirts, these coatings have not gained widespread acceptance for use on transmission components. A metallic "hard chrome" surface plating tends to improve gear fatigue life for many of the reasons given above for REM chemical polishing, but the cost to finish and treat a gear tends to be very high.

UPDATING AND BACKDATING

Most transmission manufacturers implement continual improvements to the basic design over the production life of the transmission. As engines become more powerful, or new demands are placed on the chassis, the transmission may be changed slightly to improve reliability and shift quality, among other things. Often, new parts supersede old ones in the manufacturer's parts catalog, so they can be used as service replacements for worn originals. It pays to spend the time to go through manufacturer parts lists to find new parts that can be substituted for old ones, or, in rare cases, for older, stronger parts that can be scrounged to beef up a newer transmission.

Sometimes the same basic transmission is used in more than one application, and the manufacturer has developed improved parts that can be used on lesser versions of the

For REM polishing, the parts are submerged in a tank of chemically active etching compound. Also in the tank are a lot of small ceramic tiles. As the chemical etches the outer layer of steel of the gears, the ceramic tiles remove this layer and polish the surface of the gear. REM polishing can pay big dividends in gear fatigue strength in a racing transmission—most Formula 1 transmissions use gears treated in this way.

transmission. A good example would be the steel shift forks used by Mitsubishi in EVO III transmissions, which can be installed in U.S.-market Eclipse transmissions that share the same basic design. Gear ratios are also commonly switched between transmissions to optimize the ratios for a particular use. If the transmission is destined for racing, make sure such creative parts swapping is legal (or discoverable).

BEYOND BLUEPRINTING

If blueprinting and updating a manual transmission do not improve the situation, and assuming that the original transmission must be retained, there are a number of more advanced tricks that transmission builders use to strengthen units for racing and hot street use. These vary from simple short shifters to internal changes such as case strengthening, alternative gear ratios, and full dog ring conversions for racing use.

SHORT SHIFTERS

Short-throw shifters top the list of aftermarket transmission modifications. A short-throw shifter, or "short shifter," is a linkage modification that reduces the distance the shift knob must travel to engage each gear, allowing for faster shifts (at least in theory). They are inexpensive, easy to install, and usually effective.

OEM shifters tend to have a high mechanical advantage over the shift rails and forks in the gearbox. This reduces the effort needed to get the transmission into gear, but also adds to the distance that the shift knob must be moved to shift gears. This slows down the shifting because the driver's hand must travel farther with each shift. Short shifters move the effective pivot of the shift lever to reduce mechanical advantage, and thus lever travel. Higher shifting effort is the cost of shortened shifter travel, but most performance-minded drivers won't mind the extra resistance.

Unfortunately, the shortened throw of an aftermarket shifter on a synchromesh transmission does not really reduce the time it takes to make each shift. The synchronizer blocking rings determine the delay—remember that the sleeve cannot engage a gear until the speed of the two parts matches. The blocking rings must accelerate the next gear on an upshift, and decelerate it on a downshift, which takes time. In fact, forcing the sleeve before the blocking ring allows it to move can result in a bent shift fork or damaged dog teeth.

That's not to say that short shifters are worthless. On a nonsynchronized transmission, precise, quick shifts are an absolute necessity, and the shortest, tightest shifter available should be used. Any slop or delay in the shifting process can damage the dogs on the gears and sliders. For synchronized transmissions, the biggest advantage to a short shifter is an improvement in shift feel that comes from removing factory rubber bushings and reducing play in the linkage.

Some short-throw shifters (like many of those for the TREMEC T-5) are an improvement because they incorporate adjustable stops into the shifter mechanism to prevent shift linkage overtravel and damage. Short-throw shifters vary greatly in quality, and some of the cheaper ones cannot stand up to even normal usage. A broken shifter can result in bent linkage, shift forks, and synchronizer damage, so it pays to investigate your options carefully. Many aluminum shifters are not strong enough for even casual use—aluminum is a poor choice of material for a highly stressed item like a shift lever.

If your car has vague, notchy shifting even after rebuilding and adjusting the factory shift linkage, try using a weighted shift knob before you buy an expensive short shifter. Weighted knobs improve shift feel because they add inertia to the shift lever—the initial "push" to get the lever into gear requires a bit more force, and the inertia of the knob helps snap the lever more positively into gear on each shift. Because of the differences between shift linkages and transmission detent designs, there is no one knob that will work for all transmissions. Plan on trying a few before you find one that gives the results you're after.

By the way, if you want to run a sequential shifter, a transmission swap will be necessary because it is very difficult to modify a nonsequential shift linkage to use sequential shifting. Some kind of external drum-and-ratchet assembly has to be designed, located, and attached to the shift rails or forks. There are one or two modification kits for a few (mostly Japanese) transmissions, but they are the exception rather than the rule. In addition, Quaife U.K. manufactures a kit to convert certain Ford transmissions popular in sports car racing, but the kits replace the entire extension housing, shifter, forks, rails, and top cover of the donor transmission.

CASE MODIFICATIONS

The forces created by a pair of counterrotating helical gears are constantly forcing the gear shafts apart, both radially and axially. These forces become greater as both speed and torque increase, to the point that they can exceed the mechanical limits of the shafts and case. Stock transmissions with high helical angles suffer the greatest: the higher the helix angle, the more unwanted opposing forces.

The forces produced by the gears act on the main shafts. The shafts, in turn, transfer those forces to the main bearings and then to the transmission case. If the forces become high enough, the shafts will bend slightly and the aluminum case will stretch. As this happens, the shafts move farther apart and gear mesh becomes less than ideal. The farther the centers of each gear move away from each other, the more stress is put on the thinner, weaker tips of the gear teeth. If the gears pull too far apart, one gear tooth may break off, quickly destroying both mating gears.

In addition to gear failure, some transmissions are known for splitting their aluminum cases. Any material between the main shaft bearing bores is highly stressed in tension, or pulling, by the spreading forces on the two shaft bearings. Aluminum becomes weaker with higher temperatures, making this thin area vulnerable to cracking from the combination of heat, spreading force, and vibration. Small cracks gradually grow into larger ones until the gear forces eventually rip the transmission in two.

Front-wheel-drive transaxles with helical final drive gears suffer the greatest from this problem. The pinion gear is usually quite small, and may not be well supported by bearings. It also turns at quite a high speed compared to the ring gear. All of these factors increase the deflection of the pinion shaft and reduce the mesh of these two gears. A stripped pinion gear is a common failure behind a strong engine and a lot of traction.

Since durability is related to both the forces acting on the case and the strength of the case and shafts, there are two ways to improve overall reliability. The first way is to reduce the forces created by the helical gears. Aftermarket gear sets with lower helix angles or straight teeth eliminate much of the side loads on the bearings and retainers, but they do not eliminate the loads forcing the shafts apart. The other alternative is strengthening the transmission case.

If the transmission is popular enough, an aftermarket case made from better aluminum alloy may be available. Often, factory cases are manufactured from an alloy chosen for its cheapness and easy castability rather than strength.

Transmission cases are cast from a ductile (flexible) aluminum alloy that stretches with heat and gear forces. This stretching causes problems with gear alignment and ultimately reduces the strength of the gear train, since the gears no longer mesh precisely. One fix for this problem is to increase the bearing area of the case—the original case is bored out for a steel sleeve, which is then honed out to properly fit the bearing. The resulting steel ring supports the shaft bearings, and thus the shafts, better than the transmission's original case, keeping gear alignment precise and the transmission reliable.

An aftermarket sand-cast case of a stronger alloy will help, but these are available for only some transmissions, including the rear-engine VW, TREMEC T-5, Chrysler A-833, Ford Toploader, Borg-Warner T10, and Muncie.

If your transmission has trouble with case cracking and gear damage, and you must use the original case for rules, cost, or other reasons, there are ways to strengthen it. One popular method is using steel or iron reinforcements around the bearing bores in the aluminum case. The steel flexes less than the aluminum case and keeps the two shafts together. There are several ways to do this, depending on the layout of the transmission being modified. Some transmissions have an intermediate bearing bulkhead or a separate bearing retainer that can be replaced by steel.

In more extreme cases, a large plate can be machined to replace the bearing bores and support both shafts. The case is cut out around the original bearing area and tapped for retaining bolts. A large plate is then bolted into place before the bearing bores are machined to their final diameter. In either case, the machine work must be done very accurately, or any benefit from strengthening the case will be lost to gear noise, friction, or more stress.

Yet another way to strengthen the case involves welding aluminum gussets onto the outside or inside. The success of this approach varies greatly depending on the abilities of the welder and the location and size of the gussets. If the welding is not done right, the case could warp and pinch the mainshaft bearings or end up weaker than before. In addition, haphazardly adding gussets is unlikely to make much difference. Another option is an external steel brace or girdle that holds the transmission together from the outside. The problem with both solutions is that their effectiveness varies. The stresses inside the transmission are so great that it is unlikely that an external support of any kind will be able to prevent case cracking and damage.

ADDING EXTRA BEARINGS

In older transmissions, where the mainshaft gears ride directly on the shaft with no bearing in between, the gears can gall on the shaft and cause excessive wear. There are a few ways to get around this problem, but all require some machine work. The first is to bore out the center of the gear and install a bronze bushing (as described in Chapter 4). In some cases, the gear can be bored out and have a sleeve pressed in to provide a hardened wear surface for a caged needle roller bearing. As with the other transmission machine work, a good machinist can do just about anything, but this is not a job for someone not willing to spend the time that it will take to do the setup.

Another popular location for added roller bearings is the extension housing of rear-wheel-drive transmissions. Most have a plain bushing to support the end of the driveshaft yoke. As the bearing wears, it causes the front of the driveshaft to move around and vibrate badly. To eliminate this problem, some racing transmissions use a needle roller bearing in this location. Combined with a case-hardened and ground driveshaft yoke, it can eliminate many off-balance issues with a rapidly turning driveshaft.

ALTERNATIVE GEAR RATIOS

If you intend to go racing with a production-car transmission, strength is only one factor that must be considered. Most street transmissions are designed with a wide spread of gear ratios with large gaps between them. The lower gears are set very low, while the higher gears are very high overdrive gears to reduce engine rpm on the highway. In racing, such a wide spread is not necessary. Most courses require only limited combinations of engine and vehicle speed, and an overdrive gear is not usually desirable (since it reduces torque output to the final drive).

This means that, in practice, most of the gears of a production transmission will not work in a race car. Purpose-designed race transmissions have the luxury of a wide selection of interchangeable ratios, but most street transmissions do not. Some popular gearboxes like the Honda B-series, TREMEC T-5, and older four-speeds have aftermarket gear sets available for them, with a selections of alternative ratios. Chances are good that if you are running one of these units, there is a gear set that will fit your needs; pick the set closest to what you want and use the final drive to fine-tune the power band and rpm range of the engine. If you have a transmission that is not well supported by the aftermarket, there is still hope. A machine shop could be hired to produce an entire gear set from billet steel, which could turn out to be prohibitively expensive.

If you have a three-shaft rear-wheel-drive transmission like most four- and five-speeds, you may not have to replace every gear, however. These transmissions have one advantage in this area compared to transaxles, since every gear but fourth is driven through the input shaft and countergear. An input shaft and countergear pair with a higher ratio will drive each gear slower by the same percentage—this will then reduce the distance between each gear ratio (in percent, or engine rpm drop at each shift).

As an example, we'll use an old, but very sturdy, four-speed transmission design: the Mopar A-833 four-speed used from 1964 to 1979. This transmission was built with one of about five different gear sets, but for the purposes of illustration we will use the most common, found behind most small-block V-8 engines during the late 1960s and early 1970s.

The input gear has 24 teeth, and the mating gear on the countershaft has 31 teeth for an overall ratio of 1.29:1. The first table lists the number of teeth on each gear pair and the resulting ratios (in combination with the input gears).

Gear	Tooth Count Counter	Main	Ratio	Ratio Gap
Input	31	24 (input)	(1.29)	—
1st	35	17	2.66	—
2nd	34	23	1.91	0.75
3rd	29	27	1.39	0.52
4th	—	—	1.00	0.39

Now, let's assume that we have found that the original first gear (2.66:1) is too low with our current final drive, and we want to get it closer to second gear, or around 2.25:1 for example. To figure out how much to change our input gears, figure the difference between the old and new ratios, and multiply the input gear ratio by the same amount:

$$(2.25/2.66) = 0.84$$
$$(0.84 \times 1.29) = 1.08$$

To get that ratio with the first gear pair will require an input shaft gear and countergear that are very close to the same size. There is one caveat here—don't forget that the gears in a pair are designed to mesh together at a particular center distance and tooth pitch. If we do not change those two variables, we are stuck with a total tooth count the same as when we started (that is, 55 [31 plus 24]). Within this tooth count, shooting for a 1.08:1 ratio, the closest pair are 27 and 28 teeth for a 1.04:1 ratio. Ignoring for the moment the mechanical aspects of the change, the new input gear pair will give us the following ratios:

Gear	Tooth Count Counter	Main	Ratio	Ratio Gap
Input	28	27 (input)	(1.04)	—
1st	35	17	2.14	—
2nd	34	23	1.53	0.61
3rd	29	27	1.11	0.42
4th	—	—	1.00	0.11

Notice that the gap between each gear has now been reduced. Once we have arrived at a desired gear pair, the next step is to have them made. A good gear cutter will be able to make just about anything you want, but it will not be cheap. The procedure for replacing these gears (both, unfortunately, are cast in place) is to grind or turn off the teeth until a small-diameter stub remains and then weld on the new gears (which have been bored out to match the diameter of the stub). Voilà! Instant close-ratio gearbox.

Note that this trick works best with four-speed transmissions. If the transmission includes an overdrive fifth

The dogs of a nonsynchronized transmission are much larger than the small dog teeth of synchronized transmission gears. This makes them stronger, and the elimination of synchronizers allows the gears to become wider and stronger as well. Of course a dog ring transmission would be difficult to drive on the street—every shift must be made hard and fast. This type of gear is really best for racing.

gear, that gear will also become higher, so it will be even farther from the other four gears. To get around this problem, you may have to find a new gear set for fifth gear, or possibly swap the gears on their shafts (with lots of machine work, of course!).

LIGHTENING INTERNAL PARTS

Synchronizer blocking rings must speed up and slow down the rotating parts of a transmission before they will allow a shift to be completed. The heavier the parts, including the gears, the more their rotational inertia, and the more strain they put on the synchronizer blocking rings. Shift quality and vehicle acceleration can both be improved by lightening the gears and shafts in the transmission. Shifts will be faster since the lighter internal parts allow the gear train to slow faster, shortening the time needed for each shift.

As long as lightening is not carried so far that the strength of the gears is compromised, it is a positive modification. This would not be a modification to make on a transmission known for breakage. If there is enough extra strength, the gear lightening will have minimal or no effect on reliability. Transmission mainshafts can also be gun-drilled

to reduce their weight, but the small amount of weight removed from the center of the shafts does not really make much difference in either synchronizer performance or drivetrain weight. It is definately a modification of last resort.

SYNCHRONIZER UPGRADES

Few transmissions have alternative upgraded synchronizers available, with multiple friction surfaces or improved friction material. When racing where a synchronizer is required, or street use, these upgraded synchros can improve shift quality and speed. For the TREMEC T-56, G-force installs improved triple-cone synchronizers on the third and fourth gears to match the factory first and second gears. Dual-cone synchronizers are also available for some Mitsubishi front-wheel-drive and all-wheel-drive transmissions from a couple of sources. These improved synchronizers can mean the difference between a quick shift and a grinding shift.

DOG RING CONVERSIONS

If upgraded synchronizers are not enough, the best way to make a production transmission into a racing gearbox is by eliminating the synchronizers and converting it to a dog

The easiest, and perhaps cheapest, way to get a nonsynchronized racing transmission is to build one. Kits like this one for the Mitsubishi turbo four-cylinder transmission allow the transmission builder to replace the entire gearstack and one of the shafts with sturdy, made-for-racing gears. Usually these kits are not quite bolt-in ready, since the different demands of the straight cut gears and dog ring sliders require special preparations during assembly. The manufacturer of your aftermarket gear set should be able to detail any changes that must be made.

ring box. The conversion can be performed in one of three ways: the existing gears and synchronizers can be replaced with gears and sliders machined as a unit with the dog ring; the existing gears can be modified by welding and machine work and mated to new sliders; or the existing gears and sliders can be modified to create a kind of "pseudo" dog ring transmission with some of the benefits of a full conversion.

The easiest and best way to convert a transmission to dog ring shifting is to replace the entire gear and synchronizer stack. If you have one of the dozens of transmissions with strong aftermarket support, this should be no more difficult than calling your favorite speed shop and ordering the gear set. The gears in these conversion sets are usually made wider and stronger than the transmission's original gears to take advantage of the space gained by removal of the synchronizer cones and blocking rings.

Replacement gear sets with dog rings are designed from the start with racing in mind, so they also have the benefit of closer, higher ratios and better gear design for high-performance use. Most are cut with lower helical tooth angles (or even straight teeth) to reduce heat and friction buildup, which also improves bearings and case life, making them a very good choice for building a racing transmission.

If your transmission does not have a good selection of alternative gear sets with dog ring shifting, the existing gears can be modified to provide the same benefits. To turn them into dog ring gears, several machine shops can machine off the original synchronizer cone and dog rings and weld on a dog ring. The gear hubs are honed to the proper size, and the sliders are modified by removing teeth until the spaces between the internal splines are the same width as the gear dogs. Liberty's Gears in Michigan is the best-known shop that performs this kind of work, and their "pro-shift" conversions are very popular in some drag racing classes. They are surprisingly inexpensive and a good way to get fast shifting on a budget.

Not all transmissions can be pro-shifted, but there is at least one more truly low-budget way to get synchronizer-free shifting. In the 1960s, Chrysler racing engineers figured out a way to eliminate the synchros on their drag-racing gearboxes without using any aftermarket parts (which were not allowed by the rules at the time) and still get the benefits of the large windows that allow dogs to shift quickly without grinding.

Their solution to the problem was the "slick shift" conversion. Since the old Mopar A-833 transmissions had an even number of gear dogs and synchronizer splines, the engineers simply removed every other one on both parts. This resulted in a synchronizer sleeve and gear with half the normal number of teeth and enough rotational clearance for a good shift. Enough teeth are left so that they are still strong enough not to shear off, but they are not as strong or resistant to damage as true dog rings. This only works on transmissions with an even number of dog teeth on the gears, however. If the dogs become damaged from missed shifts, some gears can be salvaged by welding on dog rings like described above.

CONVERTING TO TWO-WHEEL DRIVE FOR DYNAMOMETER TESTING

If you have an all-wheel-drive car or truck, dynamometer testing can be a challenge. Four-wheel dynos are a lot harder to find than two-wheel dynos and they are more expensive. Trucks with part-time four-wheel drive can simply be switched to two-wheel-drive mode and tested through the rear wheels. Cars with electronically controlled or viscous center differentials need to be modified to run in two-wheel-drive mode, however.

If the center differential is left connected, it will overheat if one pair of wheels is prevented from turning. The differential is designed to cope with only temporary variations in traction between the front and rear wheels and will attempt to send more torque to the stopped wheel pair. If the rear driveshaft is removed, the front wheels will not turn. All of the engine's torque will be sent to the (now-disconnected) rear wheels.

The only way to test the car on a two-wheel dyno will be to lock the center differential and remove the rear driveshaft. The locked differential will send all engine torque to whichever pair of wheels has traction—in this case, the front. The best way to lock the center differential is with a "spool" similar to those used in drag racing in place of differentials. This will be easier in some cars than others, of course.

FINAL DRIVE GEARS

If a car's gearing is too high or too low for your intended use, it is much easier and cheaper to change the final drive ratio than to change all of the transmission's ratios. The final drive ratio affects overall gearing, but not the range of gearing available. By going to a lower final drive for increased engine in rpm in the higher gears, the low gears might become too low and unusable, for example. It is a balancing act between low-speed and high-speed acceleration. The best ratio will be the one that best matches the vehicle's use, whether drag racing, road racing, or street. There is no "right" ratio, since vehicle weight, engine torque curve, and traction all play a part. Luckily, final drive ratios are cheaper than transmission gears, so it doesn't cost much to experiment.

Setting up a hypoid final drive for racing use is more or less the same as for street use, but, as with transmission bearings, differential bearings should be preloaded more than recommended for best ring gear stiffness and more ideal gear mesh. When setting up the gear mesh for racing, make the contact area heavier on the "toe" (the narrowest part) of the pinion gear teeth on the drive side. This will help with the gear mesh under power. The hypoid gear backlash can also be decreased to almost zero; however, a ring and pinion set up this way may be too noisy for street use.

If you are stuck with a hypoid gear set with a high pinion gear angle, make sure the gears have plenty of oil cooling, and use the best fluid possible. Consider using the REM treatment discussed above to reduce friction losses and heat buildup in the final drive. See the section below for a discussion of lubricating and cooling hypoid final drives for endurance road and circle-track racing. Always check the axle temperature if you suspect it is too high. On the street, the cooling effect of the oil contained in the axle is usually sufficient, but race cars using hypoid gearing almost always require an axle cooler.

LUBRICATION

The viscosity and type of oil that a transmission requires vary, but there is a wide scope for experimentation. By juggling oil base stock, additives, and viscosity, racers and transmission builders look for decreased power loss, increased wear resistance, or both. The key to experimentation with oil formulations, as with any other modification, is understanding the basic compromises inherent in any oil choice.

As we have already seen in the section on manual transmission lubricants, the EHL film thickness of synthetic oil tends to be more stable than that of mineral oil. That makes synthetic oil a very good choice for any high-performance application since a thinner oil (for less power loss) can be used with less detrimental effects on the gears, or a thicker oil can be used to provide a thick EHL film even at high temperatures in a heavily stressed transmission.

Choosing an oil for a street application is fairly simple. OEM gears have fine, small teeth that have lots of load sharing and low contact pressures, and most street driving will never heat the transmission enough to stress the oil significantly. For most stock applications, the best lubricant will be a high-quality synthetic oil in the manufacturer's recommended viscosity and API (American Petroleum Institute) rating.

If you want to experiment with different oils in a stock transmission, make sure you understand the different alternatives and make a choice based on sound principles. If any problems develop, however, be ready to swap back to the recommended fill as soon as possible. If the transmission specifies automatic transmission fluid, be sure to use it, since the synchronizer blocking rings may be damaged by anything else. Unless the transmission specifies API GL-5 lubricants only, GL-4 oil will be a better choice since it has a lower percentage of EP additives that reduce synchronizer efficiency.

For racing, the choices become much more complicated. The optimal lubricant will be the one that provides a sufficiently protective EHL film thickness at the maximum transmission temperature. Racing transmissions run at very high temperatures, so the thicker the EHL film the better—most racing transmission manufacturers recommend a very-high-viscosity lubricant. In addition, racing gear sets often make use of larger, stronger teeth that have higher contact pressures and less load sharing (from shallower helix angles and larger diametrical pitches). These teeth need thick, strong EHL films to prevent excessive surface wear and pitting.

The best lubricant for transmissions with dog rings has a high concentration of EP additives since these transmissions do not have synchronizers that depend on friction to work. These transmissions work best with a very-high-viscosity synthetic GL-5 oil. The same goes for hypoid final drives—they have very stringent oil demands and require high levels of EP additives to survive.

COOLING

Oil temperature is the other critical variable in EHL film thickness and strength, and it also has a significant role in lubricant life and durability. If the oil temperature gets too high, the EHL film thickness will begin to break down, and all the detrimental effects of a thin EHL film will appear. The higher the oil temperature, the lower the fatigue life of the gears and the shorter the life of the bearings.

Thicker oil will only do so much—once temperatures reach 250 degrees F. or higher, there is no oil that will be able to prevent gear wear and eventual damage. The oil will quickly break down and cease to do its job as a lubricant. For the transmission to last, the oil temperature will have to go down, and cooling will be required.

In general, street transmissions will never produce enough excess heat to require a cooling system. Oil coolers are only necessary when transmission temperature reaches 210 to 220 degrees F.—oil life declines very rapidly beyond this point. To determine if a cooling system is necessary, install an oil temperature gauge and watch for readings over 200 degrees. A simple light that comes on at 220 to 230 degrees F. will work in a pinch (Stewart Warner and Autometer make inexpensive National Pipe Thread (NPT) threaded temperature switches). Install the light where the driver can see it and make a note if it comes on during a race. If it does, change the oil and think carefully about cooling.

Before assuming that all of the heat is coming from the gearbox or final drive, check the car's exhaust routing. A hot exhaust header or pipe running near the gearbox can contribute significantly to transmission oil temperature. If you suspect that some of the heat is radiating into the transmission case from the exhaust, insulate the exhaust where it runs close to the transmission. Don't insulate the transmission case since that is how a transmission is cooled.

A simple plate-style oil cooler like the Aeroquip, Earl's, and Mocal units make excellent transmission coolers. To move the oil through the cooler, a pump will be needed since most transmissions depend on splash lubrication and do not incorporate a pump. Mocal makes an excellent electric pump, and there are a couple of rear end pumps used in NASCAR that are driven off the driveshaft U-joint flange.

Once a pressure oil supply has been set up, the returning oil from the cooler should be directed to where it does the most good. Since the input shaft gears in a rear-wheel-drive transmission are the most heavily loaded, the return should bathe this pair of gears in oil. In a final drive unit, the ring and pinion gears require as much lubricant as possible, so direct the returning oil to the intersection of the two gears. If the transmission was originally designed with splash lubrication and a hollow mainshaft, direct the oil to the original catch tray in the transmission so that the shafts and bearings get enough lubrication.

TRANSMISSION SWAPPING

STREET TRANSMISSIONS

If nothing in this chapter will help your transmission survive, the only alternative will be a completely different transmission. For a street car, the best choice will usually be a stronger, larger transmission from another stock vehicle because they have gear ratios and synchronizers optimized for street use. Rear-wheel-drive transmissions are generally easier to exchange than front-wheel-drive transaxles, but front-wheel-drive transmission swaps have been (and continue to be) performed by many people.

There are a few OEM rear-wheel-drive transmissions that make good candidates for swapping into another engine-and-chassis combination. The T-5 is one of the best, relatively lightweight five-speeds for swaps, but it has been well covered in the T-5 chapter. The others listed below are good street transmissions because they have overdrive fifth gears and modern synchronizer designs.

Adapting an engine to a different transmission requires a bell housing or adapter plate, custom-splined clutch disc, and possibly a custom input shaft pilot bearing. There are numerous adapters and bell housings available from the aftermarket and junkyards for most of the transmissions listed below. The easiest interchange sources have been listed, but check before assuming there is a way to mount a particular transmission to your engine. The subject of clutch linkages is covered in the clutch chapter, but be warned that some of the suggested swaps listed below will require fairly advanced fabrication skills.

TREMEC T45/T-56/TKO-500/600

TREMEC not only owns the rights to the Borg-Warner T-5 transmission, it has also developed a line of aftermarket synchromesh transmissions designed for installation into customs, hot rods, and production-based race cars. The five-speed T45 and six-speed T-56 have been used in production, but the TKO-500 and -600 are aftermarket only. These are all good transmissions for use behind large V-6 and V-8 engines, but there are some differences between the three.

The T45 is essentially a redesigned and strengthened version of the T-5 that shares some parts with other, stronger TREMEC transmissions. It has the same single-rail shifting mechanism and uses T-5 shifters. The shaft center distance is wider, however, making the transmission gears stronger. It gives up some versatility to the T-5 because it is a front-loading transmission with an integral bell housing. Unfortunately, the only widely available version bolts to only the Ford V-8 and V-6 engines.

Long before the T-5, TREMEC bought from Ford the rights to manufacture the Toploader four-speed, introduced back in 1964. TREMEC produced the Toploader (and its cousin the 3.03 three-speed) for many years. TREMEC eventually designed a heavy-duty five-speed around the Toploader, called the 3550, which has the same bearing improvements as later T-5s (tapered roller bearings on input, output, and countershaft, and needle roller bearings under the mainshaft gears). The transmission maintained the Toploader's massive 85-mm shaft center distance, but it added a new internal three-rail shift linkage.

The 3550 was designed as a truck transmission, but Ford used it in the Mustang Cobra R in 1995. Later changes to the 3550 resulted in the release of the TKO, which had stronger input and output shafts, as well as tougher gears. The 3550 and TKO were produced concurrently until 2004.

In 2004, TREMEC discontinued the 3550 and released the TKO-500 and TKO-600 five-speed transmissions for the aftermarket exclusively. They come in two different bolt patterns to replace classic Ford and Chevy rear-wheel-drive transmissions. The TKO is somewhat unique in its flexibility—it has three different shifter locations cast into the case. The TKO comes in two different versions—the TKO-600 has higher, closer gear ratios and can withstand up to 600 lb-ft of torque. TREMEC even offers a special "road racing" version of both with an .82 (as opposed to .64 or .68) overdrive gear.

TREMEC's T-56 is a modern six-speed that is also somewhat distantly related to the old Toploader. It has the 3550's three-rail shift linkage and shaft center distance, but it is not a top-loading transmission—the gears are installed through the front and back of the case. Originally used in the Dodge Viper from 1992 on, it is a stout gearbox that can be used in many street applications. It can be ordered with a T-5 front flange for retro-fitting to some T-5-equipped cars, as well as with Ford and Mopar V-8 bell housings. The transmission's wide range of gear ratios makes it best as a street transmission behind a V-8. The double overdrive ratios mean that the final drive can be much lower for better acceleration with less effect on fuel economy, and the low first gear helps heavy cars get off the line quickly.

AX5/AX15/Toyota W and R series

One of the most versatile rear-wheel-drive (and four-wheel-drive with the appropriate version) manual transmission families from an engine and transmission swap perspective is the Aisin AX5/AX15 family, also known as the Toyota W-series and R-series transmissions. Manufactured by Aisin in Japan, the transmissions have been (and continue to be) used by many manufacturers, including Jeep, Dodge, Chevrolet, and Isuzu in both small pickups and cars. While all AX5 and AX15 transmissions are five-speed, a six-speed variant of the AX15 has been used recently.

The Toyota members of the family were installed mainly in passenger cars, although both were also used in small pickups as well. The W-series/AX5 is the lighter-duty of the two and isn't really capable of coping with more than roughly 200 lb-ft of torque. It makes a very good transmission for four-cylinder and small V-6 applications. In the United States, it was originally installed in rear-wheel-drive Celicas and pickups with the R-series engines, rear-wheel-drive Corolla GT-Ss with the 4AGE engine, and nonturbo Supras with the M-series engines. The AX5 was used in many Jeep vehicles behind the Jeep four-cylinder engine for several years in the 1990s. A variant was also used in the four-cylinder Dodge Dakota pickup in the early 1990s.

The AX15 is more useful from a strength standpoint. The Toyota version, known as the R-series transmission, was used behind the Supra turbo with the 7M engine. It was also used behind four-cylinder and V-6 engines in Toyota pickups through much of the 1990s. Domestic manufacturers put this transmission behind nearly every small engine family in their stable. Jeep used it to replace the troublesome AX5 in four-cylinder vehicles, and Chevrolet used it behind four-cylinder and V-6 engines in S10 and Colorado pickups. Mopar used it as well, behind four-cylinder and V-6 engines in the Dakota pickup from 1992 to 2003.

Because of this wide usage, the transmission is easily adapted to fit dozens of engines other than the ones it was originally installed behind. The early Jeep bell housing happens to have the same bolt pattern as Chevrolet 60-degree V-6 engines, Isuzu V-6 engines, and the high-tech Northstar V-8. The late Jeep four-cylinder bell housing has the same bolt pattern as the Dodge Neon 2.0- and 2.4-liter engines, including the SRT-4 and PT Cruiser Turbo

The Aisin-Warner AX15 (front) and AX5 (rear) transmissions are modern, sturdy, five-speed transmissions that make a good choice for custom rear-wheel-drive applications. The front bolt pattern is shared by Toyota, Dodge, Jeep, Chevrolet, Isuzu, and other bell housings. The transmissions are light and have a cast-iron bulkhead to support the shaft bearings at both ends.

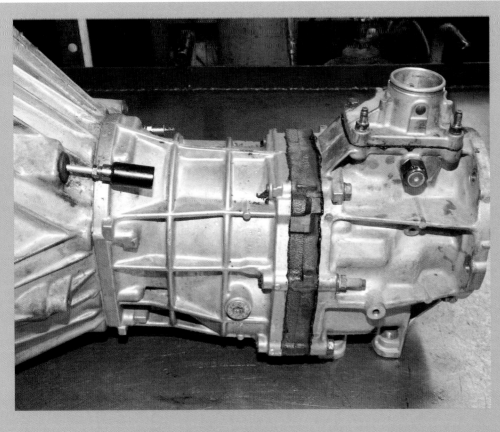

The AX5 transmission is the smaller of the two. It was used in four- and six-cylinder Jeep and Toyota applications in trucks and cars with a variety of ratios. It is a light transmission, and not really suitable for use with engines producing more than 200 or so lb-ft of torque. The transmission is known for smooth shifting, being quiet, and durability up to its rated capacity.

engine. The Jeep/Dakota V-6 bell housing shares its bolt pattern with the Dodge LA V-8 engines, including the 318, 340, and 360.

Engines that can be adapted to the Toyota W-series transmission using factory bell housings include the Toyota A-series four-cylinders, R-series four-cylinders, and M-series six-cylinders and any engine with the GM 60-degree V-6 pattern listed above.

Both transmissions are very popular in Australia, and companies have stepped in to make a wide variety of adapter plates to bolt them behind all kinds of exotic and not-so-exotic engines. Using adapter plates, the W- and R-series transmissions can be used with Chevrolet and Holden V-8s and 90-degree V-6s, Ford V-8s and V-6s, and Volvo four-cylinders, among others.

Racing Transmissions

Once you cross the line into pure racing transmission designs, there are literally dozens of different designs to choose from. The first step is deciding what is legal, and then what can fit in the budget. After these two parameters have been set, it is fairly straightforward to pick the best transmission that fulfills these requirements while

maintaining the necessary reliability. It helps if you are building a car from scratch, because the location, size, and mounting structures can be designed around the ideal gearbox.

If you are building a race car with a rear- or mid-mounted engine, there are probably only a few choices that work with your present chassis. Look at what the others in your class are running and copy them if you want to be safe, or discuss the subject with your chassis builder. If you want to strike out on your own, look at the Hewland, Quaife, and Webster boxes, and get out your checkbook. Taylor Race Engineering is probably the best bet in the United States.

For rear-wheel-drive chassis, the choices are much simpler. There are a few dozen designs out there, many of which are adaptations of production gearboxes with dog rings and closer ratios. If you are running a large American V-8, there is probably already an aftermarket bell housing that you can use to adapt your engine and transmission combination. If your chassis incorporates a motor plate between the engine and bell housing, it is a simple matter to design it with two sets of bolt holes for both the engine bolt pattern and the transmission pattern.

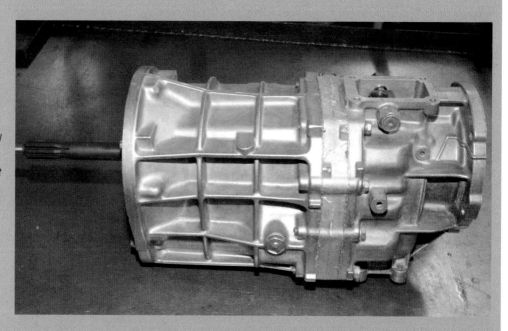

The AX15 transmission is the sturdy member of the family. It shares the same basic design as the AX5 but is larger, with a wider shaft center distance. It is also heavier and larger in every dimension. Although the front bell housing bolt pattern appears similar to that of the AX5, it is not the same and uses different bell housings. Using factory housings, it can be bolted to a staggering array of domestic and imported engines, and it makes a good choice for a street transmission. It can handle significantly more torque than the AX5.

The following is a list of some of the more common rear-wheel-drive racing transmissions available in the United States, but there are many more and this list is certainly not comprehensive.

Jerico, Muncie, Richmond T-10, Tex T101

These four-speed transmissions are very popular in circle-track and V-8 sedan road racing classes because they are simple and reliable, and may fit within some series' interpretations of "stock-based" transmissions. All four trace their roots back to 1960s production designs, but the Jerico and T101 have strayed the farthest from their OEM roots. The Richmond T-10 and Muncie are available with different gear ratios from their ancestors, but they still have blocking-ring synchronizers and helical gears in most versions.

The Jerico transmissions are based on the old Ford Toploader design, but with straight spur gears, a multi-part countergear assembly, and dog ring sliders. Each gear ratio in the Jerico is individually replaceable, so it can be set up to cover almost any combination of use and engine. The Tex T-101 is similar, but based on the Richmond/Borg-Warner T-10. The Richmond is essentially a brand-new T-10, and as such, it is the only new legal transmission in many dirt-track racing classes that ban racing transmissions.

G-force, Jerico, and Richmond nonoverdrive five-speeds

The next development of the three-shaft rear-wheel-drive transmission for circle-track and road racing is the nonoverdrive five-speed. There are at least three similar versions of such transmissions, including those built by G-force, Jerico, and Richmond Gear. All three have vertically split cases from the input to output shaft. This makes them very easy to service.

The Richmond differs from the other two in having synchronizers and a very limited selection of gear ratios. Only two complete gear sets are available. The G-force and Jerico nonoverdrive five-speeds come with dog ring shifting, no synchronizers, and a wide selection of gears. Either manufacturer can supply dogs that are optimized for drag racing or road racing.

The four-speed and five-speed American transmissions have an excellent selection of alternative ratios and years of development experience behind them. They are ideal for racing but they are very heavy—too heavy for many four-cylinder applications. If you need something smaller, look at Quaife's range of gearboxes based on the European Ford Sierra "Type 9" gearbox and European Cortina/Pinto four-speed "rocket" box. Quaife offers complete transmissions as well as dozens of alternative ratios, dog ring conversions, and most of the parts needed to build your own lightweight transmission. A T-5 rebuilt with a G-force gear set would be another great choice.

CHAPTER 8
CLUTCHES AND FLYWHEELS

Considering the clutch's vulnerable position as the mediator between the engine's torque and the drivetrain's traction, it's surprising that clutches don't fail more often. An increase in either force bears directly on the clutch, which must cope with these opposing loads without slipping. Not only does it have to withstand steady torque loads, but it must also engage and disengage smoothly and completely.

If this sounds like a lot to ask of a drivetrain component, that's because it is. Most OEM clutches do pretty well, considering all of this, although too much power and too much traction can push a marginal stock clutch to complete failure. Cars with a surplus of both are known for their voracious appetite for clutches; turbo Subaru and Mitsubishi owners certainly don't need to be reminded of the damage four-wheel-drive traction and a turbocharger can wreak on a clutch.

Depending on how you look at it, there can be a good side to clutch trouble. Some racers like to think of it as the first indicator of a good engine program. "If you don't have clutch trouble you don't have enough power" is a common refrain.

Of course, the driver has possibly the most important role in the life of clutch components—repeated hard starts like in Solo2 or drag racing kills clutches faster than anything else. A clutch that has never seen competition has a better chance of surviving than one that gets flogged on the track every weekend. Clutch trouble is completely avoidable with a bit of planning; clutches are very simple devices with many years of development behind them.

In an ideal world, a clutch would be like an on-off switch, disconnecting the engine from the transmission to allow shifting, and engaging to transfer power. No standing starts would be needed, and a sprint car's dog clutch would be the ideal solution. It would be mechanically locked together when engaged and completely separate when disengaged with no need for springs, friction, or large-diameter plates.

Unfortunately, most clutch applications require more flexibility. One of the clutch's primary functions is to allow for standing starts. At a stop, the engine is already running, and the car must be brought up to engine speed without causing the engine to stall. The clutch achieves this by transferring engine torque smoothly to the drivetrain while bleeding off the excess rpm.

It may sound counterintuitive, but even while the clutch is slipping, all of the engine's available torque (at that rpm) goes to the transmission. A clutch cannot multiply or divide torque the way a gear can—it can only eliminate excess speed (and thus power, since power is a measure of work divided by time).

In the case of a slipping clutch, the engine is making the same amount of power (the same torque, at the same rpm) as it would if the clutch were not slipping. Some of the excess engine speed (in rpm) is being bled off into heat through friction between the clutch disc and flywheel. The power going into the clutch is greater than the power coming out of it because the speed is lower, but the torque remains the same on both sides. During partial engagement, the torque transmitted through the clutch accelerates the car while the speed (in the form of heat) is radiated into the flywheel and surrounding air.

A clutch must also balance the somewhat opposing demands of low pedal effort, smooth operation, and holding ability, which can only be accomplished with high, predictable levels of friction. Clamping force supplied by the pressure plate produces friction between the clutch disc and flywheel. The disc's coefficient of friction determines how much friction will be produced by a given amount of pressure plate force and friction material diameter, and thus how much torque the clutch can transfer. This torque limit also applies when the clutch is being intentionally slipped to transfer power and accelerate the car.

One of the problems with a slipping clutch is that the friction material's coefficient of friction is affected by heat. As temperature goes up, the coefficient of friction goes down, and the total clutch capacity decreases. If you have ever slipped a clutch to failure trying to climb a steep hill or start a trailer, you have seen this principle in action. Heat reduces friction, which increases slippage, which increases heat—the cycle becomes self-limiting when the torque capacity of the clutch drops to zero.

To avoid this kind of meltdown, a clutch must have enough capacity to handle the engine's torque and enough heat resistance to handle the highest expected temperature.

A clutch uses friction to convert power, in the form of excess revs, into heat. This works great as long as the temperature stays within the heat capabilities of the clutch. If you exceed this temperature, be prepared for clutch failure. The clutch shown here is an extreme example—this clutch got so hot that the binder in the friction material burned out and the clutch disc came apart. Usually clutch failure isn't quite so extreme.

A clutch consists of a clutch disc, which provides smooth, predictable levels of friction; a pressure plate, which provides pressure to keep the disc flat against the flywheel; and a throwout bearing, to release that pressure. It doesn't make economic sense to replace just one part of the clutch system because of the work that it takes to get to the clutch. Buy a clutch kit from a reputable source and don't worry about problems later.

A pressure plate is actually a complicated assembly of several important parts. The cover is a pressed steel ring that contains the pressure of the conical spring. The spring is sandwiched between the cover and the pressure ring, with a wire pivot ring providing a friction-free bearing surface. The thin steel straps transfer torque from the pressure ring to the clutch housing, absorbing shocks and allowing the pressure ring to lift away from the disc surface.

This is where the selection of clutch parts comes in. Both main parts of the clutch system—the disc and pressure plate—have qualities that can be varied to achieve the desired combination of torque capacity and heat resistance. Disc friction material can be varied to increase heat resistance or coefficient of friction, and pressure plate load can be raised to help overall torque capacity. There are limits to this, though, so let's look at each part of the system separately.

PRESSURE PLATES

The pressure plate provides the force that holds a clutch engaged, clamping the disc to the flywheel. Most clutches in use today have a diaphragm spring pressure plate, which is very light and compact. It is also cheap to manufacture, which is probably the biggest reason for the diaphragm clutch's widespread use. Older coil spring designs such as the Long and Borg and Beck are still around, but they are not used on any modern car (with the exception of some drag cars).

At the heart of the diaphragm pressure plate is a flat spring that works like the bottom of a soup can or a wave lock washer: as the center is pressed, the spring flattens out. This so-called belleville spring is trapped between two pivot rings inside the pressure plate housing. Bolts or rivets through the whole assembly hold the pivots and spring together so that the edge of the spring pivots up and releases the clutch as the throwout bearing depresses the spring's central fingers.

Steel drive straps loaded in tension transfer torque from the housing to the pressure ring that forms the friction surface of the pressure plate. In some pressure plates, these straps also retract the ring when the clutch is released. The pressure ring can be either gray cast iron, which tends to be brittle, or ductile cast iron. Although most OEM clutches have cast rings, ductile iron is used on some high-performance pressure plates because it is less likely to explode at high rpm.

The two most important characteristics of the pressure plate are the force it exerts on the clutch disc and the effort required to release it. The force exerted by the diaphragm spring against the pressure ring and housing (which clamps the disc to the flywheel) is the **static load** of the pressure plate. This force is what keeps the clutch engaged; the higher the static load, the higher the torque capacity of the clutch if all other factors are constant.

Pedal effort is the opposing force, the amount of force needed to depress the clutch pedal and overcome static load. High pedal effort is unfortunately the flip side of high static load, and it can lead to more than a strong left leg. Excessive pedal effort strains clutch linkage parts and can damage the engine's crankshaft thrust bearings. Since the thrust bearing must withstand release force on the pressure plate, there is a limit to how high static load can be without causing excessive wear.

The problem with determining optimum static load comes when you increase the torque production of an

The most important part of a diaphragm-spring pressure plate is the conical diaphragm spring itself. The spring is a section of a cone, laser-cut from a flat sheet of steel and formed into this shape. The throwout bearing presses on the ends of the spring fingers to release clutch pressure. The thicker the spring, the stiffer—as well as the larger the diameter—of the spring.

engine. If the pressure plate load is high enough to handle torque at peak rpm, it may result in a clutch pedal effort that is too high. Conversely, if the static load is decreased to a point where clutch pedal effort is reasonable, the load may not be enough to handle the torque produced by the engine.

This was a much bigger problem with the old coil-spring pressure plates because the pedal effort of a coil-spring plate increases with increasing compression. A plate stiff enough to eliminate slipping at high rpm could result in a pedal effort beyond reasonable levels (around 50 pounds at the pedal). Both of the popular (in the United States) designs got around this problem by adding centrifugal assist weights that added load at high rpm. This was not always practical for high-rpm shifting applications, but it got the job done.

Diaphragm pressure plates alleviate this problem somewhat because the spring has a nonlinear force curve. This means that force does not necessarily increase as the spring is compressed. At first, force increases as you might expect, but past a point the force required decreases. The farther the spring is compressed beyond this point, the less force is required to depress it.

The clutch pressure plate is designed so that the installed height of the clutch is slightly past the stiffest part of the diaphragm spring's travel. As the disc wears, load increases until the diaphragm spring is at the strongest point, and then decreases as the pressure plate extends farther to clamp the disc.

With stiffer pressure plates, pedal effort is still an issue, especially for the first fraction of travel, but load can be increased with fewer negative effects. This makes it easier to balance static load and pedal effort. Optimal static load will not necessarily result in pedal effort that is too high.

One way to increase the load of a diaphragm is to form and heat-treat it so that it forms a taller cone; the resulting spring will have a higher peak force. This is the only way that a stock plate can have its load increased without changing the spring. If the stock spring is still not strong enough, it can be replaced with one of the same or a slightly larger OD or smaller ID. A thicker spring will also be stiffer, and thicker release fingers will eliminate some of the flex that increases pedal travel.

Some manufacturers stack more than one spring to increase plate load, but there are drawbacks to this approach. For one thing it means that the pressure plate is limited to double-stock capacity, which is a huge increase in static load and pedal effort. For another, the friction between the two diaphragms will add to pedal effort without increasing load.

DISCS

The clutch disc is arguably the most important part of the clutch system. The pressure plate clamps things together, but the disc provides the friction that transfers torque to the drivetrain. For this reason many of the clutch's characteristics are influenced by its design and material construction. Disc-lining material determines the clutch's initial grip, overall capacity, and ability to take heat while the design of

Above: *A sprung-hub clutch disc is the default style for most applications. There isn't much room to improve on it for a street application. Choose the highest-quality organic disc you can find and pair it with a stock-rate pressure plate, and you won't go wrong. Despite what you may have heard, the springs in a sprung-hub pressure plate are designed to absorb torsional vibrations, not shocks.* Below: *One of the interesting features of clutch discs is marcel. This refers to the wave of the steel plate between the two friction material surfaces. The greater the marcel, the softer the clutch engagement. Marcel is nice for a street application, but it isn't necessary. A clutch disc with no marcel is fine for a daily driver and a race car, especially with hard motor mounts.*

the disc and hub determine how smoothly the clutch will engage and disengage.

There are two ways the splined hub of a clutch disc can be mounted to the disc. It can either be riveted solidly or it can be attached through a spring center so that it can rotate a few degrees. If it is allowed to rotate, there are a series of coil springs that resist the relative motion of the two parts of the disc.

Despite the confusion that surrounds this feature of clutch disc design, there is really only one reason for a sprung-hub clutch disc: to dampen driveline torsional vibrations and reduce noise. If a sprung hub is replaced with a solid hub, more vibration and noise from the transmission gears will likely result. Torsional vibrations from the engine are not absorbed in the clutch hub and pass directly to the transmission gears. While this is harmless in most applications, a few front-wheel-drive road-racing cars with four-cylinder engines and stock transmissions have trouble with solid clutch discs.

One design feature that determines how smoothly a clutch disc engages is **marcel**, the wave in the disc between the friction material facings. A larger (thicker) marcel results in a disc that engages smoothly as the pressure plate squeezes the disc between the flywheel and pressure ring until the marcel flattens completely.

Marcel slightly delays clutch engagement, so it is not used in racing clutch discs, but any street or dual-purpose application should use a clutch disc with some marcel. The marcel thickness in many stock discs is more than necessary for high-performance use, however. On the street, the easier modulation and increased drivetrain life that marcel provides will more than make up for any slight loss in engagement speed.

Clutch disc weight is another important factor in choosing a clutch. While the disc represents only a fraction of total clutch weight, it is important for the life of the transmission. The lighter the disc, the less work the transmission has to do to synchronize the speed of the gears when shifting. Unless you double-clutch, the synchronizers in the transmission must slow the gear train, including the input shaft and clutch disc, to allow the gear teeth to engage.

A heavy or large-diameter clutch disc means more work for the synchronizers, which will wear out much faster. This is one of the reasons that going to a larger-diameter or multidisc clutch of the same diameter is usually a last resort. It may be fine for a racing transmission with dog rings, but it will strain the synchronizer rings of a street transmission. For the same reason, most racing applications with a synchronized gearbox should have a nonsprung hub because it

reduces the weight of the clutch disc and improves shifting performance. Beware of potential gear fatigue issues if the engine is a four-cylinder and the transmission is known to have issues, however.

FRICTION MATERIAL

Remember how we established that friction is what makes a clutch work? That friction is produced between the flywheel/pressure plate and clutch disc friction material. The coefficient of friction of the disc determines overall clutch capacity with a particular pressure plate load and diameter, while heat capacity and durability determine the clutch's suitability for a particular application.

Organic friction material is the most common of all clutch lining and is the baseline against which other materials are compared. "Organic" refers to the use of natural resin binders to hold the lining together. Ingredients as varied as fiberglass, cloth, and other fibers form the body of the friction material, with metallic wire mixed in to increase heat resistance and burst strength. Organic lining is either bonded to a thin steel backing before being riveted to the disc or is riveted directly to the marcel. Steel backing is more common in high-performance applications, and is very durable.

Your stock clutch disc is most likely organic, and this lining has a lot to recommend it, including smooth, gentle engagement and reasonable heat capacity. A good-quality organic clutch disc will outlast many "performance" clutches

The best friction material for street use has a high percentage of bronze metallic material in it. The metallic strips absorb heat from the surrounding friction material and keep the disc together despite high revs and lots of slippage. The nonmetallic components of the friction material are needed to provide gentle friction characteristics.

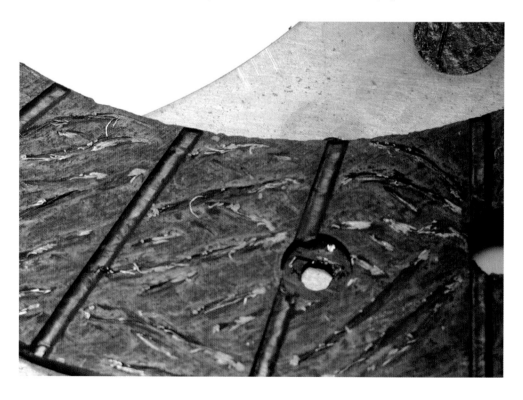

There is a dizzying array of clutch discs available from the aftermarket. They run the gamut from sintered iron to bronze, Kevlar, and carbon fiber. It's important not to choose the wrong disc for your application. Many of these exotic discs are a bad choice for a street application because of their poor release characteristics. The puck-type discs, in particular, are very unforgiving.

with much better street manners. On the flip side, organic does have less heat capacity than most other common lining material, and it wears faster than some. These two factors have influenced many racers to switch to metallic lining, but unless you have problems with an organic disc, there is very little reason to use anything else on a street car.

More-exotic materials may offer some improvement over organic linings, but there are compromises in every choice. Some of these compromises are worse than others, and you should carefully evaluate the friction material being offered as part of a clutch kit before committing yourself to something you don't need or want.

At least one manmade organic material, Kevlar, is quickly becoming popular because of its long life and easy drivability. A Kevlar-lined clutch disc will last nearly twice as long as a traditional organic disc, and it has very good street manners. This makes Kevlar a good choice for a stock replacement disc, but it may not be the ultimate racing clutch material.

For one thing, Kevlar's coefficient of friction is low and decreases rapidly at high temperatures, which means that a pressure plate with more load must be used with a Kevlar disc to maintain the same capacity. In addition, Kevlar is a very good insulator. The heat created by a Kevlar disc slipping

A clutch can fail for reasons other than wear. The splines in this clutch disc hub have been torn out. The symptom of this failure was a clutch that wouldn't disengage—the splines became locked to the transmission input shaft and could not slide on the splines to allow the pressure plate to release the clutch.

against a flywheel has nowhere to go and will burn the flywheel. An application that sees severe slippage (such as a four-wheel-drive turbo car) would probably be better off with a heavy-duty organic lining.

Inorganic or metallic linings are the ultimate in coefficient of friction and heat resistance. They are composed mostly of a sintered (compressed) metallic ingredient such as ceramic, copper, iron, or bronze and will not get "weak" with repeated abuse. Sintered metallic lining can transmit torque up to the melting point of the substrate—2,600 degrees F. for iron, for example.

Sintered iron is commonly used for tractor or truck-pulling applications, where slippage and very high torque is the rule. Unfortunately, sintered iron discs tend to eat pressure plates and flywheels and are very heavy. A sintered iron disc weighs more than two organic discs, which makes it a poor choice for synchronized transmissions.

One solution to the problem of excessive metallic disc weight is ceramic-copper friction material molded into "pucks" of about 3 square inches. Three to six of these pucks are riveted to the disc, reducing total weight when compared to an iron disc. Puck-type discs are good for high-power shifted applications with limited clutch size because of their high heat resistance and lighter weight than sintered iron.

The problem with all metallic clutch lining is the nature of its grip: ceramic and iron discs grab almost instantly with little or no slippage. This is partly due to the material itself and partly due to the "puck" shape, which concentrates pressure plate load onto a smaller area of the disc. The harsh engagement means that metallic discs have a tendency to break drivetrain parts when the car has a lot of traction. It may be the fast way around a track, but it is not the hot ticket for a street or dual-purpose clutch.

EXOTIC CLUTCHES

The formula to calculate clutch capacity takes into consideration the pressure plate load, disc friction material, disc effective diameter, and number of friction surfaces. We have already covered increasing friction coefficient and pressure plate load, which leaves us with two methods of increasing clutch capacity: increasing the effective diameter of the clutch disc and adding more friction surfaces.

The effective clutch diameter is defined as two times the distance from the center of the disc to the center of the friction material. Interestingly, this means that a clutch can be made stronger simply by decreasing the radial width of the friction material pads. The problem with this approach is that it reduces the area of the friction material, which reduces the heat capacity of the clutch and thus the disc's life, since the same forces act on less friction area.

The remaining way to increase the effective disc diameter is to install a larger clutch disc. This is more feasible for some engines and transmissions than others, since some manufacturers produce similar engine and transmission packages with different clutch diameters. For those engine/transmission combinations, installing a larger clutch is as simple as buying the larger parts and bolting them on. Assuming there is enough room in the bell housing, a larger clutch will increase clutch life and ultimate capacity before slipping. This comes with a weight penalty, of course, which affects both acceleration (rotating mass of pressure plate) and shifting (disc weight), since the disc is part of the weight that must be accelerated and decelerated by the synchronizers and blocking rings.

Multidisc clutches have been utilized by many racers looking for a way to reduce clutch diameter and lower the engine in the car while not giving up any capacity. Since there are more friction surfaces, these multidisc clutches can be made very small. Quarter Master, for example, makes a 4.5-inch-diameter, three-disc clutch that can handle 900 lb/ft of torque.

For a race car, it is hard to argue with this kind of clutch, assuming it is legal. Multidisc clutches increase total clutch capacity and reduce rotating mass at the same time. They allow the crankshaft to sit lower in the chassis, which lowers the car's center of gravity. Assuming you are using a popular engine/transmission combination, they are even easy to set up and use, since Quarter Master and Tilton make so many flexplates, bell housings, and adapters.

Like every other capacity increase there are some compromises inherent in the multiplate clutch system. For one thing, the added friction surfaces and smaller diameter mean that multidisc clutches wear out much faster than single-plate clutches, and are more sensitive to wear. Extended disengagement (like waiting for a stoplight with the transmission in gear) from street use will wear one out even faster. The problem is the radial clearance between the posts (the axial spacers between the pressure plate and flywheel that drive the metal plates) and floaters (the floating friction plates). When the clutch is disengaged, the floating plates rattle against the posts and both parts wear. The end result is notches in the posts that cause the clutch to hang up and not disengage smoothly.

In addition, multidisc clutches have no marcel and no air space. Unlike a single-plate clutch, there are no drive straps to pull the pressure ring away from the friction discs when the clutch is disengaged. This contact between the friction and floater discs causes a slight drag that makes it difficult for transmission synchronizers to slow the input shaft enough to get the transmission in gear.

If there is a synchronized (street) transmission behind the clutch, it is very difficult to use a multidisc clutch successfully. The exception to this is the Tilton carbon-carbon clutch. Since the plates are so light, the floater and friction plates do not stick together when the clutch is disengaged, which makes it much easier to shift.

This exotic clutch also benefits rotating weight and heat capacity: the carbon plates are nearly immune to heat, and the coefficient of friction actually increases as temperature goes up. The flywheel can even be made lighter since it no longer has to incorporate a friction surface—the final carbon plate does not move relative to the flywheel face.

FLYWHEELS

Flywheel size and weight are not particularly important for clutch and transmission performance, but they impact directly on the car's acceleration. A rotating weight like the flywheel absorbs power from the engine during acceleration. The heavier the flywheel, or the greater its diameter, the more power it absorbs and prevents from passing to the rest of the drivetrain. Going to a lighter or smaller flywheel can help a car accelerate faster, and a smaller-diameter flywheel allows the car builder to use a smaller bell housing and drop the engine in the chassis.

The problem with changing clutch size, either up or down to use multidisc clutches, is that it requires a different flywheel. It is physically possible to redrill an OEM flywheel, but most people recommend against it because it is almost impossible to maintain the required concentricity for balance. An error of less than .001 inch will cause vibration and unnecessary stress on the flywheel or pressure plate, not to mention the engine's crankshaft.

Whenever swapping flywheels, use the best-quality bolts you can find to hold it to the crankshaft. Always use the engine manufacturer's recommended bolts, in their original packaging, or quality aftermarket equivalents. Don't use parts store grade-8 bolts, since they have very little or no quality control. Use Loctite to hold the bolts in the end of the crank, and torque them to the required specification. These bolts are vitally important for safety and reliability, and they are not a place to save money.

LINKAGE

The last piece of the clutch system, and the one that is often left alone, is the linkage. Despite the difficulty of changing major parts, anything that reduces flex in the clutch system will result in better clutch action and less wasted movement. Even a few thousandths of an inch can make a big difference in clutch performance. Car manufacturers recognize this and have used thicker pressure plate housings, stronger actuating levers, and different clutch designs to reduce deflection.

In many cars, the hydraulic lines are very long and soft, which makes the clutch vague and "mushy" feeling. Stiffer pressure plates can make this worse since they cause the hydraulic lines to swell even more than stock. Switching to stainless braided -4 Teflon hose will alleviate the problem and reduce fluid displacement and movement loss in the hydraulic system.

The most important factor governing pedal effort in a given car is the ratio of master cylinder bore to slave cylinder. A larger master cylinder bore gives less mechanical advantage and a stiffer pedal, while a larger slave cylinder does the opposite. This is not particularly useful for most production cars since there are no alternative cylinders, but some manufacturers use different cylinders that share the same mounts.

If you choose to modify the hydraulic system to decrease pedal effort, don't forget that decreasing effort means increasing master cylinder stroke and decreasing slave cylinder stroke. If your car's clutch linkage has marginally enough stroke already, then there is not much you can do to increase it, and a smaller master cylinder will not help.

A lightweight flywheel is more of an engine performance enhancement than a clutch performance modification. These flywheels are machined from chromoly billets to be as light as possible without being as weak as aluminum flywheels. A light flywheel will have no effect on shifting or clutch performance.

Cable clutches are another matter altogether. Most of the problems found in these systems are caused by the friction of the cable and the poor materials chosen for adjusters and brackets. Cost is really the only reason to build a cable-operated clutch, and fortunately they are not very common. The most common high-performance cable clutch is found on the Mustang, and dozens of manufacturers offer improved adjusters, cables, and brackets to solve some of the problems inherent in this system.

SELECTING A CLUTCH

To decide what you need in a clutch you have to be realistic with your application and expectations. As I have tried to emphasize throughout this chapter, every characteristic of the clutch system (and any other system, for that matter) is a tradeoff. If you insist on overclutching your car, your sore left leg or neck may remind you of the poor static load or disc material choices you have made. You might also live to regret a stiff clutch when you have to rebuild your engine to replace a damaged thrust bearing or crankshaft, or rebuild your transmission to replace worn synchronizers.

It may not sound as cool to have, but a new stock OEM clutch may be the best clutch for most applications. A good-quality replacement clutch disc with an organic friction lining having a high percentage of metallic content (like the ones supplied in OEM-quality replacement clutch kits) will take just about all you can throw at it. There are plenty of 10-second drag cars and nationally competitive road racers that have unsexy sprung-hub organic discs and good-quality OEM pressure plates. Only when you have trouble with this kind of clutch should you consider upgrading.

If you do have trouble with the stock parts, or you insist on upgrading your clutch, you should be honest about your engine's torque output and the intended use of your car. Take this information and compare it to what you know about friction material, pressure plate load, and disc construction, in that order.

For example, if your car is used only for track or autocross and it has a sturdy drivetrain, you will be able to get away with much harder friction lining and no marcel. If you have to drive it to work every day, make sure you have some marcel and a decently smooth friction material. Most of the metallic linings are best used on track-only cars because of their aggressive action and lack of marcel.

A slightly stiffer pressure plate will increase clutch holding capacity in any application without affecting drivability very much. An extremely stiff pressure plate is necessary only with serious power levels and hard launches, and even then only when you are prepared to deal with the increased pedal effort and thrust bearing wear that they can cause.

You should avoid multidisc and large-diameter clutches on a street car, or a race car with synchronized transmission, unless you have no other choice. A car with a dog ring transmission, like a Liberty or Hewland box, can use any clutch successfully since there is no friction involved in changing gears. Going even further, a road race car that will see constant maintenance can get away with a smaller clutch than a street car, since road racing doesn't usually involve clutch-punishing standing starts.

FLYWHEELS AND BELL HOUSINGS

The bell housing between the engine and transmission is another often overlooked but important part of the drivetrain. There are a few different styles of bell housing in use, made of either cast aluminum or steel. Most OEM bell housings are cast aluminum. Many transaxles have cases that incorporate the bell housing on one half of the split case. Aftermarket racing bell housings for rear-wheel-drive transmissions are made of steel and SFI certified to prevent exploding pressure plates from injuring the driver.

No matter what material the bell housing is made from, it should be inspected periodically for cracks and checked for squareness and concentricity with the end of the crankshaft.

When replacing your clutch, carefully check the throwout bearing pilot surface on the input bearing retainer. If this surface becomes scored and damaged from a bad throwout bearing, it will cause the clutch to hang up and release poorly. If, as in this case, the pilot is made of aluminum, it will become scored much faster, and much worse, than if it is made of steel.

SFI CERTIFICATION

The SFI Foundation is a nonprofit organization that sets safety and other standards for aftermarket parts. The safety of flywheels and other clutch parts is very important—the rotating speed of these parts gives them enormous force if there is an explosion or something breaks. A clutch explosion can destroy the bell housing, body sheet metal, transmission input shaft, and injure the driver. For this reason, SFI certification is very important for these rotating parts.

The following list details the SFI specifications associated with drivetrain parts and the parts that they cover. For more information on each of these, check the SFI website at www.sfifoundation.com.

Specification Number	Product	Recertification Period
1.1	Replacement Flywheels and Clutch Assemblies	2 Years
1.2	Multiple Disc Clutch Assemblies	2 Years
1.3	Nitro-Methane Drag Race Multiple Disc Clutch Assemblies	1 Year
1.4	Alcohol Drag Race Multiple Disc Clutch Assemblies	1 Year
1.5	Multiple Disc Clutch Assemblies for Supercharged, Nitrous Oxide-Injected, and Turbocharged Vehicles	1 Year
6.1	Containment Bellhousing for SFI 1.1 & 1.2 two disc maximum Clutch Assemblies or SFI 1.1 & 1.2 three disc (8-Inch disc maximum) Clutch Assemblies used ONLY on naturally aspirated vehicles	5 Years
6.2	Containment Bellhousing for SFI 1.3 & 1.4 Clutch Assemblies	2 Years
6.3	Containment Bellhousing for SFI 1.2 GREATER THAN TWO DISC Clutch Assemblies used on naturally aspirated vehicles or SFI 1.1 & 1.2 Clutch Assemblies used on supercharged/nNitrous injected vehicles	2 Years

A bell housing that is not square to the end of the crankshaft will cause the transmission input shaft to bend and put side loads on the input shaft bearing. This can cause hard gear shifting and even damage the transmission bearings and shafts. In the worst-case scenario, the bending loads could damage the engine's rear crankshaft bearing.

To check the concentricity and squareness of the bell housing, bolt it up to the rear face of the block and install a dial gauge on the back of the crankshaft. Indicate off the center bore of the bell housing and rotate the crankshaft. For the very best transmission life and clutch performance, the total runout should be zero, although most transmission manufacturers recommend less than .010 inch. Using the same setup, place the dial indicator tip against the back of the bell housing on the transmission mounting surface. Again turn the crankshaft, and note any runout.

If the transmission mounting face of the bell housing is not absolutely flat with respect to the rear face of the engine block, most machine shops can quickly set it up in a mill to correct the error. Problems with concentricity are corrected with eccentric bell housing dowel pins, which are easily available from bell housing manufacturers (such as Lakewood) and engine manufacturers. If the engine has only one bell housing this job is a good sight easier since the bell housing only needs to be set up once. Making more than one bell housing fit the same engine is a chore, but it can be done. One way is to enlarge the bell housing dowel pin bores and rebush them with eccentric bushings that are welded or pressed in place. A good machinist can be a real asset for situations like this.

APPENDIX

T-5 Tag Numbers and Applications

T-5 Tag Number	Vehicle	Class	Gear Ratio Key (see below)
1352-001	AMC 1982-83 Passenger Car 258 L6	NWC	
1352-002	AMC 1982 Jeep CJ 258 L6	NWC	20
1352-004	Nissan 1983 280z 2.8 L6 Turbo	NWC	9
1352-005	GM 1984-86 Chevette 1.6 L4	NWC	8
1352-006	AMC 1982 passenger car	NWC	
1352-007	AMC 1982 Eagle 258 L6	NWC	
1352-008	AMC 1982 Eagle 2.5 L4	NWC	20
1352-010	GM 1982 S-Truck 4-6 Cyl.	NWC	20
1352-012	GM 1982 S-Truck 2.4L Diesel	NWC	20
1352-013	GM 1983 T-Truck 4-6 Cyl.	NWC	20
1352-014	GM 1983 T-Truck 4 Cyl.	NWC	20
1352-015	GM 1983 Camaro/Firebird 2.8 V6	NWC	9
1352-016	AMC 1982 Jeep CJ 2.5 L4	NWC	20
1352-017	AMC 1982 Jeep CJ 258 L6	NWC	20
1352-018	Ford 1983-84 T-Bird/Mustang 2.3 L4 turbo	NWC	18
1352-019	AMC passenger car	NWC	
1352-020	AMC Jeep	NWC	20
1352-021	AMC passenger car	NWC	
1352-022	AMC 1982 Jeep	NWC	20
1352-023	AMC Jeep	NWC	20
1352-024	AMC Jeep	NWC	20
1352-025	AMC Jeep	NWC	20
1352-026	AMC Jeep 2.1 L4 Diesel	NWC	20
1352-027	GM 1983 Camaro/Firebird 2.5 L4	NWC	9
1352-028	GM 1983 Camaro/Firebird 5.0 V8	NWC	1
1352-029	AMC 1983 1/12 Jeep XJ 2.5 L4	NWC	20
1352-030	AMC 1983 1/12 Jeep XJ 2.8 V6	NWC	20
1352-031	Ford 1983 T-Bird/Mustang 2.3 L4	NWC	18
1352-032	Nissan 1983 280ZX Europe 2.8 V6 Turbo	NWC	9
1352-033	GM 1983 S-Truck 2.0 L4 / 2.8 V6	NWC	20
1352-034	Ford 1983 Mustang 5.0 V8	NWC	2
1352-035	AMC 1983 Jeep CJ 2.1 L4 / 2.2 L4 Diesel	NWC	20
1352-040	AMC 1983 Jeep XJ 2.5 L4	NWC	20
1352-041	AMC 1983 Jeep SJ 2.8 V6	NWC	18
1352-042	GM 1984-85 S-Truck 2.8 V6	NWC	18
1352-043	GM 1984-85 S-Truck 2.8 V6	NWC	18
1352-044	AMC 1983 1/12 Jeep CJ RHDrive 2.1 L4 Diesel	NWC	20
1352-045	AMC 1983 Eagle 2.5 L4	NWC	20

T-5 Tag Number	Vehicle	Class	Gear Ratio Key (see below)
1352-046	AMC 1983 Jeep CJ 2.5 L4	NWC	20
1352-047	Nissan 1984 280ZX 2.8 L6 Turbo	NWC	8
1352-048	AMC 1984 Eagle 258 L6	NWC	
1352-049	AMC 1984 Eagle 2.5 L4	NWC	20
1352-050	AMC 1984 Jeep CJ 2.5 L4 / 258 L6	NWC	20
1352-051	AMC 1984 Jeep CJ 258 L6	NWC	20
1352-052	AMC 1984 Jeep CJ 2.1 L4 / 2.2 L4 Diesel	NWC	20
1352-053	AMC 1984 Jeep CJ RHDrive 2.1 L4 Diesel	NWC	20
1352-054	GM 1984 Camaro/Firebird 2.5 L4	NWC	10
1352-055	GM 1984 S-Truck 1.95 L4 (Isuzu)	NWC	20
1352-056	GM 1984 S-Truck 2.0 L4	NWC	20
1352-057	GM 1984 S-Truck 1.95 L4 (Isuzu)	NWC	20
1352-058	GM 1984 S-Truck 2.0 L4-2.8 V6	NWC	20
1352-059	AMC 1984 Jeep XJ 2.5 L4	NWC	20
1352-060	AMC 1984 Jeep XJ 2.5 L4	NWC	20
1352-061	GM 1984 Camaro/Firebird 2.8 V6	NWC	10
1352-062	GM 1984 Camaro/Firebird 5.0 V8	NWC	1
1352-065	Ford 1984 Mustang/Capri 5.0 V8	NWC	2
1352-067	Ford 1984 SVO w/Hurst shifter 2.3 L4 Turbo	NWC	11
1352-068	Nissan 1984 300ZX Europe	NWC	8
1352-069	Nissan 1984 300ZX Europe	NWC	8
1352-070	GM 1984 1/2 Camaro/Firebird 5.0 V8	NWC	1
1352-071	GM 1985 Camaro/Firebird 2.8 V6	NWC	18
1352-072	GM 1985 Camaro/Firebird 5.0 V8	NWC	10
1352-074	AMC 1985-86 Eagle 258 L6	NWC	
1352-075	AMC 1984 1/2 Eagle	NWC	
1352-076	AMC 1985-86 Jeep CJ 2.5L4 / 258 L6	NWC	20
1352-077	AMC 1985-86 Jeep CJ 258L6	NWC	20
1352-078	AMC 1984 1/2 Jeep CJ	NWC	20
1352-079	AMC 1985-86 Jeep CJ 2.1 L4 Diesel	NWC	20
1352-080	Nissan 1985 300 ZX TC 3.0 V6	NWC	8
1352-081	Nissan 1985-86 300ZX Europe 3.0 V6 Turbo	NWC	8
1352-082	AMC 1985 Eagle	NWC	
1352-083	GM 1985 Camaro/Firebird 2.5 L4	NWC	13
1352-084	GM 1985 Camaro/Firebird	NWC	10
1352-085	AMC 1984 Jeep XJ	NWC	20
1352-086	AMC 1984-85-86 Eagle 2.5 L4	NWC	
1352-101	GM 1985 M-Van 4.3 V6	NWC	11
1352-102	GM 1985-86 2.5 L4	NWC	13
1352-107	GM 1985 S-Truck 2.2 L4 Diesel	NWC	13
1352-108	GM 1985-86 T-Truck 2.5L4 / 2.8 V6	NWC	13

T-5 Tag Number	Vehicle	Class	Gear Ratio Key (scc bclow)
1352-110	GM 1985 S-Truck 2.5 L4 / 2.8 V6	NWC	13
1352-114	Ford 1985-86 T-Bird/Mustang 2.3 L4 Turbo	WC	19
1352-115	Ford SVO 5.0 V8	WC	1
1352-116	Ford 1985-86 SVO Mustang 2.3 L4 Turbo	WC	9
1352-126	Ford 1985 Mustang/Capri 5.0 V8	WC	4
1352-134	Ford UK 1986 Sierra 2.0 L4 Turbo	WC	3
1352-136	GM 1985 S-Truck 2.2 L4 (Isuzu)	NWC	13
1352-141	Ford 1986-87 Mustang/Capri 5.0 V8	WC	4
1352-145	GM 1985-86 S-Truck 2.5 L4 / 2.8 V6	NWC	13
1352-146	GM 1985 S-Truck 2.8 V6	NWC	20
1352-148	GM 1985 M-Van 4.3 V6	NWC	11
1352-149	GM 1986 M-Van 4.3 V6	NWC	11
1352-150	GM 1986 Camaro/Firebird	NWC	10
1352-151	Nissan 1986 300ZX North America 3.0 V6 Turbo	NWC	8
1352-154	Ford 1987 Mustang/Capri 2.3 L4	WC	20
1352-155	Ford 1987 T-Bird Cougar 2.3 L4 Turbo	WC	15
1352-156	GM 1986 Camaro/Firebird 2.8 V6	NWC	18
1352-157	GM 1986 Camaro/Firebird 5.9 V8	NWC	10
1352-158	GM 1986 Camaro/Firebird 2.5 L4	NWC	13
1352-159	GM 1986 Camaro/Firebird 5.0 V8	WC	10
1352-160	GM 1986 F Cars 5.0 V8 L69	WC	10
1352-161	GM 1986 Camaro Berlinetta 2.8 V6	NWC	18
1352-162	Ford 1987 Mustang/Capri 2.3 L4	WC	15
1352-164	GM 1986 M-Van 4.3 V6	NWC	11
1352-165	Ford 1986 Mustang 5.0 V8	WC	4
1352-166	GM 1987 Camaro/Firebird	NWC	10
1352-167	Ford 1986 1/2 T-Bird/Cougar 2.3 L4 Turbo	WC	15
1352-168	Ford 1986 1/2 SVO Mustang 2.3 L4 Turbo	WC	10
1352-169	Ford 1986 1/2 Mustang/Capri 5.0 V8	WC	4
1352-170	GM 1988 M-Van 2.5 L4	NWC	
1352-174	Ford UK 1985 Sierra 2.0 L4 Turbo	WC	3
1352-175	GM 1988 Camaro/Firebird Racing 5.0 V8	WC	1
1352-176	GM 1988 Camaro/Firebird 5.0 V8 TBI	WC	1
1352-177	GM 1988 Camaro/Firebird 2.8 V6	WC	18
1352-178	GM 1987 Camaro/Firebird	NWC	
1352-179	GM 1989 M-Van 4.3 V6	NWC	
1352-180	GM 1989 M-Van 2.5 L4	NWC	
1352-181	GM 1987 Camaro/Firebird V6	NWC	18
1352-182	GM 1987 Camaro/Firebird 5.0 V8	NWC	10
1352-183	GM 1987 Camaro/Firebird	NWC	10
1352-184	Ford UK 1988 Sierra 2.0 L4 Turbo	WC	3

T-5 Tag Number	Vehicle	Class	Gear Ratio Key (see below)
1352-185	GM 1987 Camaro/Firebird V8	NWC	10
1352-186	GM 1989 S-Truck 2.5L	NWC	17
1352-189	GM 1989 M-Van 4.3 V6	NWC	
1352-190	GM 1989 M-Van 2.5 L4	NWC	
1352-191	GM 1989 T-Truck 2.5 L4	NWC	17
1352-192	GM 1989 S-Truck 2.8 V6	NWC	
1352-193	GM 1989 S-Truck 2.5 L4	NWC	17
1352-194	Ford 1989 Mustang 2.3 L4	WC	15
1352-195	GM 1989 Camaro/Firebird L89 5.0 V8	WC	1
1352-196	GM 1989 Camaro/Firebird LO3 5.0 V8 TBI	WC	10
1352-197	GM 1989 Camaro/Firebird LB8 2.8 V6	WC	18
1352-198	Isuzu Rodeo	WC	
1352-199	Ford 1990 Mustang 5.0 V8	WC	6
1352-200	Ford 1989 SVO Mustang/Aftermarket	WC	1
1352-201	GM 1990 S-Truck	NWC	
1352-202	Ford SVO/Aftermarket	WC	3
1352-203	Panther Solo	WC	
1352-204	Ford Mustang 5.0 V8	WC	4
1352-205	Melroe Spray Coupe	WC	
1352-206	GM 1992 S-Truck 2.5 L4	NWC	
1352-207	Ford 1991 Mustang 2.3 L4	WC	15
1352-208	Ford 1992 Mustang 5.0 V8	WC	6
1352-209	Ford 1992-93 Mustang 2.3 L4	WC	15
1352-210	GM 1993 Camaro/Firebird 3.4 V6	WC	18
1352-211	GM 1992 S-Truck 2.5 L4	NWC	
1352-212	GM 1992 1/2 Camaro/Firebird	WC	10
1352-213	GM 1992 1/2 Camaro/Firebird	WC	10
1352-214	GM 1992 1/2 Camaro/Firebird 2.8 V6	WC	18
1352-215	Isuzu 1993 Rodeo 2.0 L4	WC	
1352-216	GM 1993 S-Truck 2.2 L4	WC	20
1352-218	Ford 1993 Mustang GT 5.0 V8	WC	6
1352-219	Ford 1994 1/2 SN95 Mustang 5.0 V8	WC	6
1352-220	Ford 1994 1/2 SN95 Mustang 3.8 V6	WC	5
1352-221	GM 1993 S-Truck 2.5 L4	WC	20
1352-222	GM 1993 S-Truck 2.8 V6	WC	13
1352-223	BW 4x4	WC	
1352-225	Ford (Aftermarket) Mustang V8	WC	3
1352-226	Ssangyong FJ 4x4	WC	20
1352-227	Ford SVO No reverse brake	WC	1
1352-228	GM 2.8 V6	WC	
1352-229	Melroe Sprayer	WC	5

T-5 Tag Number	Vehicle	Class	Gear Ratio Key (see below)
1352-232	GM 1993 S Truck 2.8 V6	WC	
1352-233	GM 1993 S-Truck 2.5 L4	WC	13
1352-234	GM 1993 S-Truck 2.5 L4	WC	13
1352-236	Ford 1994 1/2 SN95 Mustang 3.8 V6	WC	5
1352-237	Ssangyong	WC	16
1352-238	Ford Mustang 3.8 V6	WC	5
1352-239	Ford 1992-93 Mustang 5.0 V8	WC	6
1352-240	TVR 1999 Griffith 4.3 V8	WC	3
1352-242	Ford 1994 Mustang Cobra 5.0 V8	WC	6
1352-243	Ssangyong 4x4	WC	20
1352-244	Ssangyong 1994 Korenda Diesel	WC	16
1352-245	GM 1994 Camaro/Firebird V6	WC	13
1352-246	Ford 1994 Mustang 5.0 V8	WC	6
1352-247	GM 1996 Camaro/Firebird V6	WC	13
1352-248	TVR	WC	3
1352-249	Ford Mustang All 5.0 V8	WC	1
1352-250	Isuzu 1996 Rodeo 2.6 L4	WC	14
1352-251	Ford (Aftermarket) pre-1993 Mustang 5.0 V8	WC	1
1352-252	Isuzu 1995 1/2	WC	14
1352-253	Ford (Aftermarket) 1994-95 Mustang 5.0 V8	WC	6
1352-254	P/Tech Megastar 4x2 Lotus 2.2 TB	WC	7
1352-255	Ssangyong	WC	16
1352-256	Ssangyong	WC	16
1352-257	Nissin 4X4 w/ 1354 Transfer case mount	WC	20
1352-260	Ford 1999–2001 Mustang electronic speed sensor 3.8 V6WC		6

Gear Ratio Key

Key	First	Second	Third	Fourth	Fifth
1	2.95	1.94	1.34	1	0.63
2	2.95	1.94	1.34	1	0.73
3	2.95	1.94	1.34	1	0.80
4	3.35	1.93	1.29	1	0.68
5	3.35	1.93	1.29	1	0.72
6	3.35	1.99	1.33	1	0.68
7	3.35	1.99	1.33	1	0.83
8	3.35	2.10	1.38	1	0.76
9	3.50	2.14	1.39	1	0.78
10	3.50	2.14	1.36	1	0.78
11	3.50	2.14	1.39	1	0.73
12	3.55	1.99	1.32	1	0.68
13	3.76	2.18	1.42	1	0.72
14	3.76	2.18	1.42	1	0.81
15	3.97	2.34	1.46	1	0.79
16	3.97	2.34	1.46	1	0.85
17	4.03	2.37	1.49	1	0.72
18	4.03	2.37	1.49	1	0.76
19	4.03	2.37	1.49	1	0.81
20	4.03	2.37	1.49	1	0.86

SOURCES

Advanced Clutch Technology
Manufacturer of high-performance clutches
206 East Avenue K-4
Lancaster, CA 93535
www.advancedclutch.com

Albins Off Road Gear
Custom gear manufacturer
24 Wiltshire Lane
Delacombe 3356
Ballarat, Victoria
Australia
www.albinsgear.com.au

Anaheim Gear
Manual transmission rebuilding and modifying
1271 South Talt Avenue
Anaheim, CA 92806
www.anaheimgear.com

Andrews Products, Inc.
Manufacturer of racing transmission gears
431 Kingston Court
Mount Prospect, IL 60056
www.andrews-products.com

ATS USA
Manufacturer of gears and differentials for mostly Honda applications
10 West Main Street, 1-B
Elmsford, NY 10523
www.a-t-s-usa.com

Brewer's Performance
Supplier of parts and services for classic Mopar four-speed transmissions
2560 South State Route 48
Ludlow Falls, OH 45339
www.brewersperformance.com

D&D Performance
Suppliers of TREMEC transmissions and parts—T-5 specialists
47901 Anna Court
Wixom, MI 48393
www.ddperformance.com

Dan Williams
Supplier of parts and services for Ford Toploader four-speed transmissions
206 East Dogwood Drive
Franklin, NC 28734
www.toploadertransmissions.com

David Kee Toploader Transmissions, Inc.
Supplier of parts and services for Ford Toploader four-speed transmissions
San Antonio, TX 78266
www.davidkeetoploaders.com

Drivetrain Specialists of Las Vegas
Supplier of transmission and final drive parts and services
Las Vegas NV, 89102
www.drivetrain.com

EMCO Gears, Inc.
Manufacturer of racing transmissions and transaxles
703 South Girls School Road
Indianapolis, IN 46231
www.emcogears.comindex.htm

Evans Performance Products, LLC
Metal treatment specialists—source for Cryogenic and REM surface treatments
5166 Performance Drive
Cumming, GA 30040
www.evansperformance.com

Gearspeed
Honda transaxle specialists
9251 Archibald Avenue
Rancho Cucamonga, CA 91730
www.gear-speed.com

G-Force Racing Transmissions
Manufacturer of racing transmissions and gearsets, including T-5 dog ring gears
150 North Grant Street
Cleona, PA 17042
www.gforcetransmissions.com

Glebe Engineering, Ltd.
Manufacturer of racing gearsets for transmissions,
including the T-5 and Mitsubishi EVO
Edensor Works
Greendock Street
Longton, Stoke-on-Trent ST3 2NA
UK
www.glebe.co.uk

Hanlon Motorsports
Suppliers of TREMEC transmissions and parts—T-5
specialists
3621 St. Peters Road
St. Peters, PA 19470
www.hanlonmotorsports.com

Hewland Engineering Limited
Manufacturer of racing transmissions
Waltham Road
White Waltham
Maidenhead, Berkshire SL6 3LR
UK
www.hewland-engineering.co.uk

Houseman Autosport
Manufacturer of custom transmission gearsets, including
for Honda and Toyota applications
6564 Decker Drive
London, Ontario N6P 1J5
Canada
www.housemanautosport.com

Jerico Racing Transmissions
Manufacturer of RWD racing transmissions
443 Pitts School Road Northwest
Concord, NC 28027
www.jericoperformance.com

Kajun Enterprises
Muncie and T-10 specialists
P.O. Box 2195
Whitney, TX 76692
www.kajunjon.com

Kennedy Engineered Products
Manufacturer of engine adapters for air-cooled VW
transaxles
38830 17th Street East
Palmdale, CA 93550
www.kennedyeng.com

Keisler Automotive Engineering
Manufacturer of kits to adapt T-56 transmissions to
classic Mopars and others
2216-B West Gov. John Sevier Highway
Knoxville, Tennessee 37920
www.keislerauto.com

Layne Machine Work, Inc.
Parts and services for racing Muncie four-speeds
1151 North Chestnut Trafficway
Kansas City, MO 64120
www.laynemachine.com

Lenco Equipment Company
Manufacturer of drag racing planetary gear transmissions
6470 Federal Boulevard
Lemon Grove, CA 91945
www.lencoracing.com

Liberty's High Performance Products, Inc.
Racing transmission specialists—inventors of the "pro-
shift" welded dog conversion
6390 Pelham Road
Taylor, MI 48180
www.libertysgears.com

Long Enterprises
Air-cooled VW transaxle specialists
2475 Morse Road
Sebastopol, CA 95472
www.longenterprises.com

Medatronics Corporation
Supplier of RWD street and racing transmission parts and
services
208 North U.S. Highway 1 Unit #1
Tequesta, FL 33469
www.5speeds.com

Mendeola Transaxles, Inc.
Manufacturer of racing transaxles for air-cooled VWs and
off-road cars
290 Trousdale Drive, Suite J
Chula Vista, CA 91910
www.mendeolatransaxles.com

Modern Driveline
Conversion kits to install modern TREMEC
transmissions in older Mustangs
www.moderndriveline.com

MRT Performance
Manufacturer and distributor of dog-ring conversions for the Subaru WRX
1 Averill Street
Rhodes, New South Wales 2138
Australia
www.mrtrally.com.au

Novak, Inc.
Manufacturer of transmission, engine, and transfer case adapters for Jeep vehicles
P.O. Box 3367
Logan, Utah 84323
www.novak-adapt.com

Old Man Engineering
RWD racing transmission parts and service
230 Longfield Street
Mooresville, NC 28115
www.oldmanengineering.com

Opak Racing
U.S. Distributor of Spoon Sports gears and other parts for racing Hondas
355 San Bruno Avenue East
San Bruno, CA 94066
www.spoonsports.us

Passon Performance
Supplier of parts and services for classic Mopar four-speed transmissions
309 Turkey Path
Sugarloaf, PA 18249
www.passonperformance.com

Phantom Grip
Manufacturer of LSD conversions and Honda transaxle strengthening plates
www.phantomgrip.com

PowerHaus II
Distributor of custom gear ratios and other racing parts for Porsche transaxles
6270 Arapahoe, Unit 7
Boulder, CO 80303
www.phii.net

Quaife America
Distributor of Quaife differentials, transmissions, and gearsets in the U.S.
32240-E Paseo Adelanto
San Juan Capistrano, CA 92675
www.quaifeamerica.com

Red Line Synthetic Oil Corporation
Manufacturer of popular synthetic oil formulations for manual transmissions
6100 Egret Court
Benicia, CA 94510
www.redlineoil.com

Richmond Gear
Manufacturer of transmissions, final drives, and differentials including the T-10 four-speed
1208 Old Norris Road
P.O. Box 238
Liberty, SC 29657
www.richmondgear.com

Road/Race Engineering
Mitsubishi Turbo Parts and Tuning
13022 La Dana Court
Santa Fe Springs, CA 90670
www.roadraceengineering.com

Rockland Standard Gear, Inc.
Supplier of transmission and final drive parts and services, including racing rebuilds
150 Route 17
P.O. Box 13
Sloatsburg, NY 10974
www.rsgear.com

Taylor Race Engineering
Supplier of racing transmissions, parts, and service
2010 Avenue G, Suite 914
Plano, TX 75074
www.taylor-race.com

Team Rip Engineering
FWD Transaxle parts and rebuilding services—specializing in Mitsubishi turbo transaxles
Basement Level
508 East Frank Street
Kalamazoo, MI 49007
www.teamrip.com

Tex Racing
Manufacturer and supplier of RWD racing transmissions
and driveline parts
2268 Alternate U.S. Highway 220
North Ether, NC 27247
www.texracing.com

Tilton
Manufacturer of racing clutches, bell housings, and
drivetrain parts
25 Easy Street
P.O. Box 1787
Buellton, CA 93427
www.tiltonracing.com

Transmission Technologies Corporation (TTC)
U.S. sales and marketing division of the manufacturer of
TREMEC transmissions
23382 Commerce Drive
Farmington Hills, MI 48335
www.tremec.com

Uchiyama Motor Sport
Manufacturer of gearsets for the Subaru WRX and
Mitsubishi EVO
1678-1, Hanakawa-cho
Hamamatsu City
Shizuoka, 433-8109
Japan
www.umsrally.com

Windrush Evolutions, Inc. (Wevo)
Distributor of Porsche racing transaxle parts and dog ring
conversions
952A Washington Street
San Carlos, CA 94070
www.wevo.com

The Wright Gearbox
Air-cooled VW sand and off-road racing transmission
specialists
9820 Indiana Avenue
Riverside, CA 92503
www.wrightgearbox.com

ZR51 Performance
Specialists in the Corvette ZF 6-speed transmission
5612 East Almeda Court
Cave Creek, AZ 85331-6405
www.zfdoc.com

Zumbrota Bearing and Gear Inc
Supplier of transmission and final drive parts and services
622 West 1st Street
Zumbrota, MN 55992
www.zbag.com

INDEX

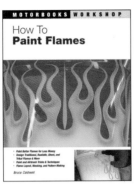

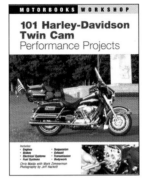
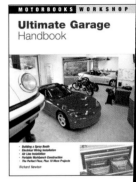